"This is the most comprehensive book on the civic society to date. It studies, with great conviction and rich command of the literature, the elements and dynamics of the civil society. Above all, the book takes us forward; we need to ask not merely if a society is civil, but also inquire into the substantive values it nourishes. Nobody is clearer on this important issue than Eberly and few are his peers."

—Amitai Etzioni, author of *The New Golden Rule*

"No one who cares about the future of America's civil institutions, no one who has a head and a heart for the plight of our most truly needy fellow citizens and young people, can afford to miss Don Eberly's masterful new book *America's Promise.* Eberly bridges all of the usual partisan and ideological divides, not by being all things to all readers, but by blending solid empirical evidence with sound practical ideas and morally compelling prescriptions. To those who know Eberly and his years of work, this extraordinary book—a grand summation of years of intellectual sweat and personal toil—will come as no surprise. Eberly is one of our few true intellectual and moral statesmen, and *America's Promise* is his blueprint for civic renewal."

—John DiIulio, professor of politics and public affairs,
Princeton University, and senior fellow,
Manhattan Institute and Brookings Institution

"An enormously helpful volume surveying the civil society debate. Eberly helps us to understand why a concern with the condition of our common political and social life focuses so intensely on the nature, status, and fate of a democratic civil society. He demonstrates decisively that what is at stake in the outcome of the civil society debate is not only our collective self-understanding but, indeed, our well-being as citizens."

—Jean Bethke Elshtain, author of *Democracy on Trial*

"If you want to know what civil society means, and why the concept is so important, by all means read this book. Wise, lucid, and extremely informative, it is an indispensable guide to the civil society debate."

—David Popenoe, professor of sociology, Rutgers University,
and author of *Life Without Father*

Previous Books by Don E. Eberly

Restoring the Good Society

Bulding a Community of Citizens: Civil Society in the 21st Century

The Content of America's Character: Recovering Civic Virtue

America's Promise

Civil Society and the Renewal of American Culture

Don E. Eberly

ROWMAN & LITTLEFIELD PUBLISHERS, INC.
Lanham • Boulder • New York • Oxford

ROWMAN & LITTLEFIELD PUBLISHERS, INC.

Published in the United States of America
by Rowman & Littlefield Publishers, Inc.
4720 Boston Way, Lanham, Maryland 20706

12 Hid's Copse Road
Cumnor Hill, Oxford OX2 9JJ, England

British Library Cataloguing in Publication Information Available

Library of Congress Cataloging-in-Publication Data

Eberly, Don E.
    America's promise : civil society and the renewal of American
culture / Don E. Eberly.
        p.   cm.
    Includes bibliographical references and index.
    ISBN 0-8476-9228-0 (cloth : alk. paper). — ISBN 0-8476-9229-9
(paper : alk. paper)
    1. Citizenship—United States.   2. Civil society—United States.
3. Political participation—United States.   4. Values—Political
aspects—United States.   I. Title.
JK1759.E15   1998
301'.0973—dc21   98-35504
                                                                   CIP

Printed in the United States of America

⊖™ The paper used in this publication meets the minimum requirements of American
National Standard for Information Sciences—Permanence of Paper for Printed Library
Materials, ANSI Z39.48–1984.

Contents

Acknowledgments   ix

Part One
The Emergence of Civil Society

Chapter 1   Civil Society: A New Solution   3

Chapter 2   The Movement   19

Part Two
Civil Society's Component Parts

Chapter 3   Social Institutions, Social Regression   37

Chapter 4   Civil Society and the Welfare State   59

Chapter 5   Community Building and Civic Engagement   75

Chapter 6   Renewing the Public Realm: Public Space
              and Democratic Deliberation   95

Chapter 7   Cultural Cleanup: Manners
              and Re-Moralization   105

Chapter 8   Recovering Individual Character and Ethics   125

Chapter 9   Toward a New Public Philosophy:
              Common Ground and the Common Good   133

Part Three
Civil Society: Its Promise and Limitations

Chapter 10   Civitas Limited: The Limitations of
              Civil Society   151

Chapter 11   The Fragility of Civil Society   163

Chapter 12   Civil Society Plus: America's Civic and
              Transcendent Creeds   181

Chapter 13   Toward Moral Realism and
              Republican Character   201

Chapter 14   *A Call to Civil Society*: Why Democracy
              Needs Moral Truths   217

Select Bibliography   245

Index   249

About the Author   255

Acknowledgments

By the time a book such as this gets into the hands of the reader, literally dozens of people have made invaluable behind-the-scenes contributions to help make it possible. I am deeply grateful for the thoughtfulness and professionalism of the staff at Rowman & Littlefield, and for the confidence that entire publishing family has placed in my work over the years.

I am grateful to the grant-making foundations that make my work possible. This book was produced in conjunction with the Institute for American Values, which received a grant from the Earhart Foundation for the project. I also wish to thank the Templeton Foundation for a direct grant for the book project.

I am indebted to the staff assistance of Stephen Piepgrass, a friend and former intern, who did an enormous amount of copyediting and adjusting during the early stages; to my colleague Peter Barwick at the Civil Society Project, who also worked on sections and offered helpful substantive feedback throughout the project; and to Clifford Frick, an able editor who has worked with me on previous book projects and who pulled through again on this one.

Special thanks goes to David Blankenhorn and Jean Elshtain for their cutting edge work through the Council on Civil Society, on which I have been privileged to serve, and to former Senator Sam Nunn and former Education Secretary Bill Bennett, whose work at the National Commission on Civic Renewal helped enormously to sharpen my focus.

I am especially indebted to those thinkers on the American scene whose inspiration and friendship have played a key role in the development of my thinking in this subject area, some of whose endorsements adorn the jacket of this book; and to hundreds of allies, acquaintances, and collaborators in the civil society movement described herein, many of whose labors are making America a much more civil and humane place.

Finally, my deepest debt of gratitude goes to my own "little platoon" consisting of my wife Sheryl, my son Preston, and my daughters Caroline and Margaret. It is this little voluntary association that has produced the most intimate, satisfying, and enduring bonds of human affection a man could hope to possess in this life, and whose daily nourishment makes my productivity possible.

Part One

The Emergence of
Civil Society

Chapter 1

Civil Society: A New Solution

As the world inches toward a new millennium, never before has a nation and its people had more reason to be proud and confident than the United States. In many ways, no civilization has ever stood taller. By any measure of success, the United States leads the world. It is the unrivaled economic and military heavyweight. Its creative genius in areas of commerce, science, and technology are the envy of the globe. Exploding breakthroughs across numerous scientific fields continue to make life safer, cleaner, healthier, and longer for its citizens. Despite its faults, no nation in human history has enjoyed more freedom and prosperity, experienced more uninterrupted progress, or maintained a more successful democracy.

Americans have always been bullish about their future. Their uniquely optimistic outlook strikes much of the world as peculiar, but the expectation many Americans possess of the continuous unfolding of a more ideal society has at least partial roots in our own spectacular success as a nation. The idea that America believes in itself, rallies together in the face of adversity, and confidently conquers problems is more than a national myth—it has a basis in experience.

The most dominant and enduring feature of America's self-concept is the idea that America works. In this century, the United States won two world wars and helped clean up after them, stabilized the global economy following a calamitous economic depression, and contained the threat of nuclear-armed totalitarianism.

The childhood memories of this generation's leaders include preparing for nuclear holocaust by crawling under school desks or climbing into bomb shelters. These dangers now seem remote. Instead of containing foreign adversaries, America now pours its energies into exploring space, running the best university system in the world, curing diseases, and producing more Nobel Laureates than most other nations combined—all this by a country that, by historical comparison, is still an infant nation.

Given this extraordinary record of success, one would expect the twenty-first century to be greeted with high hope and expectation, yet the national mood is marked more by melancholy and self-doubt than optimism. Rather than smiling contentedly, a remarkable number of Americans appears to be frowning.

Citizens have serious doubts about the health of their nation. They ask: Why does a nation that is the unrivaled democratic, military, and economic leader of the world, also increasingly lead the world in many categories of social dysfunction? Why do so many urban centers increasingly resemble third-world slums, and why does the United States lead the industrial world in child poverty? Why, in the midst of prosperity, do the problems of crime, drugs, teen pregnancy, and family fragmentation persist? Why does having so much knowledge leave us feeling so uncertain, or having so much opportunity leave us feeling powerless?

Dangers from outside are now a distant memory. The threats Americans sense today are different, though no less debilitating—they have little to do with foreign aggression and everything to do with internal regression. Today's challenges have to do almost exclusively with the pervasiveness of social disease. Large numbers of Americans uncharacteristically believe that the nation is permanently and irreversibly in decline. More than anything, they sense something important has been lost. That "something" is hard to articulate, but it evokes memories of values and beliefs once held in common and which many fear may now be gone forever.

The problems the United States faces today make yesterday's challenges seem easy by comparison. The nation has had great success in building military, economic, and administrative structures and systems, but Americans feel helpless, by comparison, in confronting problems that are inherently social and moral. External threats produced social cohesion and a sense of common purpose. Today, citizens are forced to confront conditions that have little to do with the state of national security and a lot to do with the state of their own souls. In the most fundamental way, Americans seem to be groping for direction and purpose in their lives.

A New Term in the Cultural Debate

As the twenty-first century draws near a new term has surfaced in America's cultural debate, carrying with it all of the collective longing of a nation looking for new direction. That term is civil society. The very words *civil society* seem to embody the hope that things need not remain as they are. An entire movement has arisen to recover civil society. Though diverse in its makeup, this movement is commonly described as having several related objectives: It reflects a search for a new citizenship that is less self-centered, more civil, and civically engaged. It is an attempt to draw Americans together again at a time of isolation and fragmentation, to restore community institutions, to transcend political differences in order to become neighbors again, to recover the spirit of volunteerism, and more.[1]

This book attempts to raise our understanding of what civil society is, considers why it is important, and describes various attempts to restore its vitality. It analyzes the state of the debate and provides a map of where the debate should go from here. The book advocates a "civil society plus" position, suggesting that the movement be grounded in a deeper foundation of objective moral principles. The argument set forth in these pages raises doubts about the ultimate potential of appeals to "civic participation" to curb America's powerful tendency toward a corrupted individualism and materialism. America, since its inception, has operated on both a civic creed and a transcendent creed, and both are required to sustain a healthy republic.

Although the purpose of this book is not to recite the now familiar litany of America's social woes—detailed data on the plight of the families and children of this nation are now known to all but the most detached citizens, and images of the corrupt culture confront Americans daily—in order to arrive at viable solutions, it is necessary to look at those social and cultural problems that are directly implicated in the weakening of civic America.

No simplistic theory of the origins of the nation's current condition is advanced, for there are many factors that have played a role in social fragmentation—economic dislocation, social mobility, the decline of religion, the rise of television, the displacement of civil society's functions by government, and especially changing moral norms, to name just a few. All of these factors and more are the subject presently of a robust debate among academic researchers and practitioners alike. Whatever explanatory factor one settles on, however, most observers acknowledge that the solution to the social ills of civil society must be found in civil society itself.

The Civil Society Movement's Prospects and Limits

While there is much to cheer in the emerging civil society movement, it does have limitations. Aspirations for renewal are not enough. The type and magnitude of social change the nation now needs will require more than soft and shallow sentiment to achieve. Though new desires for a more civil and humane society are consistently registered by large majorities, prospects for achieving social change must be evaluated in light of many obstacles to progress that exist today, including rather profound contradictions in the public mind itself. These obstacles include the corrosion of such basic ideas as freedom, authority, and the nature of community itself, a corrosion that has had real consequences for American society.

Few doubt that American society has weakened to an alarming degree. In poll after poll, overwhelming majorities of Americans express their belief that the United States has lost its moral center, that responsibility and accountability have become rare commodities, and that the most important social institutions no longer hold the respect they once commanded. Civility and manners have given way to behavior that ranges from discourteous to cruel. Politics continues to search in vain for ways to reconnect with the basic hopes and aspirations of the American people, as the public debate staggers from polarization to trivialization and, in the minds of many, to irrelevance.

Recently, attention has been drawn to the possibility of a precipitous withdrawal from the networks of civic engagement, suggesting that in addition to being disconnected from the political process, Americans are separated from each other.[2] Isolated and cynical, disconnected and unconcerned, individuals hole up in the minifortresses of gated communities or in bristling "identity groups." When people do face each other, their encounters are tenuous and fragile, often degenerating into acrimony.

Most Americans are old enough to know that, although America has always had its faults, society was not always this strained. Scanning the scarred social landscape, they wonder what happened. More important, most citizens want to understand how to reverse these troubling trends. Beyond their often overwhelming sense of loss and dismay, there is a feeling of danger and anxiety. No society, and surely no democracy, can continue on this centrifugal course. Isolated and cynical individuals are fitter candidates for a mob than they are for citizenship in a democratic society.

The source of these disturbing undercurrents has partly to do with the deep transformation that is under way in our social and economic structures. But just as consequential, if not more so, has been a deep philosophical change that has affected the way Americans live. The very idea of freedom, for example, which has always been the core value of American democracy, has been increasingly redefined to accommodate private, autonomous individuals.

Americans are in love with freedom, and on the surface, any proponent of democracy would be inclined to cheer this circumstance. Freedom, however, can evolve into license and when it does it corrupts our civilization and weakens the very foundations of democracy.

Americans are innately driven to expand boundaries, to think and move beyond established categories. Limitations cause a restless society of free-wheeling individualists to chafe. The pursuit of freedom—freedom to express, acquire, affiliate, disagree, or rebel—is part and parcel of the American experience, and it accounts for many of the astonishing achievements of American culture. Our deep and enduring attachment to freedom explains the genius of America, from scientific discovery to industrial innovation to soaring cultural achievements in art, music, and entertainment. In short, the greatness of our civilization has been made possible by freedom. It could not possibly be seen any other way in America.

The problem, however, is that freedom, as a concept, *can* evolve and be understood in new and different ways. Certainly there were competing visions of freedom operating in America from the beginning, but it is fair to say that the notion of ordered and responsible freedom—the freedom to pursue what is right and good—was, until fairly recently, the widely accepted operating definition. The more libertine definitions of freedom currently holding sway in America—views of freedom as absolute—may ultimately make freedom unsustainable.

Today the culture is dominated by a tendency by some elements on the left and right toward a new conception of freedom as boundless and absolute: on the left for expressive freedoms, and on the right for acquisitive freedoms. Each seeks maximum autonomy in the areas of morals or money, respectively. This recent distortion of freedom may be the single greatest obstacle to renewing civil society, and for this reason, it must be confronted. At issue is not the legitimacy of the American idea of ordered liberty, but the sufficiency of this new understanding of freedom. When culture has embraced a concept of freedom that is out of balance, it undermines the prerequisites for, and thus the possibility of, a free and functional society.

Maintaining a balance between rights and responsibilities, freedom and restraint, pluralism and consensus is difficult. The embrace of positive new social ideals often requires the tempering of other equally attractive social ideals. Just below the surface of the current debate over civil society are age-old tensions between liberty and order, the individual and the community, tradition and change.

These are not merely philosophical tensions, fought out between intellectuals and ideological adversaries in the rarefied regions of elite American society; they are living dichotomies that every American struggles with each day. Inside each of us, indeed lodged deep within the American character itself, is a split personality. Each of us has our libertarian and communitarian personalities, and our traditionalist and progressive selves, each voicing its hopes and desires discordantly. These incongruous tendencies, challenging and testing each other, individually and collectively, frequently leave the modern American feeling ambivalent in his or her response to events. If finding balance in national life is difficult it is because finding balance on a personal level is just as daunting.

Trade-offs: Freedom versus Community

As the economist contends, there are no true solutions, only trade-offs. It remains to be seen whether many Americans will actually be prepared to confront these internal divisions and accept the trade-offs that are inevitably required; for example, between personal autonomy and the call of community. No society on earth has made a greater range of personal choices available to individuals than America, making choice probably the most dominant and popular impulse operating in the culture today. One searches in vain for examples of employers, educators, or politicians who have gained broad favor by seeking to limit the range of personal choice. Absent the existence of war, economic calamity, or newfound religious fervor, the call to community rarely trumps the more powerful impulses toward personal choice.

Perhaps no one has captured this pursuit of short-term personal gains without regard for long-term collective consequences better than Allen Ehrenhalt, author of *The Lost City*. Ehrenhalt's study compares life in the Chicago neighborhood he grew up in with life in that same community today. The author remembers neighborhoods where most people were poor, but they held jobs, married and raised families, and kept the streets safe. In these same neighborhoods today, he sees open-air drug markets, teens fighting over sneakers with AK-47s, and 30-year-old grandmothers.

"How on earth," Ehrenhalt asks, "did we arrive at this pass?" when none of these neighborhoods were like this even a generation ago. Shedding light on today's ideological divisions, Ehrenhalt adds, "If you know what side somebody chooses to take on 'Who Lost Bedford-Stuyvesant?' the odds are you know what he thinks about a whole range of political and moral issues." This question of what exactly has been "lost" and who is responsible for our losing it, plays a central role in the civil society drama.[3]

Ehrenhalt maintains that there are only two, utterly incompatible explanations for the collapse of urban communities. One is that the characters in the urban nightmare are victims of residual racism and "white flight." The other is that "the squandered lives of the inner city are the plain fault of those who squandered them who lack the character and personal responsibility to conduct themselves in civilized fashion."[4]

Ehrenhalt favors the character argument, but without absolving the broader American society of responsibility. The urban ghetto, he says, is only living out the tragic consequences of the flawed values that have been widely embraced by middle America. Ehrenhalt concludes that "there may be a welter of confused values operating in the 1990s, but there is one point on which all Americans speak with unity and unmistakable clarity." We have become, he says, "emancipated from social authority as we once used to know it."[5]

Ehrenhalt reveals that

> The worship of choice has brought us a world in which nothing we choose seems good enough to be permanent, and we are unable to resist the endless pursuit of new selections—in work, in marriage, in front of the television set. The suspicion of authority has meant the erosion of standards of conduct and civility, visible mostly in the schools where teachers who dare to discipline pupils risk a profane response.[6]

Daniel Yankelovich, drawing on survey research data, sums up the cultural changes of recent decades this way:

> The quest for greater individual choice clashed directly with the obligations and social norms that held families and communities together in earlier years. People came to feel that questions of how to live and with whom to live were a matter of individual choice not to be governed by restrictive norms. As a nation, we came to experience the bonds of marriage, family, children, job, community, and country as constraints that were no longer necessary. Commitments were loosened.[7]

In short, nothing animates American popular culture and mass society quite like the idea of personal choice. Whether registered in election cycles, Nielsen ratings, the Dow Jones Industrial Average, or quarterly profit and loss statements, choice sells, and it drives American society. But Americans are discovering that having boundless personal choice is hardly a sufficient basis for civil society.

American Ironies

One of the things Americans now want on their menu of personal choices is a collective good called community. However, polls also show a fairly consistent unwillingness on the part of majorities to embrace measures that might limit private choice and thus make communal values and considerations possible. Citizens either do not think measures to elevate community over self will work or, more frequently, they see such measures as an unwarranted intrusion into their private lives. This preoccupation with private choice and aversion to collective decision making leads ultimately and inevitably to the elimination of community as a collective possibility.

There are many ironies in our sudden quest for community. One is that our obsession with private choice has made choosing and attaining community a near impossibility. Most Americans now desire a better society, but they are unwilling to make the choices necessary to bring it about. For example, most people decry the divorce revolution and its impact on children, but few seem willing to make divorces harder to come by. The public is repulsed at debauched television programming, but large segments of viewers compulsively tune in, not out. When it comes to family values, people believe their own are fine while others' are lacking. Parents say they want to restore standards and order to schools, but are quick to challenge the school principal when the child being disciplined is their own.

Most Americans believe in two incongruous propositions with equal fervor. On the one hand, they believe that choice is a good thing—the more of it the happier and better off they believe they will be. On the other hand, they also believe that society is in trouble, owing largely to bad choices by many individuals. As Americans travel this cul-de-sac in their consciousness, they often end up simply hoping that people will change and social conditions will improve while refusing to make available the collective means to achieve it. Civil society becomes little more than a vague longing or a wish, and a frustrated one at that.

In another irony, the very demographic group that now seems to yearn the most for social coherence and stability, namely the baby boom generation, is the generation that bears much responsibility for undermining social authority and delegitimizing institutions in the first place. In this generation's youth, the modus operandi was basically to tear down institutions and democratize all sources of authority. Values were considered repressive, manners were for hypocrites, and rules were for small-minded tyrants.

This huge post-World War II generation is now parenting America's children and has suddenly turned communitarian, even moralistic, but it nevertheless remains deeply ambivalent about taking measures to shore up social order. The idea introduced to society through this generation—that authority is inherently suspect—has taken deep root in America's social consciousness and shows few signs of abating.

Most baby boomers grew up with parents who reminded them frequently that there is no free lunch—that objects of desire come at a price.

To acquire things, one must work and save, they were told. These same baby boomers now want social goods. Like material goods, these social goods come at a substantial price as well. They require less individualism, more rules, and more authority. Social cohesion requires at least some conformity to moral norms, even if they are updated to reflect contemporary circumstances. There is simply no other way to produce stable relationships, extended families of moms and dads and grandmothers and grandfathers, safe streets, and orderly schools where discipline is the norm than for some price in personal autonomy to be paid.

But words like *authority*, *rules*, and *institutions* now grate on Americans deeply. They conjure up pictures of bondage and repression in a society of narrowly drawn boundaries. On election day 1996 the author asked his audience at a major university to choose between two alternative hypothetical candidates. The first hypothetical candidate pledged to pursue a "good society" consisting of shared values, civility, community, and common ground. The description was hardly completed and hands were already jutting up to signal enthusiastic approval. It all sounded very appealing.

The author went on to describe the second candidate as proposing precisely the same society, but by way of more rules, greater authority, stronger institutions, and reasonable restraint on "rights talk." Suddenly, the mood took a sullen turn. Like most audiences, these students voiced strong approval of civility and shared values, yet viscerally reacted to the kind of institutional authority required to maintain and mediate those claims and desires.

This is the rub. According to Ehrenhalt, to worship both choice and community "is to misunderstand what community is about." It is impossible, he says, to have an orderly world without someone making the rules by which order is sustained. "Every dream we have about creating community in the absence of authority will turn out to be a pipe dream in the end."[8]

Ehrenhalt is doubtful that many will choose to pay the price. He maintains that once people taste of choice and have freed themselves from rules and regulations, they may never return to a more ordered world. "Once they have been told that they no longer have to stay married—to their spouses, communities, careers, to any of the commitments that once were made for life—they will be on the loose forever."[9]

This holds important ramifications for the civil society debate. Some wrongly assume that because unbounded freedom has supplied society with energy and creative dynamism, that it is an unalloyed positive, but this is not so. Freedom must be combined with some elementary agreement over the purposes to which freedom is directed. When vastly different notions of the good and the right guide the use of freedom, society loses its cohesion.

Without the moral consensus that comes from an embrace of transcendent forms of ethical authority, life in society becomes a matter of continuous conflict—what Michael Sandel has termed "the procedural republic."[10] Nothing is settled, everything is continuously negotiated. Society becomes bogged down in civic dissonance. Life in community feels more and more like an engine running low on oil—things heat up. Institutions lose their legitimacy. The space in society that is truly voluntary and consensual shrinks. The handshake gives way to the omnipresence of law, and the legal apparatus becomes overworked and arbitrary. The state creeps in where moral consensus retreats, creating the society Tocqueville predicted, where "an immense and tutelary power . . . absolute, minute, regulate, provident, and mild [covers] the entire surface of society with a blanket of small complicated rules."[11]

Facing and Embracing Modernity

Other limits to the renewal of civil society must be acknowledged. In one of the earliest and most profound treatments of community, Robert Nisbet describes the trends of modernity that have played a powerful role in unraveling the moral and civic fiber of the country. From below, he says, the authority of family, church, neighborhood, and school is quietly eroded by the proliferation of individual rights and forms of self-expression that act with disregard for civil society. From above, civil institutions are pressured to surrender authority to the professional managers of the bureaucratic state. Caught between these "pincer" movements, the intermediate associations of civil society languish.[12]

Modern and postmodern philosophies make the achievement of moral consensus dramatically harder, even as it is most acutely needed. An older form of modernist thinking continued to cling to such universal transcendent norms as justice, beauty, truth, freedom, and equality, even while embracing reason as the grounds for society. This notion of transcendent principles, rooted in reason and prudence and often based on belief in the divine, now seems to have lapsed in many quarters of society.

In the absence of a body of universal, objectively discovered truth, the very notion of truth becomes extinguished. There are no universal principles, only preferences and opinions. There are no proven or privileged values, only personal tastes. There is no concept of justice, only private interests and personal rights. There is no concept of the common good, only self-maximizing individuals.

It is impossible to consider the debate centering on "the good" without taking into account the toll modernist notions have taken on such an enterprise. Modernity has created what British sociologist Os Guinness calls a crisis of "cultural authority." The great conflict of the age is between cultures: an older one that, in spite of all of its faults and rigid boundaries, demanded character, self-restraint, and social obligation as the price of freedom, and a newer one that demands little of the individual and everything for him.

This new culture substitutes feelings for facts; it replaces substance with images, style, and personality. Sociologist Philip Reiff has said that Americans no longer model themselves after the political man of the Greeks, the religious man of the Hebrew and Christians, or the enlightened economic man of the eighteenth-century Europeans. The new model for the conduct of life is psychological man—his prime objective being convenience, individuality, and unrestrained freedom.

The purpose of culture is really to regulate and order lives through informal and noncoercive means. Social regulations include such things as manners and moral norms. In a nonstatist society, culture must play the lead role in establishing boundaries around the individual granting or denying permission to do and say things.

There are only two forms of restraint. One is internal and voluntary, based upon religious belief, personal disciplines, and moral conscience. The other is external and imposed, either by society in the flexible form of moral norms and taboos, or by the state in the form of inflexible rules. The expectation of the founders was that the more voluntary self-control man possessed, the less external control would be required. The Constitution, as John Adams put it, was designed for a "moral and religious" people, and inadequate for any other. Freedom, in other words, was linked to self-mastery.

The founders had a pessimistic view of man, yet an optimistic outlook regarding the possibilities of harnessing man's corrupted nature for the common good through the right mix of moral norms and institutional arrangements. Man was not thought to be an angel and thus was not prepared for perfect freedom. He was thought to be prepared for freedom in exact proportion to his willingness to place controls upon his demands and passions.

Modernity has essentially reversed this skepticism about man's nature, casting doubt instead on the necessity of social rules or institutional mediation of any kind. Rules, and especially the social rules that should gently govern individuals, have become difficult to agree upon and even harder to enforce. The result of this loss of social authority, in yet another irony, is a greater reliance on an intrusive state, the ultimate destroyer of private choice.

The social reformers of this age have no choice but to live with the fruits of modernity and attempt to make improvements in whatever way they can. Modernity cannot be repealed, but reformers can seek wherever possible to limit its more harmful tendencies. This is not an easy task, for the simple reason that few would voluntarily part with the many advances offered by modernity, and opt for life in a tradition-bound community. Even where tightly bound communities remain, the settled life is now invaded by technology, and the intimate world of face-to-face relationships—what Jürgen Habermas called the "life world"—is replaced by ties and forms of interaction that are more distant, tenuous, and anonymous.

A final reality that will impede the renewal of civil society is the sheer recalcitrance of secularism, the essence of modernity. Even as growing numbers of Americans are reported to be searching for spiritual meaning, the truth is that religious life rarely flourishes unless imbedded in and practiced in community. Modernity's technical and material abundance undermines the force of the mystical and moral, and feeds our faith in the secular and rational. As a result, modern social reform movements must operate without a "broadly accepted, culturally centering worldview connecting religion, politics, and social change."[13]

The movement to renew civil society is essentially a social reform movement. However, because of the predominance of secularism, today's social movements cannot draw the same power from religious belief as many similar movements of the past did. Religion and social change have traditionally been powerful allies. Social movements have been the vehicle by which the larger society profited from moral renewal. Historically, says Hugh Heclo, "the revitalization produced by awakenings follows upon repentance." A recent example of this is the early civil rights movement, inspired by Martin Luther King's appeal to moral conscience.

According to some observers, the 1960s ushered in a dramatic shift in social movements away from religious motivation. "The New Light of the sixties," says Heclo, brought about an inversion: the self as aggrieved rather than "repentant and surrendered before a higher law." With sin passé, "self-blame was out and system-blame was in."[14]

Accommodating this shift, many modern social movements tend not to invoke conscience but rather seek to tap each person's desire, even sense of right, to satisfy his or her own perceived needs for fulfillment. In the world of modern and postmodern confusion, contradictions abound. Many search for answers for society while harboring the firm conviction that there are no answers outside of the individual self.

All of these factors and more shape society's values and core ideas. It is uncertain how these changes will affect prospects for renewing civil society. The sheer speed, scale, and constancy of change frustrate most attempts at predicting or generalizing. Many question whether older models of analysis can even capture the complex patterns of development in today's rapidly changing society. The information explosion has produced a search for new theories of history that can accommodate chaos, discontinuity, and cultural incoherence.

The Scope of the Civil Society Debate

The unfolding debate over civil society raises many important topics for discussion. These include calls for a new public philosophy emphasizing the need to elevate the common good over private self-interest, renewing social values and institutions, encouraging wider civic participation, and cultural cleanup.

This book explores the terrain of the civil society debate, its themes, its goals, and the major people and institutions behind the growing movement to promote it. It will also invite an honest debate about moral certitudes. As polls indicate, the flood of interest in civil society on the public's part is driven by a legitimate and urgent worry about the state of public morality.

The rise of incivility and the collapse of moral consensus reflect more than a decline in civic institutions. They manifest a deeper breakdown in the basic agreement of citizens—what can be called a social covenant—over a set of moral propositions. Civility and civil society are ultimately moral concepts. To succeed, the civil society movement must bring about the recovery and modern application of the nation's highest moral ideals.

Revitalizing American civil society is a necessary first step toward moral and cultural renewal. However, in the final analysis, the civil society movement in its present state of development does not go far enough. It does not seriously confront the deterioration of the moral values that have undergirded the American project.

The quality of American life will not be restored by merely promoting civic mindedness. Real prospects for change will require that the nation once again embrace the larger civic and moral principles that sustain a well-ordered democratic society. In its current formulation, the civil society solution takes the debate only so far, and risks denying America the larger and more lasting cultural renewal it needs.

A "civil society plus" position is necessary, then, for real consequential social change to be achieved. The recovery of civil society will be aided by, and indeed will require, the recovery of America's tradition of moral realism. Civic institutions are important, but just as important are the ideas and moral values that become embedded in those institutions. Moral relativism has severely weakened the community institutions that must be rebuilt to reestablish a civil society. In fact, the pervasive moral skepticism and doubt of our time are among the chief causes of the collapse of the authority and legitimacy of these institutions.

This moral skepticism and outright hostility was, until very recently, pervasive especially in educational fields, as schools and universities could find no basis for including a place for morality within the secular sciences. Morality was assumed to constitute little more than the expression of personal preferences and parochial attitudes. Many concluded that belief in values was essentially unscientific and akin to religious faith. Others simply feared that moral education involved indoctrination or concluded that holding to an objective standard of right and wrong was inconsistent with cultural diversity.

Today, however, there are some signs that this aversion to morality in the name of science is changing. Moral belief is being recovered as a defensible intellectual posture. Confidence that there are moral facts, which can be discovered, approved, and broadly applied within the human community, is returning. Historical evidence shows that core values are indispensable to the functioning of society, and that across civilizations certain fixed moral propositions have been and still are regarded as true.

The broad acceptance over the course of human civilization of these self-evident facts and their rediscovery may prove to be the coup de grâce for the moral subjectivism of recent decades. The movement toward ethical relativism has few ardent advocates left, both because old philosophical schools are dying out and because members of even the most insulated intellectual circles are increasingly realizing that society, untethered from moral principles, can sink into the Hobbesian swamp where all are at war with all others, and life is "solitary, poor, nasty, brutish and short." Life in America certainly has not approached this point, but the raw cynicism and anger that many detect in the streets have caused even moral agnostics to suddenly discover some utility in ethical finalities, whatever they may ground it in.

Politician and moral philosopher Vaclav Havel has spent his life searching for ways to recover moral transcendence, first as a writer and now as president of the Czech Republic. Human civilization will only be possible, he believes, if "we all accept a basic code of mutual coexistence, a kind of common minimum we can all share, one that will enable us to go on living side by side."[15]

Conclusion

After defining the term *civil society* and laying out the groundwork for discussion, this book provides an overview of the civil society movement in its public, intellectual, and grassroots dimensions. The many public projects that seek to reestablish a sense of commonality, shared purpose, and moral responsibility are identified and analyzed. In a candid look at the many civic and cultural enterprises that seek to tackle some aspect of public improvement (i.e., civility, cultural cleanup, character, improvements in public discourse, and attempts to forge anew the nation's basic public philosophy), this book points out that each of these intellectual and grassroots movements has its limits, but is not to be dismissed. Each point to broader possibilities for advancing toward a new moral consensus in this postmodern and pluralistic age.

Following this survey of the civil society movement, the book then attempts to show how the civil society debate can respond in concrete ways to the more fundamental concern registered consistently by large majorities of Americans—the erosion of core values. The book argues that the civil society movement should be guided more explicitly by specific moral and philosophical objectives. Specially, it should seek to recover the ingredients of a free and ordered society within liberal political theory, and search for greater balance between the extremes of order absent freedom and freedom without order that have presented themselves on the American scene.

The book concludes with a call for a fresh embrace of the core principles of individual character as a practical and attainable goal for our schools, institutions, and places of work and worship in every community in America, and argues for a renewal of the older American public philosophy of civic republicanism that seeks to promote the common good centering in character.

Notes

1. Deb Reichman, "Let's Be Civil," *Associated Press*, 5 February 1997.
2. Robert D. Putnam, "Bowling Alone: America's Declining Social Capital," *Journal of Democracy* 6, no. 1 (January 1995).
3. Allen Ehrenhalt, "When Moral Agency Disappears," *The Weekly Standard*, October 1996, 32.
4. Ehrenhalt, "When Moral Agency Disappears."
5. Allen Ehrenhalt, "Learning from the Fifties," *Wilson Quarterly*, Summer 1995, 19.

6. Ehrenhalt, "Learning from the Fifties," 8.

7. Henry J. Aaron, Thomas E. Mann, and Timothy Taylor, eds., *Values and Public Policy* (Washington, D.C.: Brookings Institution, 1994), 37.

8. Ehrenhalt, "Learning from the Fifties," 21.

9. Ehrenhalt, "Learning from the Fifties," 25.

10. See Michael Sandel, *Democracy Discontent: America in Search of a Public Philosophy* (Cambridge: Harvard University Press, 1996).

11. Alexis de Tocqueville, *Democracy in America* (Garden City, N.Y.: Doubleday Anchor Books, 1996), 692.

12. See Robert Nisbet, *The Quest for Community* (San Francisco: Institute for Contemporary Studies, 1990).

13. Hugh Heclo, "The Sixties' False Dawn: Awakenings, Movements, and Postmodern Policy-making," *Journal of Policy History* 8, no. 1 (University Park: Pennsylvania State University Press), 46.

14. Heclo, "The Sixties," 46.

15. Address by Vaclav Havel, Harvard University, Cambridge, 8 June 1995.

Chapter 2

The Movement

Defining the Term

The term *civil society* has made a sudden and dramatic reappearance, after near complete abandonment in American public discourse. In reality, the term is older than the Republic itself and is only now reemerging after a period of extended neglect. The concept has a rich history in both political theory and sociology.

Because the concept of civil society is unfamiliar to many, and because the postmodern culture tends to empty language of any fixed meaning, a definition for this newly rediscovered term is called for. In addition to rhetorical confusion and widespread conceptual ambiguity surrounding the term *civil society*, recent political interest in the subject has done little to clarify its meaning and purposes. As the civil society debate has shown, the masters of political debate are often more adept at appropriating freshly minted language such as civil society to capture public support and to score a few quick points for their side than they are at deepening public understanding.

As the term *civil society* has been used thus far in the cultural debate, it is more suggestive than precise. Many use it as an adjective to describe the kind of decent society that we collectively long for. Used in this sense, the term merely serves as a hopeful catchword for prescribing civility and manners as an antidote to the harsh edge of contemporary American society and public debate. This application of the term offers little substantive guidance on how to achieve the society that so many are hoping for. Mere talk of civility lacks a sufficient foundation for more consequential change in American society.

While civil society implies civility for some, for others it is virtually synonymous with the private sector, implying that the term's major attraction is its usefulness in a larger attempt to curb the state and expand the private market. For congressional conservatives, for example, civil society consists mostly of replacing public welfare with private charity, volunteerism, and service.

By contrast, political liberals frequently embrace civil society, not to hem government in as much as to "strengthen" it, perhaps to reform it, but most importantly to restore its public acceptance. Liberals are quick to emphasize the virtues of strong civic communities in boosting public support for government, as Robert Putnam discovered in his research on regional government in Italy. Harvard Professor Theda Skocpol casts a slightly different but no less approving light on the role of the government in generating civic life. She argues that growth in the federal government has actually spurred the development of voluntary associations and that without active government, volunteerism and civic membership would be weaker today, not stronger.[1]

For most, however, civil society entails ingredients of many of the above, blended together and served up in the modest hope of restoring balance and health in what was once a vibrant, multisector society.

Civil society is perhaps best understood as a noun—as a real flesh and blood "thing"—consisting of people and institutions with moral substance and function. Understood this way, the path to constructing a civil and humane society lies in erecting institutions that socialize and civilize.

Any discussion of civil society draws upon a constellation of related terms including citizenship, community, civic participation, social institutions, and social capital. Though there are more, these are the descriptive terms most commonly used in public conversation and scholarly treatment of the subject. In order to organize important work around the renewal of a concept termed civil society, the conceptual foundation of the phrase must be better laid out

Civil Society as Voluntary Association

Above all, civil society denotes that realm of society in which non-political institutions operate—families, houses of worship, neighborhoods, civic groups, and just about every form of voluntary association imaginable. Always implied in the term *civil society* are activities and associations that are free and voluntary. Michael Walzer describes civil society as "the space of uncoerced human association" and also "the set of relational networks—formed for the sake of family, faith, interest, and ideology—that fill this space."[2]

To Tocqueville, civil society described civic associations: the legions of charities, lodges, mutual aid societies, fraternal orders, civic leagues, and religious associations. According to the French political theorist, Americans formed associations "of a thousand kinds: religious, moral, serious, futile, general or restricted, enormous or diminutive." Nothing was more deserving of attention, he said, than these associations that dotted the United States' unique civic landscape. They were indispensable to the functioning of American democratic society, for they were the "necessary" foundation upon which "the progress of all the rest depends."[3]

Just as in Tocqueville's time, some of today's civic associations are large, some are small; some are local and some national; some serious and some not so serious—all serving a myriad of purposes. Many of the most prominent of today's voluntary associations, such as the Scouts, the Salvation Army, and the Parent-Teacher Association (PTA), serve important civic and charitable purposes. Others, from hobby groups to choral societies, simply provide a richer social life and a sense of neighborly regard.

The central point, however, is that these associations are voluntary and serve larger social purposes. They arise spontaneously from the aspirations and desires of free people. Civil society is thus an important space where citizens meet each other voluntarily, work toward common purposes, and learn the essential habits of collaboration and trust.

A healthy civil society yields by-products necessary for sustaining democracy. The institutions of civil society mediate between the individual on the one hand and the state and the market on the other, tempering the negative social tendencies associated with each. Civil society also builds social ties and obligations by weaving isolated individuals into the fabric of the larger group, tying separate individuals to purposes beyond their private interests.

Through simple acts of connection made in the realm of civil society, the private individual's perspective is widened and he or she learns what it means to be a citizen. Democracy finds its source of strength in habits of the heart. As Alexis de Tocqueville recognized, the reciprocal ties nourished in civil society are the wellspring of democratic life. Through civic participation, he said, "feelings and opinions are recruited, the heart is enlarged, and the human mind is developed."[4]

Civil Society and Economic Associations

Some argue that civil society must include the economic market within its conceptual boundaries. The economic realm of society is, after all, a voluntary and spontaneous order. Much like civil society, it is a sphere of human exchange that enjoys considerable freedom from government control. The market also overlaps with civil society in its function as a transmitter of ideas and intellectual goods.

However, while similar in some ways to the market, civil society runs on a different set of impulses. It operates, not like government, on the basis of compulsion, nor like the market, on the basis of competition or the profit motive. Though in many ways private, civil society self-consciously serves public purposes as it calls people beyond the minimalist obligations of the law and the narrow self-interest of the market's bottom line to a higher plane of social cooperation and generosity.

As we will see again and again, the subject of the modern economy and its relationship to civil society unavoidably arises. Alan Wolfe, one of the most prominent theoretical contributors to the civil society argument, has effectively raised to new levels of concern the matter of modern capitalism's corrosive effects on the sphere of civil society and its bonds of loyalty, friendship, and trust.

The difficulty in finding the exact place of the economic realm in relationship to civil society demonstrates the challenge of establishing broadly shared boundaries and definitions. One could argue, for example, that civil society must include some forms of economic activity, while perhaps excluding other forms.

As used by Tocqueville, civil society appears to possess boundaries of scale as well as scope. The term *civil society* frequently connotes the idea of local community and small-scale associations. Tocqueville spoke frequently and fondly of the idea of local "township" because it captured a great deal of freedom for the individual but also cultivated attachment to the interests of others. To Tocqueville, civil society fostered an ethic of cooperation, not merely unfettered competition.

Tocqueville wrote that the citizen is attached to his township because "the well-being it affords secures his affection; and its welfare is the aim of his ambition and of his future exertions."[5] It is through this bond of personal attachment and significance that the individual is rendered more willing to act on behalf of his fellows, to "sacrifice some of his private interests to save the rest." Self-interest becomes self-interest "rightly understood" when it is moderated by human cooperation and tethered by virtue.

Civil society, therefore, might include the economies of the local grocer, dentist, and shopkeeper, but probably not the international corporate conglomerate. While the local trades possess personal loyalties and membership—local merchants usually are woven into the social fabric of the community as active and permanent members of civic life—by contrast, large corporate interests find it nearly impossible, by virtue of their scale, ownership, and function, to permit local loyalties to affect the bottom line.

Civil Society and Political Associations

If the term *civil society* does not apply predominantly to economic interests and activity, neither does it encompass political interests. Recently politicians, policy activists, and political interest groups have rediscovered the notion of civil society, and their interest is certainly welcome. To a large extent, public debate in America takes shape through the political process. However, it is very doubtful that the reconstruction of civic order will be led by politicians or political lobbies.

A healthy political system is more dependent upon a strong civil society than it is capable of creating it. Healthy civic life directly nourishes a robust democracy. As Tocqueville saw it, civic customs bind the nation together and, in so doing, make important political contributions. Civil associations, he said, facilitate political associations.

But few believe politics can cure a weakened civil society. Says Robert Royal of the American Unum Project, "Barring a truly great spirit in the White House—someone like Lincoln, who would understand the shape and limits of what the state can do to encourage a healthy civil society—we must look elsewhere for moral and civic reconstruction." Civil society is not mostly about politics and it is not, according to Royal, about "democratic machinery or the well-managed bureaucratic state." "Civil society," he says, "is precisely a human order that is larger and richer than the state."[6]

While the civil society debate frequently includes discussion of such problems as declining voter participation, flawed public debate, and political corruption, the institutions and functions of civil society must not be understood primarily in relationship to the political realm. In many ways, civil society entails activity that is pre-political or that transcends politics. In the well-ordered society, politics plays a peripheral, not central, role in the lives of the people.

Today, as part of the outgrowth of civil society, many citizens are discovering ways to improve their world by turning away from what Chris Gates of the National Civic Leagues calls big "P" politics of conventional electoral activity to the small "p" politics of organizing neighborhoods and communities. In a very real sense, Americans see these small-scale and local forms of engagement in civic action as the means for taking back a public agenda that was largely lost to politicians and government managers.

Clearly, Tocqueville did not intend to confuse civic associations with political factions and interest groups. If modern political action organizations were included in the definition of civil society, the United States would be one of the most civically well-endowed societies in history. In recent decades, Americans have joined political organizations in record numbers. They may not turn out on election day, but they have certainly attempted through grassroots organizations to keep a watchful eye on their interests.

Mass membership organizations such as the American Association of Retired People (AARP), the Sierra Club, the National Rifle Association (NRA), or the Christian Coalition may have legitimate and important political roles, but they do not directly or primarily serve civic purposes. Harvard professor and civil society expert Robert Putnam places such groups in a "tertiary" category of associations because for most members, "the only act of membership consists in writing a check for dues or perhaps occasionally reading a newsletter." For associational membership to be considered a form of social capital, he argues, it must contribute to increased social trust. This trust, however, cannot be achieved when members of an organization never meet one another.[7]

To take this argument one important final step farther, civil society is not merely about economic, social, or political associations—the call to civil society involves much more than an invitation to join for the sake of joining. If civil society is no more than a morally neutral term to describe the realm of voluntary human associations, organizations like the Mafia, militias, and racist enclaves must, against our better judgment, be included within the scope of this definition.

Civil Society as Incubator of Citizenship

If civil society is not mostly about economics, politics, or the state, it *is* mostly about the character and qualities of citizenship. It is about the individual in civic association with his fellows. The citizen in civil society is not a political subject, a client, or a marketplace customer. The citizen is, instead, an inhabitant of a neighborhood, town, city, or state with all the rights and reciprocal obligations inherent to those relationships. The key ingredient in citizenship is social sympathy and regard for others and for the common good. Though citizenship certainly entails advancing private wants and interests, the citizen advances his interests through collaboration, which takes into account the well-being of others.

When people reach for the language of civil society, they typically do so to express the hopes and desires of the individual as citizen, not as client or consumer. Civil society advocates call for greater social trust and collaboration, broader civic participation, stronger social institutions, deeper loyalties to legitimate authority in society, and a willingness to yield to the claims of community for the sake of the common good. These are the concerns and objectives of citizens.

Civil society, whether acknowledged or not, is an inherently moral term that implies the existence of social and moral obligations that exist independent of the individual and operate upon him. The term not only points to purposes beyond the private self, it directs the individual to specifically positive social ends. Civil society, therefore, unavoidably touches upon matters of philosophy, morality, culture, and even religion.

Civil society involves a new way of thinking and talking about this world. It dwells less on government, raises more doubts about the magic of unfettered markets as a social panacea, and expresses far more interest in the civic sector of "little platoons," voluntary associations, and functional neighborhoods.

Different Views of the Movement

Demarcating the many schools of opinion and projects that aim to strengthen civil society is just as difficult as defining the term. Scores of new organizations have arisen to promote various aspects of civil society, and many older institutions, from policy think tanks to universities to charities, have enlisted the term to better define and promote their work.

Civil society has attracted adherents from across the entire political spectrum: progovernment, antigovernment; promarket, antimarket; from neocons and cultural conservatives to neoliberals and communitarians. On the one hand, this near universal embrace of civil society may signal an unprecedented search for a renewed consensus over shared ends in society. On the other hand, civil society may become so vacuous a term that it leaves the debate largely unchanged, locked within the existing confines of liberal individualism, whose core assumption is that society exists primarily to offer individuals expanded moral or market choices under a neutral government, not to serve any understanding of the common good.

Civil society, rightly understood, directly challenges the political status quo, taking issue both with the uncivil conduct of politics and the assumptions that have governed the two parties for decades. Despite a political debate that still frequently lurches toward rancor, partisans from across the political spectrum now extol the concept. Half a dozen major national commissions and councils now exist to study the problem of incivility, and have attracted leaders ranging from centrist Bill Bradley to conservative Bill Bennett to liberal former Congresswoman Patricia Schroeder.

From the podium of the National Press Club, retiring Senator Bill Bradley calls Americans to help recover civil society, without which, he says, the American system "is not stable and cannot provide support for a vital America." The "familiar ruts" of the American debate, he adds, like a preoccupation with either the government or the market, are not enough to create and sustain civilization. Instead, the nation needs a "healthy robust civic sector," where "the bonds of community can flourish." But, Bradley continues, echoing the central thesis of the civil society movement, this civic sector—this third leg of the American system—is in trouble. "[L]ike fish floating on the surface of a polluted river, the networks of voluntary associations in America seem to be dying."[8] Suddenly, the prosaic world of civic participation, family dinners, PTA meetings, and Youth Soccer has taken on profound social significance, and phrases like Robert Putnam's "bowling alone," which describe the intense individualism of the modern-day United States, have entered the cultural parlance.

From the same platform, former Education Secretary Bill Bennett announces the creation of a National Commission on Civic Renewal to study the problem, and asks plaintively, "[W]hy, when we have so much material wealth, are Americans so cynical, so distressed, so angry with each other, so untrusting, so ticked off about so many things? Why, when so many things are so good, do we feel so bad?" Why the rudeness, litigiousness, increased stress, drugs, and suicide, he wonders.[9]

From Independence Hall in Philadelphia, Retired General Colin Powell calls together the nation's top philanthropic, corporate, and civic leaders to organize a new volunteer army to confront at-risk children and youth in the communities of the United States. Joined by the current and all former presidents or their spouses, half the state governors, and dozens of mayors, the former general announces his effort to "rescue" two million at-risk kids by the year 2000 through volunteerism and private sector charity.[10]

The idea of civil society appears to have arrived with all the hoopla of the Great Society initiatives of the sixties and seventies, the supply side revolution of the eighties, and the devolution initiatives of the nineties. Civil society is touted as the latest wonder drug—a social Prozac—to treat a host of debilitating problems from fragmenting families to the underclass to a decline in civic engagement.

Many observers are not sure whether to dismiss the movement or embrace it. Some see it as little more than the misplaced angst of a privileged dual-career class, or the latest cultural convulsions of a bulging baby boom generation finally coming of age. Like a pig moving through a python, they think, this generation has progressed predictably through the life cycle and now views with distaste the cultural license it helped foment. To this generation that once rebelled against authority but now carries the responsibility for society on its own shoulders, the once reviled fifties don't seem so bad after all.

Others do not see the civil society debate as a promising new direction at all but rather as a diversion from the hard work of achieving economic justice for the disadvantaged. For them, civil society is a convenient justification for the government to abandon the underclass. These critics note that the ostensibly moral embrace of civil society conveniently coincides with budget-cutting priorities.

Critics are divided over whether to view the phenomenon as another intellectual fad that will follow the familiar pattern of trendy public ideas, in accordance with which it will surface, briefly scintillate, then just as surely slip off the United States' social screen. The provocative political talk show host, John McLaughlin, asks his panelists whether civil society is just another fad? In a word, yes, they say.

Not so, says *Washington Post* columnist E. J. Dionne, a frequent observer and occasional contributor to the civil society debate. The civil society debate "is not a flash in the pan," he says, because it responds to "problems inherent in other ideas" that have been competing for the attention of Americans. Its rise and continued popularity is explained, he insists, by three developments with deep roots. One is a movement among thinkers on the left and right to "reflect on the failures of their respective sides and face evidence that may be inconvenient to their arguments." The second is a widespread sense that changes in the economy and in the organization of work, family, and neighborhood have outpaced older forms of civic and associational life. The third factor that will ensure the continued popularity of civil society, Dionne maintains, is "the impact of an anti-government mood that has been part of American life since the 1970s."[11]

Certainly there are reasons to be skeptical. In contemporary American society enthusiasm for "paradigmatic shifts" is usually as big as the shifts are brief. For example, an instant sense of expectation was raised previously with such terms as "empowerment," "reinventing government," "public-private partnerships," and more recently, "the new citizenship." Social historian Gertrude Himmelfarb, a substantial contributor to the civil society debate, warns that civil society risks becoming just another mantra—a trendy term expressing merely a superficial desire, passing like previous social and political fads as quickly as it arrived.[12]

Whether the movement toward civil society represents a Copernican shift carrying with it dramatic promise, or whether it proves to be little more than a momentary mood swing and a minor correction of course for our widespread cultural extravagance, or something in between, remains to be seen. Nevertheless, most will acknowledge that new and important developments are under way.

The current civil society debate shows a great deal of promise despite its potential limits. Contrary to the objections of many pessimists and skeptics in this discussion, unprecedented efforts are being made to renew the social realm. The social landscape is coming alive with new movements to recover character, ethics, sexual responsibility, fatherhood, marriage, and a less corrupt popular culture.

Thanks to the arrival of the civil society debate the public conversation about values has also changed for the better, shifting significantly from the language of personal rights to that of social responsibility. Instead of concentrating exclusively on individual fulfillment, the conversation now focuses on community well-being; instead of the "Whose values?" language of moral relativism, people increasingly speak the "our values" language of common ground. This is a new and potentially durable development that, even five years ago, could not be clearly discerned.

Not all welcome the arrival of the civil society debate, as mentioned, much less view it as a social elixir. In fact, some observers from both ends of the political spectrum hope the issue proves to be the short-lived fad its skeptics predict it will be.

The Left: Civil Society as Social Reaction

Voices on the left dismiss the movement as repressive or reactionary. Feminist author Camile Paglia believes that the entire civil society debate is an attempt to restrain discourse and stifle dissent. Rather than viewing the movement as an attempt by citizens to regain direction in a society careening out of control, Paglia takes the opposite view. She sees it as a last-ditch attempt by an old guard establishment to retain control of the social debate in the United States.[13]

Jean Cohen, an academic adviser to the National Commission on Civic

Renewal, contends that the entire debate over civil society, with its focus on the alleged decline of intermediary bodies is "theoretically impoverished and politically suspect." Cohen maintains that this conceptualization of civil society, which nearly everyone now "equates with traditional forms of voluntary associations (including 'the' family)," when combined with the discourse of civic and moral decline, "undermines democracy instead of making it work, threatens personal liberty instead of enhancing it, and blocks social justice and social solidarity instead of furthering them." Cohen criticizes conservatives in the debate for assuming that "we can have a vital, well-integrated, and just civil society without states guaranteeing that universalistic egalitarian principles inform social policy."[14]

For many feminists, according to Alan Wolfe, "the whole idea that civil society is in decline can be interpreted as part of the backlash against women's entry into the workforce, since it was women historically who assumed the burdens of family and communal life." Feminists are not alone, however, in this critique, says Wolfe. In many ways, he says, the response of feminists only mirrors that of others who are prepared to defend "modernity against nostalgia." Civil society, in other words, appears to be a backlash against the great control individuals have gained over their lives since the 1950s. Wolfe is among those who believe that a revival of civil society is required, not in order to reject modernity, but "to complete its trajectory." He maintains that civil society in today's world will be found in the workplace, in cyberspace, and in forms of political organization, and that we should resist the yearning for older forms of civic association.[15]

Other voices on the left dismiss it as a nostalgic movement of those who long for an imaginary golden age of "father knows best" traditionalism and small-town Norman Rockwell parochialism. Their message is basically, "Get real! If that world ever actually existed, it certainly isn't worth defending, much less recovering."

Jean Bethke Elshtain, a leading theoretician in the civil society movement and one of its most powerful defenders, says that "The Accusation of Nostalgia" is one of the most common charges against civil society that is "indiscriminately shot skyward." According to Elshtain, civil society's critics view the current debate as "at best a big evasion, at worst, a pernicious invitation to triumphant localism." Elshtain, like most civil society advocates, is quick to point out that the federal government sometimes is needed to override localism and that a robust civil society "isn't a cure-all and never was." But, she adds, the real nostalgia in the debate is felt among those who yearn for an unquestioned "triumphant progressivism" that stubbornly refuses to accept the fact that "the federal-government-centered solutions don't solve all problems or even, more disturbingly, that not all of our problems are fixable."[16]

Much of the nostalgia accusation appears tied directly to assumptions about the role of the federal government in guaranteeing certain social conditions for all Americans. Government can either help or hinder, says Elshtain, but the core tasks of democracy falls to "the overlapping, plural associations of civic life in which citizens build and pass on those formative institutions—families, schools, churches, unions, and all the rest, including state and local governments—without which there is not democratic culture and, indeed, nothing for the federal government to either correct or curb or serve."[17]

This reaction by "progressives" to talk of civic virtue and local voluntary associations fits a well established pattern. The progressive drive of the twentieth century, as scores of conservative civil society advocates allege, was animated by suspicion of the very private, voluntary associations civil society theorists are now trying to revive. These associations were dismissed by progressives as regressive and reactionary enclaves that had to be brought under the enlightened supervision of the bureaucratic state.

James Morone, writing in the liberal journal *American Prospect*, adds another criticism often heard coming from the left. Morone blasts the civil society movement as a familiar moralistic reflex that stands in "a long, unhappy American political tradition." The moral diagnosis, he says, "is wrong and its political consequences are pernicious." Moralizing "divides Americans into a righteous 'us' and a malevolent 'them,'" he says.[18]

Morone worries that civil society talk replaces discussion of the cold, hard facts of declining economic prospects for American workers and the poor with homilies about private virtue and "blame the victim" theories. Morone alleges that "when economic and social problems are transformed into declining moral standards, the hunt is on for immoral people who threaten the public good."[19]

The Right: Civil Society as Political Distraction

The civil society movement's critics are not all on the left. If liberals worry that civil society abandons public action, some conservatives fear the opposite. Some on the right can be heard quietly voicing the concern that the civil society movement distracts from the far more important work of dismantling the welfare state, which, according to these detractors, is the primary source of the social decay now alarming many civil society advocates. Reflecting the criticisms of many of his conservative colleagues,

David Frum worries that talk of renewing civic community is taking the fighting spirit out of the antigovernment revolution. According to Frum, the federal government's massive welfare machine constitutes "a colossal lure tempting citizens to reckless behavior."[20]

To libertarian conservatives, civil society basically means going soft. David Brooks of the conservative *Weekly Standard* notes disapprovingly the shift away from the conservative ideology of the Reagan years, which celebrated such virtues of the entrepreneur as audacity, high ambition, and self-sufficiency. The virtues held up by civil society conservatives, he maintains, are not those of the rugged individualist but the quieter and softer virtues of the communitarian: fairness, caring, responsibility, respect, and trustworthiness.[21]

Other more traditional conservatives like Gertrude Himmelfarb believe civil society virtues are too soft and ungrounded in another way. In stark contrast to civil society critics on the left, Himmelfarb maintains that civil society invokes too few references to "morality and moral sanctions without any reference to one of its most important institutions, the churches." The function of civil society, she says, is "to encourage moral behavior and discourage—which is to say stigmatize—immoral behavior." For civil society to carry out these functions, it must be "a tougher civil society," promoting "vigorous virtues" such as shame.

In a revealing indicator of the potential implications for existing political coalitions, the criticism of the libertarian right is frequently similar to that of the left. David Brooks responds to the civil society movement's emphasis on restoring community bonds and local authority with a question Paglia, the feminist liberal, could have asked: "Do I want local busybodies with piddling township posts exercising their petty powers by looking into my affairs?"[22] Libertarians on the left and the right alike sense in the civil society movement a challenge to their expansive views of freedom from social authority.

What does all of this mean for the future of democratic governance? It may be too early to tell. Naturally, civil society is not about to cancel out existing ideological nostrums—the abundance of polarizing public issues will see to that. Nevertheless, the civil society debate is likely to represent some challenge to existing left-right coalitions, each of which has an "order" wing and a "freedom" wing.

For some, civil society will simply be seen as a means of cleaning up politics. For others, it offers the framework for transcending politics altogether. Bill Bennett captured this sentiment this way: "Society places far too much hope in politics to solve moral, cultural and spiritual afflictions."

We should take a step back from politicization, he says, think about who we are, and make adjustments in our behavior, "because at the end of the day, behavior follows attitude, and attitude follows belief."[23]

Conclusion

Instead of following the familiar path from obscurity to intellectual and political popularity and then back to oblivion, the nation's interest in civil society may signal a unique chance for the kind of renewal that growing majorities of Americans say they want. What else can explain the sheer range of civil society adherents, from grassroots leaders to intellectuals and public leaders?

From across the political spectrum, a chorus of concern can be heard warning that social institutions, the foundation of a free and democratic society, are in urgent need of repair. Bipartisan experts acknowledge that society cannot thrive, perhaps not even survive, without strong social institutions, a vibrant moral order, and an active, engaged citizenry. For this reason alone, civil society is worth defending and developing.

If the civil society movement proves to be more than a fad it may do so because it did not originate in official political circles. In fact, the concept only recently entered political debate after years of germination in spheres well beyond the beltway. The most consequential and durable social change in America tends to bubble up from below and is well beyond the din of the partisan Washington debate. The civil society movement possesses many of the characteristics of a durable movement. From its inception, it has percolated in grassroots citizens groups, animated the minds of a new generation of social movement architects, and coalesced a diverse group of public intellectuals who have grown weary of shopworn ideologies.

For this reason, the civil society phenomenon should not be examined through normal political or journalistic lenses. Its leading advocates are public figures who are among the least inclined to exploit its arrival in order to perpetuate an existing public debate that has grown tedious and sterile.

Also unique about the civil society debate is its international scope, which reflects a global preoccupation with the need to sustain and give new birth to nongovernmental institutions, especially in the formerly totalitarian east block. Although the form of civil society developed in eastern Europe cannot be transported directly to the American situation, the fact that the movement proved revolutionary in that section of the world shows that it is not merely a fad among American intellectuals and policy activists.

Finally, the civil society conversation is unique because it is not primarily focused, like most social movements, merely on reforming government. The leading voices in the civil society debate are rarely heard fulminating over flawed public policies. On the left and right of center, these leaders agree that policy reforms are important but see them as dramatically insufficient for social renewal. The focus of civil society advocates is instead on the state of community and culture.

For these reasons and more, the civil society movement must be encouraged and supported. The ideas of the movement, as they are currently formulated, are insufficient for wider cultural renewal, but by setting more ambitious goals, namely the recovery of moral and ethical certainties, the civil society movement could very well lead to broad-based cultural rebirth.

Notes

1. See Theda Skocpol, "Civic Engagement in American Democracy" (testimony prepared for the National Commission on Civic Renewal, Washington, D.C.).

2. Michael Walzer, "The Idea of Civil Society," *Kettering Review,* Winter 1997, 8.

3. Alexis de Tocqueville, *Democracy in America*, trans. Henry Reeve (New York, 1954), 2:114, 129.

4. See Alexis de Tocqueville, *Democracy in America*, vols. 1, 2 (New York: Alfred A. Knopf, Inc., 1945).

5. Alexis de Tocqueville, *Democracy in America*, ed. Philips Bradley (New York: Vintage, 1990), 68.

6. Robert Royal, "Reinventing the American People," *The American Character*, published by the Ethics and Public Policy Center, Fall 1993, 3.

7. Robert D. Putnam, "Bowling Alone: America's Declining Social Capital," *Journal of Democracy* 6 (January 1995), 71.

8. Senator Bill Bradley, "America's Challenge: Revitalizing our National Community," National Press Club, *Federal News Service,* 9 February 1995, 3.

9. William J. Bennett, "Moral Decline and the Fraying Social Fabric," National Press Club, *Federal News Service*, 18 November 1996, 2.

10. Mark Stricherz, "Any Volunteers?" *The New Republic*, 5 January 1998, 12.

11. E. J. Dionne, "Why Civil Society? Why Now?" *The Brookings Review*, Fall 1997, 6.

12. Gertrude Himmelfarb, "Second Thoughts on Civil Society," *The Weekly Standard*, 9 September 1996.

13. Deb Reichmann, "Let's Be Civil," *Associated Press*, 5 February 1997.

14. Jean L. Cohen, "America's Civil Society Talk," from Paper no. 6, an unpublished paper presented to the National Commission on Civic Renewal.

Part Two

Civil Society's Component Parts

Chapter 3

Social Institutions, Social Regression

Introduction:
Something is Wrong with Society

Nothing drives the debate about American culture and society more than a concern for the basic health of the nation's core institutions. It is the sense, as E. J. Dionne put it, that "contemporary society is missing something." Words like fraying, fracturing, and fragmenting are typically used to describe this phenomenon, and they portray a culture torn apart.

"What chills me about the future," writes one citizen, "is a general sense of the transformation of our society from one that strengthens the bonds between people to one that is, at best, indifferent to them." There is "a sense of an inevitable *fraying* of the net of connections between people at many critical intersections, of which the marital knot is only one. Each fraying accelerates another. A break in one connection, such as attachment between parents and children, puts pressure on other connections [such as] marriage." With enough fraying, individuals lose "that sense of membership in the larger community which grows best when it is grounded in membership in a small one."

Journalist Kenneth Woodward of *Newsweek* laments,

[A]ll of the core institutions that once transmitted moral education are in disrepair. The family has *fractured*; neighborhoods have disappeared or turned surly; many schools can barely educate, and even many churches wonder what to teach.[1]

"The historic idea of a unifying American identity is now in peril," worries author Arthur Schlesinger, Jr. This, he says, leads to "the *frag-mentation*, resegregation, and tribalization of American life"[2] (emphasis added).

Fraying communities, fractured families, a fragmenting nation—journalists, scholars, and citizens alike seem to agree that American society is, in too many ways, pulling apart at the seams.

The Paradox of Progress

Americans are having to come to terms with the paradoxes of their own progress. The United States, the unrivaled democratic, economic, and military leader of the world, increasingly leads the globe in many categories of social dysfunction, including crime, family breakdown, and teen pregnancy. The nation's problems of child poverty and urban blight stand out as ugly scars, especially when compared to other less prosperous western industrial nations.

These internal social problems continue to grow, even in the face of astonishing scientific advancement, technological innovation, and vast economic improvement. The United States' inability to generate social gains commensurate to its economic progress and the realization that for the first time in the nation's history succeeding generations may actually do worse than those that went before have eroded national self-confidence. Throughout their history, Americans have had a high sense of purpose and have been sustained by the belief that in their many successes, they had much to offer the world. Yet today, while most nations admire America's technical and material successes, few are rushing to adopt America's culture.

Georgie Anne Geyer, a lifelong foreign correspondent, and author of the recent book *Americans No More: The Death of Citizenship*, believes that the United States' global reputation will suffer from its internal decay. She describes the American paradox—the West has triumphed over totalitarianism, the United States enjoys relative peace and prosperity, and democratic capitalism is sweeping the world, yet the world looks at American society and culture with deepening dismay.[3]

The United States may have proven to be good at everything except building a sustainable society. Americans have not matched the astonishing accomplishments of their hands and heads with a comparable development of their hearts. Robert Bellah, editor of *Habits of the Heart*, maintains that we have not learned to unite our technological achievement with a coherent pattern of living together.

Social Regression

The concept of societal decline is difficult to capture, and even harder for many to admit. Some stiffly resist the very thought of "decline" and consider it inadmissible in a society that is determined to approach the future with optimism. For example, Alan Wolfe demands that the one term in the discussion of civil society that ought to be obsolete is "the notion of decline." Such talk, he maintains, only feeds a forbidden nostalgia. We should "abolish from our language dealing with social institutions and practices," he says, a way of thinking which compares the present with some "mythical past as well as some hopeful future."[4]

Terms like *social recession* or *social deficits* are frequently used, but even they fail to capture the erosion of social well-being that has spawned a civil society movement. Finding the right descriptive terminology is difficult because of a broad ignorance of the workings of society, which has been fed by a public debate that has for decades focused almost exclusively on the machinery of government, public policy reforms, and economics.

American society has done a good job of maintaining a consciousness of individual rights. It has done such a poor job of preserving the vitality and moral authority of its institutions that few individuals can even describe the basic functions of society and its various sectors. Few would be able to clearly describe any sphere separate from the state or the economy. For most, the only real components of our nation worth talking about are the private sector consisting mostly of the economic marketplace, and the public sector consisting mostly of the state.

Civil society, or the nation's social sector, has its own characteristics, and its own strengths and weaknesses. It is a separate and important sphere, often referred to as the third sector or the third leg of a three-legged stool. To illustrate this, let us imagine ourselves to be a group of physicians around an examination table assigned to evaluate several patients. The first patient brought before us is the national economy. Our evaluation points to several sector and regional weaknesses. Some of us are concerned about wage stagnation and a growing gap between the "haves" and "have-nots," but the patient looks reasonably healthy. The economy is approaching full employment, so much so that in many areas of the country there is severe competition for available workers.

The second patient brought to the examination table is the body politic, or the state of our democratic union. Here our examination points to strong antipathy among the people toward their government, especially the central government. This antipathy occasionally spills over into angry populism and radical militia movements. We worry about a lack of accountability and responsiveness within mainstream politics to basic problems. But as we examine the entire body, we do not see anything that would represent a grave or immediate threat to the union—nothing approaching advanced cancer.

Then the third patient is brought before us and laid on the examination table. This patient is American society and culture. As we carefully examine this patient's vital organs, we detect acute illnesses and worrisome malignancies.

Here, the picture becomes harder to confront, because society is essentially about each of us as Americans. Unlike our economic and political maladies, worsening social conditions do not readily lend themselves to blame theories or scapegoating. They represent values and personal choices made by millions of Americans. Social regression describes the condition of our own private lives as well as our public lives and institutions. If we are to take seriously our own feedback to national pollsters, we paint a portrait of ourselves as a nation made up of citizens incapable of self-governance.

Social regression is, above all, about a breakdown of social institutions, especially of the family. A breakdown of such primary social institutions erodes the psychological and spiritual strength necessary for a free society and a democracy to function properly. Many Americans are averse to institutions, preferring solitary individualism instead, but it is in and through strong institutions that self-governing individuals are made.

Social regression reflects the collapse of public manners and civility, which in many communities has produced a visible nervousness and a palpable fear. Terms once used to describe environmental degradation are now applied to the culture. Phrases like "toxic society" and "hole in the moral ozone" speak to the corrosive affects modernism has had on the nation's moral and social ecology.

Finally, like social progress, social regression develops a cumulative momentum. It has dynamics of its own that may or may not be affected significantly by government policy, technological advances, or an expanding economy.

The Limits of Social Policy

The growing realization of the limits of government and economics reflected in the civil society debate may eventually shake conventional approaches to social problem solving. For much of the twentieth century, social analysts and planners placed an almost unbounded faith in technical expertise, public policy refinements, and improved economic incentives to solve social problems. Unfortunately, renewing society is not as simple as reforming impersonal systems and structures. Society is more organic and requires solutions that are more complex than building or repairing infrastructure.

Much of the current public debate centers on the actions of government. The designers of the modern welfare state sincerely and earnestly believed they could eliminate poverty, reduce unemployment, and achieve racial justice through government intervention. Though the public debate has shifted recently toward a more critical view, it still revolves around the role of government: Some still demand government do more, others demand it do less, and still others simply want things done differently. These different schools of "governmentalism" have much in common. Each prescribes structural changes to combat social and moral problems, hoping that when government is properly configured and the economy freed, forces of renewal will gush into America's homes, schools, and neighborhoods.

There is little evidence, however, that changes in government structure or activity will make more than a dent in the most costly and consequential social problems. Policy changes have undeniably affected some social problems such as crime and safety. Still, it is difficult to imagine significant breakthroughs coming from federal or state lawmakers to reduce teen pregnancy, family fragmentation, dependence on drugs, or the decline in manners and morals. Reversing social pathologies will require changing attitudes and behaviors, which is tied to curbing cultural excesses and renewing moral foundations.

A recent report by the Carnegie Council on Adolescent Development shows the limits of government social policy. Of the 19 million children in the United States between the ages of 10 and 14, two-thirds has tried alcohol, a third has used drugs, and another third has contemplated suicide. Certainly government will be called upon to address these issues. But can a failure in federal drug policy really account for so many kids using drugs? Or, when one in 40 Americans over the age of 18 is on probation, parole, or in prison, are joblessness, racism, or lenient deterrents really to blame? When nearly 40 percent of American kids fall asleep in a household without their biological father, and one in every two will spend some time before the age of 18 in a father-absent household, can these troubling facts really be laid entirely at the feet of an overindulgent welfare system?

The familiar and convenient response of blaming government is not entirely groundless. However, it is dramatically insufficient to explain the behavior of many Americans, especially the young. Many adolescent girls have sex early, frequently with older men, because they lack a father's love. Girls have babies while still children themselves because this is the only form of companionship they know. Young men turn to violence and predatory behavior because of a subconscious rage against the father who was never there to show them how to be a man. Lives are often disordered because of moral and behavioral factors that lie largely well beyond the reach of policymakers.

When public debate does not concentrate on government, it focuses on economics. For many decades now, society has measured its general well-being by economic indices like the gross national product. It is tempting to assume economic progress can pull social progress in its wake, or that prosperity will ensure strong and resilient social institutions.

Unfortunately, these assumptions collapse in the face of mounting social data. Social problems have become like uncoupled freight cars, severed from the engine of economic success. Researchers at Fordham University have found a startling 20-year-long trend showing that the freight train of economic progress no longer pulls along with it social progress as it once did. In fact, they're moving on separate tracks and in opposite directions—with economic progress moving up, social trends moving down, like "a crocodile's jaws opening."[5]

Newspapers from October 1996 captured this disheartening picture as separate stories on the same day reported the height of U.S. economic achievements and the depths of the nation's social conditions. In the first story, the Dow Jones Industrial Average soared to a record 6,000 (it has since gone much higher), while in the second the nation's social well-being was reported to have fallen to its lowest point in almost 25 years. Ominously, four of the most serious problems facing the nation's children—child abuse, teen suicide, drug abuse, and the high school dropout rate—had worsened.

Though government and economics play important roles in society and must be taken seriously, social problems are more complex, and often require social, not political, solutions. The nation's social deficit is directly linked to nongovernmental factors like the collapse of character-forming institutions, the weakening of social norms, and the psychological fallout from family disintegration.

There are signs that players on both sides of the public debate are beginning to realize that governmental tinkering and economic progress produce, at best, minor changes at the margins of these fundamental and intractable social problems. On the political left, President Clinton has boldly proclaimed that "the era of big government is over," acknowledging that government activism is often powerless to raise individuals out of poverty and despair. On the political right, many have come to doubt that simply eliminating government programs or relaxing market constraints can solve the nation's social problems.

None of these measures, by themselves, transform the person as a moral decision maker. They seek to free up, or empower the individual, without overcoming the limits of individual autonomy or restoring the person to moral community. As Jean Bethke Elshtain has said, " We have become so entranced by the notion that the self is merely the sum total of a person's choices that we have lost any moral framework for evaluating those choices."[6]

Boston University Professor Glenn Loury, a skeptic on the renewing powers of social policy, recently explained in testimony before Congress,

> People are not automata; their behavior in matters sexual may not be easily manipulated by changing their marginal tax rates or their recipiency status under welfare programs. It is my conviction that the problem of illegitimacy and family breakdown are, at base, cultural and moral problems, which require broad societal action in addition to legislative change.[7]

This breakthrough could forge new alliances around fresh strategies for revitalizing communities, where real solutions are waiting to be found. As Loury says:

> [I]n every community there are agencies of moral and cultural development which seek to shape the ways in which individuals conceive of their duties to themselves, of their obligations to each other, and of their responsibilities before God. These mainly, though not exclusively, religious institutions are the natural sources of legitimate moral teaching—indeed, the only sources.[8]

Community: The Reservoir of Social Capital

If neither governmental changes nor economic expansion by themselves will rejuvenate society, the United States must turn to the social sector for renewal.

The civil society movement, for many at least, operates on the assumption that democratic viability as well as continued economic prosperity depend on maintaining the moral vitality of the civic sector. The values necessary for the success of both economic and democratic life flower in the soil of vibrant communities and functional families. These institutions work together to temper individual interests, to cultivate bonds of affection among citizens, and to inspire loyalty toward the larger group.

Recent research by Robert Putnam of Harvard University, Francis Fukuyama of the Rand Corporation, and a number of other leading social scientists points to an unbreakable link between strong social institutions and the healthy function of both democratic government and the market economy. Putnam, whose research focused on the relationship of regional governments in Italy to robust civic life, found that democratic government is far more effective when surrounded by strong civic communities.[9]

Citizens in civic communities, Putnam says, "are helpful, respectful and trustful toward one another," in effect, taking upon themselves much of the work of democratic deliberation and consensus building. These individuals are bound together, not by rigidly enforced rules or "vertical relations of authority and dependency," says Putnam, but by "horizontal relations of reciprocity and cooperation."[10] Strong communities, in other words, are voluntary, consensual, and mutually, trustful.

Francis Fukuyama has looked at the role that trust and collaboration now play in empowering individuals to compete in a rapidly changing and interconnected global marketplace. Economic life, he says, is maintained by "moral bonds of social trust," an "unspoken, unwritten bond between fellow citizens that facilitates transactions, empowers individual creativity, and justifies collective action."[11] Fukuyama concludes that societies with strong bonds of social trust and collaboration will gain important advantages over those characterized by individual isolation and social fragmentation.

To succeed, market capitalism must be more than an arena of crass self-advancement pursued by utility maximizing individuals. Durable prosperity depends upon a vibrant moral and social order, not simply upon unfettered markets. Like the success of democracy, the success of capitalism depends upon a rich supply of social capital, including knowledge, aptitude, skills, and positive social habits. This social capital is vital in a postindustrial age where softer forms of human capital emerge as dramatically more important than hard capital assets such as factories, tools, and machines. Tragically, at the very time when American society needs social capital the most in order to compete in an unregulated, rapidly changing, global information economy, that capital has been severely depleted.

Trust

Few topics have generated more interest in the civil society debate than the subject of trust. Trust is widely viewed as both a core requirement of civic life and one of its chief by-products. People who do not trust their neighbors are less likely to cooperate and are more prone to conflict and litigation. Studies have not found a definitive cause for distrust, but most acknowledge that trust in other people is a major determinant in civic membership; basic civic habits and personal trust are causally linked.

Trust is a principle form of social capital. A nation's reserves of social capital can be drawn down just like its more tangible stock of economic capital. The phrase "living on borrowed capital" has been used to refer to the failure of one generation to renew and pass on to the next the social endowments it has inherited. Trust is delicately acquired and tenuously maintained over the course of generations based through the thousands of deeds carefully recorded by the human mind and rationally transferred to personal attitudes and actions. The result is a decline in what Fukuyama calls "spontaneous sociability," rooted in the loss of social trust. This decline portends worrisome consequences for a democratic society.

The absence of trust throughout society increases the transaction costs in the economy as elaborate efforts must be made by individuals and corporations to protect against fraud and deceit. When private transactions are no longer regulated by morality, the regulatory state that Tocqueville described as "absolute, minute, regular, provident and mild" inevitably emerges to fill the void.[12]

Both Putnam and Fukuyama emphasize the primacy of trust as a social good, because it is the glue that holds social life together and the lubricant that smooths social transactions. Trust is an intangible asset, preserved through unwritten and unspoken habits and customs. It is immeasurably consequential, difficult to build up, hard to preserve, costly to lose, and deeply challenging to replenish once depleted.

There are many reasons for declining trust. Frequently cited are political corruption, crime, economic dislocation, racial discrimination, and a lack of roots for a large segment of American society. Distrust can produce civic withdrawal, but so is the reverse also true: Uninvolvement in civic life can cause declining trust. Wendy Rahn, a political science professor at the University of Minnesota who has pioneered research into the causes and consequences of personal mistrust, contends that a lack of participation breeds suspicion and distrust, which in turn decreases people's sociability and community involvement. "This 'vicious cycle' results in communities being less well off and their inhabitants less satisfied both with their personal and public lives."[13]

Perhaps the most frequently identified factor in the loss of trust is the declining performance of government. For many years, large majorities of Americans have distrusted such powerful public institutions as the press, the government, and the courts. While in 1964, three quarters of the American people trusted the federal government all or most of the time, today, only one quarter trusts the government.[14]

Governmental inadequacies, however, represent only part of the picture. More recently, U. S. citizens have grown distrustful and suspicious of each other. Contrary to convenient myth, discontent is not confined to governmental malfeasance and feckless politicians. Rather, the decline in trust in government has tracked the collapse of personal trust. Though many blame politics for the cynicism and distrust in the United States, many social experts see the blame flowing in the opposite direction. According to University of Maryland political scientist Eric Uslaner, "The reason politics is behaving so badly is . . . the whole country is behaving badly."[15]

Just how untrusting Americans have become is one of the many topics of study and debate among civil society scholars. However, when the American people themselves are surveyed on the question of trust, little doubt remains that distrust is widespread. In a four-part series on the decline of trust in February 1996, reporters Richard Morin and Dan Balz presented the results of an extensive *Washington Post* social survey. The United States, they concluded, is becoming "a nation of suspicious strangers," and declining trust is the major reason for the loss of confidence in major institutions. According to Morin and Balz, "Every generation that has come of age since the 1950s has been more mistrusting of human nature." A transformation in outlook, they maintain, has "deeply corroded the nation's social and political life."[16]

Trust in fellow citizens has fallen precipitously over the past two decades. In 1994, only 34 percent of Americans told pollsters that they could trust people most of the time,[17] and according to recent polls, only 18 percent of graduating high school seniors agreed that most people can be trusted most of the time.[18]

The *Washington Post* series captured the decline of trust through the words and images of citizens themselves. "It's like living in the cave man age," says Michael Callecoat, 29, a self-employed contractor living in New Jersey with his wife and three-year-old daughter. "Nobody cares anymore. Nobody cares." Lesvia Hernandez, the 23-year-old manager of a retail store in Windsor, Connecticut, says, "They will no sooner run you down and run away than to spit in your face. I can't trust anyone. We aren't willing to trust other people, even people who live next door to us." She added that her mother's purse was stolen by her next-door neighbor.[19]

Family: The Incubator of Trust

Most civil society advocates believe that democracy more or less depends for its success upon those institutions that socialize infant individuals into adult citizens. At a time of social disintegration then, the central social task for older generations is to transform self-interested private individuals into public-spirited members of the community. Creating a good society made up of involved citizens requires healthy socializing institutions, starting with the family.

The late sociologist James Coleman used the term "social capital" to describe a range of personal strengths cultivated in the family, especially cooperation in working toward a common goal.[20] As we will see, social capital means different things to different people in the civil society debate. For Coleman, however, the term applied to qualities that were generated mostly by the family.

Social capital has many intangible characteristics. As inherently social and meaning-seeking creatures, human beings need membership, connection, and coherence in the context of community. When these needs are not met, society atrophies and individuals experience painful isolation and acute unease, a condition sociologist Emile Durkheim called "anomie."

There are many reasons people feel distant from each other, as discussed, including the uprooting effects of our increasingly fast-paced and anonymous society. Fear and distrust are also common, even rational, responses to the frequent offenses and even occasional assaults that are now nearly commonplace in the nation's public spaces. These other factors have played important roles in causing antisocial behavior, but many acknowledge that the leading culprit in American distrust and cynicism is the rupture of primary relationships within the family.

No human bond is more intimate or perceived by children to be more naturally durable than the parent-child relationship. Unlike more fragile social ties, the bonds of family are rooted in nature. An adult will be less trusting and cooperative if, as a child, he or she experienced a painful loss of trust in his own parent—the one person in whom he believed he could surely place his trust. Sadly, for many children growing up today in the United States, this betrayal occurs not once, but several times before adulthood. The nation's high divorce rate contributes to the cynicism and isolation of those injured by the family rupture.

It must be said that not all civil society scholars accept the importance of stable families. To some, family life represents the private realm that should lie beyond public scrutiny or debate. But it is simply not possible to discuss social institutions without focusing heavily on the family. Alexis de Tocqueville, the foremost observer of American democracy, believed that this basic institution is largely responsible for maintaining the democratic regime. The prerequisites of democracy—the habits of the heart, as Tocqueville put it—are nourished and transmitted from generation to generation through the family. Mediating associations are important, but even they draw important resources from the family.

Many civil society proponents, though certainly not all, believe that the unique socializing role of parents, both mothers and fathers, is paramount to the preservation of civil society. Human socialization occurs mostly through patterns of trust and interdependency that are developed within the family structure. Families cultivate a spirit of compromise, a capacity for trust and trustworthiness, a tendency toward helpfulness and empathy, and capability for self-restraint and respect for others.

Trust, as it turns out, is acquired in early childhood. According to Professor Wendy Rahn, "If the young are not growing up with a sense of generalized trust, there's really not any hope that they will really develop it." She maintains that trust diminishes with time and experience, and if it does not develop in the young, their capacity for trust will decline faster and farther than usual.[21]

The State of the Family Debate

Healthy families are the most indispensable institutions of civil society because they are the primary incubators of trust. The capacity of the human infant to grow into a caring citizen, capable of self-control and empathy toward others, is largely supplied through the child's early attachment to caring and competent parents. In bonding with the child, the parent ensures that "a strong, mutual, irrational, emotional attachment" is put in place between the child and the one who is "committed to the child's well-being and development, preferably for life."[22]

Family structure has been the focus of intense interest and sharp debate in political and intellectual circles for decades. The current debate was sparked, in large part, by Daniel Patrick Moynihan's 1965 study for the Johnson Administration, *The Negro Family: The Case for National Action*. The study issued dire warnings about the impact of the deteriorating black family on the African-American community.

Moynihan argued that

> a community that allows a large number of men to grow up in broken families, dominated by women, never acquiring any stable relationship to male authority, never acquiring any set of rational expectations about the future—that community asks for and gets chaos. Crime, violence, unrest, disorder—most particularly the furious, unrestrained lashing out at the whole social structure—that is not only to be expected; it is very near inevitable.[23]

Moynihan's fiery eloquence generated controversy well into the nineties, but his analysis also became a wellspring for a stream of debate linking social order to the health of the core social institutions that socialize young males.

Other major milestones in the family debate include: Charles Murray's 1984 book, *Losing Ground: American Social Policy, 1950-1980*; Bill Moyer's 1986 television documentary on family breakdown; William Galston's 1990 essay, "A Liberal-Democratic Case for the Two-Parent Family"; the 1991 National Commission on Children, chaired by Jay D. Rockefeller IV; Dan Quayle's "Murphy Brown" speech in 1992; Barbara Dafoe Whitehead's 1993 *Atlantic Monthly Magazine* essay, "Dan Quayle Was Right"; Charles Murray's 1993 newspaper column, "The Coming White Underclass"; and David Blankenhorn's 1995 book, *Fatherless America*.[24] Each of these landmark presentations took the American family debate to a higher level of awareness regarding the scale and consequences of disruption.

For many years, the family debate was regarded by many as more polarizing than constructive. Although the family has had strong intellectual and political support from across partisan lines, many believe the family has been used as an ideological club that sets back the serious work of forging a new national consensus in the broader cultural debate. Irving Kristol, for example, wrote in the fall of 1992 that family values are not a political issue, but are instead predominantly a religious and cultural issue. He added that many of the changes in family structure are side effects of affluence, not outgrowths of flawed policies.[25] Efforts to strengthen the family, therefore, should not be cast in narrowly partisan terms.

Though still occasionally rancorous and partisan, the public debate over the family has matured in recent years. The question of the family's preeminence in society and the inescapable importance of parents is largely settled within mainstream debate. Many across the political spectrum agree that the irreducible components of family include parents committed to the care and nurture of their children.

Scholars and commentators now routinely cite the large number of single-parent households, most lacking fathers, to explain numerous negative trends among children. Recently, the family debate has pinpointed the relationship of father absence to such specific social pathologies as crime, drug abuse, and teen pregnancy. Family sociologist David Popenoe, a leading figure in this debate, argues:

> [T]he decline in fatherhood is a major force behind many of the most disturbing problems that plague American society: crime and delinquency; premature sexuality and out-of-wedlock births to teenagers; deteriorating educational achievement; depression, substance abuse, and alienation among adolescents; and the growing number of women and children in poverty.[26]

Conflicting visions of the family will continue to generate important debate, especially over public policies, but now the arguments are mostly over means rather than ends. Policy and social science experts are now generally coalescing around the argument that family fragmentation is the chief contributor to many forms of maladjustment among children.

University of Maryland Professor Bill Galston, a leading shaper of this new bipartisan consensus on the family, states that there is more agreement than ever over the basic fact that "the family disintegration that we are currently experiencing—in some respects, at an accelerating pace—is harming our children. It is harming them deeply. It is harming them dreadfully."[27]

Galston, who was a domestic policy advisor to President Clinton during the president's first term, reports confidently that the "old debate is over. . . . There is no disagreement between the current President of the United States and the former Vice President of the United States, Dan Quayle, on the desirability of stable, intact, two-parent families." He adds, the new debate addresses "why we are so far from where we want to be, and how we can move closer to it." [28]

Galston also asks the question that is central to the civil society debate: What is required for a nation to make further progress on a proposition that enjoys the support of 83 percent of the American people? The answer to this question may be the civil society movement. Instead of hampering or replacing the family debate, the civil society movement has encouraged important discussion. As issues of trust and other core ingredients of citizenship continue to come to the fore, the family becomes seen as all important in raising civic-minded, trustful, and trustworthy citizens.

The Family and Civil Society

The more recent framework of civil society tends to examine the institutions of marriage and family in a new light and with a greater urgency than the debate of a decade ago. The family becomes seen as an indispensable seedbed of civic trust and thus is linked to social regeneration, not merely to ideological agendas.

Jean Bethke Elshtain, chair of the Council on Civil Society, maintains that there is a powerful reciprocal effect at work in the relationship between families and communities. Because the family is nested in "a wider network of social institutions, . . . civil society surrounds the family in a way that either helps to sustain, or helps to undermine, parental commitment and accomplishment."

Elshtain believes that

> Marriage and family are the most fundamental forms of civic association. We know that mothers and fathers are essential to the life of the child, the community, and the wider civil society. And we know that strong and perduring marriages—strong family stories if you will—preserve and protect some of our own most cherished democratic ideals: pluralism, plurality, our distinctiveness.[29]

Although interest in the family has always run high among conservative family policy advocates and right-leaning think tanks, it took the arrival of new institutional players to achieve progress both in the debate and in organizing new forms of cultural support for a pro-family agenda. The most notable contributor to these developments is the Institute for American Values, which has produced numerous books, publications, and conferences on the connection of marriage and the family to civil society. The institute and its allies cast the debate in nonpartisan terms and move beyond rhetoric to offer solutions.

The institute's Council on Families, cochaired by Elshtain and David Blankenhorn, has drawn together a diverse collection of family scholars from across the political spectrum to inform the debate with firm evidence from the social sciences, especially from sociological and cultural perspectives. Facts and arguments produced by this group have had considerable effect throughout America because of extensive media coverage.

The council has had an especially strong impact in heightening awareness of the importance of marriage. Its books and critical reports on the subject include one report entitled *Marriage in America*, which received broad coverage in the popular press. In the report, the council says the divorce revolution, with its steady displacement of the marriage culture with a culture of divorce and unwed parenthood, has been a destructive failure.

In detailing divorce's many negative effects on child well-being—abuse, neglect, psychological and behavioral disturbances, poverty, crime, and declining educational achievement—the report states that unless the decline in marriage is reversed, no other achievements will be powerful enough to reverse the negative trends in child well-being. Marriage is losing its meaning because it no longer embodies commitment and obligation to others, becoming reduced instead to a vehicle for the emotional fulfillment of adults. Failure to reverse the culture of divorce, the report argues, may result in "cultural suicide."[30]

The *Marriage in America* report includes five pages of recommendations to reclaim marital permanence, with applications for those who influence values, including clergy, social workers, employers, civic leaders, attorneys, judges involved in family law, entertainers, and, of course, policymakers.

In a subsequent and widely reported study, the council released information indicating that the vast majority of undergraduate marriage and family textbooks convey "a determinedly pessimistic view of marriage." The report added that most current textbooks, "both by what they say and, sometimes even more importantly, by the information they omit, repeatedly suggest that marriage is more a problem than a solution." [31]

Recent years have witnessed a dramatic rise in academic research focusing on the many benefits of marriage to adult health and well-being and to children. Public intellectuals, including David Popenoe, Maggie Gallagher, and Barbara Dafoe Whitehead, regularly make pro-marriage arguments before public audiences.

Numerous policy and advocacy groups have responded to improvements in the popular debate by advancing the renewal of marriage with greater confidence. Literature and data on marriage and divorce circulate widely, and an explosion of motivational books on building stronger marriages provides evidence of increasing popular interest in the subject.

Operating in tandem with, and often as an outgrowth of, this academic work has been a new grassroots movement to restore marriage. Leading the movement is Michael McManus, religious journalist and head of Marriage Savers, an organization that develops "community marriage policies" through cooperating church congregations. In his book, also called *Marriage Savers*, [32] McManus argues that with 90 percent of all marriages still taking place in churches and synagogues, these religious institutions can and must do more to improve the success rate of the unions they bless.

Through a marriage savers "covenant," religious and civic leaders agree to basic preparation requirements for couples seeking to be married in a community church. Couples are given extensive marriage counseling—consisting of a "relational inventory" and conflict resolution training—before the ceremony. They are then supported by older and stronger couples through the early years of their marriage. Although the movement remains young, McManus has documented how divorce rates have declined in dozens of communities where congregations have worked together to that end.

Marriage has been made a greater priority at a number of important institutions, such as the American Enterprise Institute, which long focused exclusively on economic policy concerns. The May/June 1996 edition of its magazine, *The American Enterprise*, entitled "It Takes a Marriage," was almost completely dedicated to the subject of renewing the institution, featuring many well-recognized voices on the issue.

A growing number of scholars points to a decline in cultural reinforcements for courtship and marriage. Leon Kass, writing in the *Public Interest*, says that we live in an utterly novel and unprecedented period in this regard. "Until what seems like only yesterday," he says, "young people were groomed for marriage, and the paths leading to it were culturally well set out, at least in rough outline." The young man was required to court or woo the young lady under conditions set by society. Today, Kass says, there are "no socially prescribed forms of conduct to help guide young men and women in the direction of matrimony." [33]

Kass describes a wide range of cultural influences that stack the deck against successful marriages. These social pressures include the sexual revolution, which largely destroyed the mystery and awe of sexual matters, the divorce revolution, which causes marriages to take place among the young less frequently and less successfully, and the near complete de-stigmatization of out-of-wedlock childbearing.

The cultural influences that eroded the strength of marriage in the 1960s, gained enormous momentum during the 1970s when most states passed laws to make the marriage contract less binding. The no-fault divorce revolution essentially enabled either spouse to break up the marriage without his or her partner's consent.

Now, a new network of state-based family advocacy groups, known as state-family policy councils, are calling for marriage reform laws to reverse the no-fault revolution. A no-fault reform bill is currently making headway in Michigan, and similar initiatives are beginning to generate interest in several other states, including Georgia, Kentucky, Illinois, and Washington.[34] In Louisiana, a public law has recently been passed to create a new "covenant" marriage policy that enables parties to a marriage contract to choose a fault-based contract that is harder to escape.

Working in tandem with this policy reform movement are similar movements to both strengthen existing marriages and to prepare partners for future marriage. These operate primarily within the faith community. In addition to McManus' Marriage Savers movement, Promise Keepers, an evangelical men's movement, seeks to shape their millions of attendees at football stadium rallies into "men of integrity." Preachers at their rallies admonish men to honor and remain faithful to their wives. These movements and other evangelical groups, together with publishing houses like Focus on the Family, have spearheaded new efforts to fortify marriage across the nation.

Fatherhood and Socialization

What the family debate really boils down to is the presence or absence of fathers, since the vast majority of broken or never formed families results in children being raised apart from their biological fathers. The growing movement to renew fatherhood in the United States is one of the most active and promising areas of cultural renewal. As anthropologist Margaret Mead recognizes, "[T]he supreme test of any civilization is whether or not it can teach men to be good fathers."

Father absence is in many ways the most consequential factor in a wide range of negative outcomes in children, including teen pregnancy, drug abuse, adolescent violence, and crime. As columnist William Raspberry, a prominent journalist and advocate of fatherhood, states, "[T]here's as strong an association between fatherlessness and anti-social behavior as there is between cigarettes and lung cancer."[35]

Perhaps no factor is more relevant to the civil society debate than the role fathers perform in socializing children. Wade Horn, president of the National Fatherhood Initiative, explains that proper socialization must include developing the ability to delay or inhibit impulse gratification. According to Horn:

> [W]ell-socialized children have learned not to strike out at others to get what they want; under-socialized children have not. Well socialized children have learned to listen to and obey the directions of legitimate authority figures, such as parents and teachers; under-socialized children have not. [36]

He notes that studies demonstrating the differences between the parenting styles of fathers and mothers indicate that fathers are essential to developing impulse control in the young.

Here the reciprocal relationship between family roles and civil society could not be stronger. Fatherhood both strengthens civil society and is held together by it. Fathering, unlike mothering, which has a more biologically determined role, is heavily influenced by the wider culture. Social norms and reinforcements have a powerful effect on the attitudes and behaviors of fathers.

The emerging fatherhood movement is fueled by a conviction that a decline in fathering, whether through physical absence or emotional disengagement, results in psychologically underdeveloped children. Not only do these children frequently engage in destructive behavior; many become socially underdeveloped citizens, incapable of participating in society. Fathers, therefore, become either powerfully negative or positive agents in child development and in the making of responsible citizens.

The National Fatherhood Initiative, a four-year-old bipartisan civic initiative, has single-handedly placed the reality of father absence and its social consequences on the public agenda, and is arousing a response from within the many social sectors that affect male attitudes and behavior, including religious, civic, educational, and community groups. The initiative has influenced the public debate by contributing to thousands of news stories and radio and television broadcasts, public service advertising campaigns, and local and nationwide projects.

A host of other national and local groups has also emerged to strengthen the skills of individual fathers and their community support networks. Organizations like the National Center for Fathering and the National Institute for Responsible Fatherhood provide outreach, training, and educational literature to individual fathers.

Books on fatherhood are so plentiful that many bookstores have opened new sections featuring books on this subject and other men's issues. Other more analytical books, such as David Blankenhorn's *Fatherless America*, [37] and David Popenoe's *Life Without Father*, [38] have received extensive reviews and wide circulation among social and political analysts.

A dozen or more major philanthropies are also pouring sizable contributions into projects including academic research, practitioners' networks, and educational and public awareness initiatives.

Conclusion

The civil society movement has arisen to address the multiplying evidence that the nation's social institutions have become battered by neglect. Among those institutions that produce a nation's vital social capital are an array of local character-shaping entities, at the center of which is the family. For the family restorationists, social capital originates predominantly if not exclusively in the family.

It remains to be seen whether all this fresh attention will produce large-scale shifts in social trends. Many indicators are sending mixed signals. The long steady rise in illegitimacy rates appears to have finally stabilized and divorce rates are actually falling. Overall teen pregnancy rates are declining, although the percentage of teen births to unmarried mothers continues to rise. Least promising of all is the continued doubt among the young regarding the importance of marriage as a necessary condition for child rearing. Among those American households in which children are being raised, the number that contain a married mother and father continues to decline.

In many ways, the approach that individual Americans bring to the family reflects the deeper conflicts within the wider culture. Across the nation the debate continues over whether to favor traditional attitudes toward family, centering on the virtue of sacrifice, or to embrace the more recent trends of expressive individualism and freedom from the constraints of family and community.

Regardless of the eventual outcome of the discussion on the family in the United States, the civil society debate is shedding fresh light on the primacy of this basic institution as a source of social capital. The civil society debate is taking aim at a variety of deficiencies in the nation's social sector, including civic stagnation and declining trust. But few factors have generated more concern or more action than America's fragmenting family system.

Notes

1. Kenneth L. Woodward, "What is Virtue?" *Newsweek*, 13 June 1994.
2. Arthur Schlesinger, *The Disuniting of America: Reflections on a Multicultural Society* (New York: W. W. Norton and Company, 1992), 17.
3. Georgie Anne Geyer, *Americans No More: The Death of Citizenship* (New York: Atlantic Monthly Press, 1996).

4. Alan Wolfe, "Is Civil Society Obsolete?," *The Brookings Review*, Fall 1997, 11.

5. *The Index of Social Health 1995: Monitoring the Social Well-Being of the Nation. Special Section: Comparing Social Health and Economic Growth*, Fordham Institute for Innovation in Social Policy (Tarrytown, N.Y.: Fordham University Graduate Center, 1995).

6. Jean Bethke Elshtain, "Bad Seed," *The New Republic*, 9 February 1998, 9.

7. Glenn C. Loury, testimony before the U.S. Congress, House of Representatives Human Resources Committee of the Ways and Means Committee, 20 January 1995.

8. Loury.

9. Robert D. Putnam, *Making Democracy Work: Civic Traditions in Modern Italy* (Princeton: Princeton University Press, 1993).

10. Putnam.

11. Francis Fukuyama, *Trust* (New York: The Free Press, 1995), dust jacket, see also 10.

12. Alexis de Tocqueville, *Democracy in America* (Garden City, N.Y.: Doubleday Anchor Books, 1996), 692.

13. Wendy Rahn, "An Individual-Level Analysis of the Decline of Social Trust in American Youth," unpublished paper presented to the First Plenary Session of the National Commission on Civic Renewal, Washington, D.C., 25 January 1997.

14. Richard Morin and Dan Balz, "Americans Losing Trust in Each Other," *The Washington Post*, 28 January 1996, 1.

15. Morin and Balz, 1.

16. Morin and Balz, 1.

17. *The Index of National Civic Health*, (College Park, Md.: National Commission on Civic Renewal, May 1998), 9.

18. Urie Bronfenbrenner, Peter McClelland, Elaine Wethington, Phyllis Moen, and Stephen J. Ceci, *The State of Americans* (New York: The Free Press, 1996).

19. Morin and Balz, 3, 4.

20. James S. Coleman, "Social Capital in the Creation of Human Capital," *American Journal of Sociology* 94 (1988), 95-120.

21. Rahn.

22. Mitchell B. Pearlstein, *From Moynihan to "My Goodness": Tracing Three Decades of Fatherlessness in the United States* (Minneapolis: Center for the American Experiment, August 1995).

23. Daniel P. Moynihan, "Family Policy for the Nation," *America*, 18 September 1965.

24. Pearlstein.

25. Irving Kristol, "'Family Values'—Not A Political Issue," *The Wall Street Journal*, 7 December 1992.

26. David Popenoe, "A World Without Fathers," *Wilson Quarterly*, Spring 1996, 12.

27. William Galston, "Beyond the Murphy Brown Debate," speech to the

Institute for American Values, 10 December 1993, 4.

28. Galston, 5.

29. Jean Bethke Elshtain, "What Makes Democracy Possible? Marriage in Civil Society," *Family Affairs* 7, no. 1-2 (Spring 1996), 3.

30. *Marriage in America: A Report to the Nation*, Council on Families in America (New York: Institute for American Values, March 1995).

31. "Closed Hearts, Closed Minds: The Textbook Story on Marriage," A Report to the Nation from the Council on Families, Norval Glenn, Research Director (1997).

32. Michael J. McManus, *Marriage Savers* (Grand Rapids, Mich.: Zondervan, 1995).

33. Leon R. Kass, "The End of Courtship," *The Public Interest*, Winter 1997, 40.

34. Rob Gurwitt, "The Crisis of Divorce," *Governing,* May 1996, 40.

35. William Raspberry, "Social Cancer," *The Washington Post*, 5 October 1994.

36. Wade Horn, "Character and Family," in *The Content of America's Character*, ed. Don E. Eberly (Lanham, Md.: Madison Books, 1995), 80.

37. David Blankenhorn, *Fatherless America* (New York: Basic Books, 1995).

38. David Popenoe, *Life Without Father* (New York: The Free Press, 1996).

Chapter 4

Civil Society and the Welfare State

If the family is the core concern for some civil society advocates, the destructive influence of the nation's welfare system is the animating issue for another group of advocates. Any large movement to recover civil society carries with it a burden to address the well-being of all communities, including those wracked by poverty and dysfunction. A move to restore civil society must do more than alleviate the anxieties and alienation of the middle class; it must also reverse the disorder and despair of poor communities. The civil society movement is therefore unavoidably linked to the debate over social welfare policies.

Another segment of the civil society movement sees the recovery of civil society predominantly as an opportunity to replace a costly and ineffective federal welfare system with state, local, and community programs. With the passage of comprehensive welfare reform legislation in 1995 and 1996 ending welfare as an entitlement, significant changes are occurring at the state level.

In fact, the social welfare reform segment of the American civil society movement has already scored impressive accomplishments in dramatically altering the nature and scope of the welfare system. Since Congress acted to eliminate welfare as a basic entitlement in 1995, many states have adopted sweeping reforms that have cut the roles by as much as 55 percent in some locations. Nationwide, the number of cases has fallen by more than a quarter, although it must be said that many of these reductions merely decrease the current caseload to levels slightly below those of the early 1990s, immediately before a dramatic rise in caseloads in 1992.

Most of these states, in transforming their policies, have emphasized civil society themes and embrace a new "cultural" ethos when it comes to delivering human services. In some cases, social service programs have been renamed to emphasize work, family, and community as opposed to income support. One welfare office in Colorado, for example, renamed itself the Family Independence Center. Even welfare caseworkers have seen their titles change to signal a shift away from the "welfare culture" to civil society. A welfare recipient is now likely to meet, not with a welfare caseworker, but with a "work assessment specialist" or a "job placement officer."[1]

Welfare reformers argue that the dramatic reduction in welfare numbers proves that a welfare state is not the answer. Though the federal government has spent trillions of dollars on welfare in its war on poverty, the number of poor has either remained the same or increased. This criticism of the welfare state centers on its cost, its ineffectiveness in reducing poverty, and its dependency-producing features.

According to these critics of welfare, civil society has atrophied primarily because government has supplanted many of its functions, eroding private responsibility. One leading advocate of this position, Charles Murray, states bluntly:

> I strongly believe that if we got rid of the welfare state entirely—not just cut payments 10 percent or create workfare requirements—that this would create a moral revolution. Once the state stops masking the costs of these problems you'd once again see stigma attached to things like parenting children out of wedlock.[2]

Though this radical premise lies at the core of welfare-cutting revolution, even Murray doubts that the nation will embrace such a sweeping and risky experiment.

What the civil society movement's welfare reformers really want is to replace welfare with private solutions. Washington conservatives praise the "little platoons" of neighborhood associations and civic fraternities, hoping to reengage these local groups to perform those welfare functions that the state has supplanted. For the welfare reformers, social capital refers essentially to local charitable and voluntary aid societies.

Private Charities

Conservatives want to reinvigorate the moralizing functions of community by returning the current duties of the welfare state to nonprofit, and especially faith-based charities. These local private and religious charities deliver more personalized compassion, often accompanied by reciprocal requirements designed to develop character and self-reliance.

Private and community-based programs are variously praised as personal, challenging, flexible, innovative, community centered, results-driven, and often spiritually renewing. In contrast, government programs are seen as undemanding, rule-bound, distant, unaccountable, impersonal, and hypersecular.[3]

Citing examples of charities that have shown long-term success rates that greatly exceed those of government-run programs, proponents of these private charities argue that their organizations are simply more effective than their government-run counterparts. Teen Challenge, for example, is a network of faith-oriented drug treatment programs that has gotten into trouble with government agencies for keeping minimal paper work, hiring staff without professional degrees, and operating facilities that fall short of government standards. Studies show, however, that the program achieves long-term cure rates of 67 to 85 percent, compared to rates for government programs that rarely exceed the single-digit range.[4]

Stories of successful local charities like Teen Challenge abound and conservatives are confident that more programs like this can fill the vacuum in American charity left by a retreating government. Senator Dan Coats (R-Ind.), a leader in this movement, has organized support in Congress for a legislative package centering on community-based charity called the Project for American Renewal. The proposal includes 18 separate initiatives to reform public housing, promote the two-parent family, support religious charities through welfare set-asides and deductions, and experiment with a host of minor projects to boost character and responsibility.[5]

Through tax breaks, subsidies, and statutory reforms, the Project for America Renewal seeks to expand the role of private charities and individual giving as an alternative to governmental intervention. A similar package of initiatives to expand charitable giving, boost mentoring, and support other socially valuable activities by individuals has been introduced by Representatives J. C. Watts and Jim Talent.

The movement to reform American charity has more than government replacement in mind; it seeks to return major philanthropic institutions to their roots as providers of local aid to the poor. Established and funded by the Bradley Foundation and chaired by former GOP presidential candidate Lamar Alexander, the National Commission on Philanthropic and Civic Renewal ranks among the top initiatives established in recent years to renew civil society. It was founded to assess "how private giving in the United

States can help revive our poorest communities and promote self-sufficiency and independence among citizens."

The commission's final report levels multiple criticisms against the charitable sector, calling it, for example, "ineffective, sometimes wrongheaded, and occasionally counterproductive." Most important, major corporate and foundation philanthropies are faulted for systematically overlooking worthy local charities that are "radically different from the government sponsored social-service model that has also become the model of many large charities."[6]

Conservatives were among the first to criticize Colin Powell's "President's Summit on Volunteerism" for being too much like government-sponsored charity. The summit basically called for corporate funders to give more to existing charities while presumably sidestepping small but effective faith-based charities. As both the Alexander report and the criticism of Powell powerfully illustrate, the conservative critique of government and its failures extends well beyond the state to the institutions of civil society.

Intellectual and Institutional Foundations

The move to revitalize civic community by replacing costly and ineffective welfare programs with a network of community-based nonprofits has received powerful intellectual and institutional backing by major Washington-based policy groups. To most of these groups the revival of civil society is tied to their long-standing objective of rolling back the state. The Heritage Foundation, one of the oldest and largest conservative think tanks in the nation, has adopted a new emphasis on citizenship and institution building. Its flagship journal, *Policy Review*, has been reconfigured with a new subtitle, *The Journal of American Citizenship*, and now seeks to "illuminate the families, communities, voluntary associations, churches and other religious organizations, business enterprises, public and private schools, and local governments that are solving problems more effectively than large, centralized, bureaucratic government." By "chronicling success stories, exposing obstacles and opportunities, and debating the policies that will best invigorate civil society," the journal places itself in the service of a "new citizenship movement."[7]

Conservatives are not newcomers to the intellectual tradition now being recovered by the civil society movement. Indeed, the revival of interest in the concept of civil society in the twentieth century, which is today at its peak, received its initial spark in the late 1970s when Peter Berger and Richard John Neuhaus published *To Empower People*, urging policy reforms to strengthen the intermediary institutions and associations of civil society. Their small booklet, now virtually a classic, was recently republished by the American Enterprise Institute.[8]

Berger and Neuhaus undoubtedly drew much of their insight from another towering figure in the conservative intellectual tradition, Robert Nisbet. Nisbet's 1953 book, *The Quest for Community*, also a classic in most circles, set forth the idea that the greatest challenge of modern society is "protecting, reinforcing, and nurturing where necessary, the varied groups and associations which form the true building blocks of the social order."[9]

Sparking renewed interest in civil society was a speech delivered by civil society intellectual and philanthropist Michael Joyce in the early 1990s, first before the Heritage Foundation, and later before many influential policy and civic groups. The speech was a bold call to recover a larger and more encompassing concept of the American citizen, to roll back government incursion into society via the "helping" and "caring" professions, and to restore "a robust, vigorous" civil society with its "rich, vital web of civic life." Joyce was interested in more than changes in federal welfare policy. For Joyce, civil society entails an "expansive field of human endeavor," encompassing "all of the institutions through which individuals express their interests and values," including our places of employment, families, schools, churches, neighborhood associations, clubs, fraternal and sororal lodges, and ethnic and voluntary associations of all sorts.[10] The United States, according to Joyce, needed a comprehensive turn away from decades of hostility and indifference to an entire sector.

Other conservative institutional players and intellectuals who have contributed to the social policy debate include the Capital Research Center, specializing in the reform of philanthropies, the Acton Institute, promoting the recovery of a morally grounded society and culture, especially through religious charities, the National Center for Neighborhood Enterprise, a self-help action group that trains local entrepreneurs in neighborhood reclamation, and the Center for Effective Compassion, chaired by political columnist and philanthropist Arianna Huffington. On the center-left, a similar movement toward reform has been organized by the Progressive Policy Institute. Each of these programs contributes intellectual, policy, and practical tools to the movement to recover private charity.

Standing well above his contemporary peers in the debate over civil society and private charity is historian Marvin Olasky, whose book on social history, *The Tragedy of American Compassion*, has been championed by conservative policy wonks and Speaker of the House Newt Gingrich. Olasky shows how charity workers in the nineteenth century understood the problems of idleness, drunkenness, crime, and promiscuity to be related to issues of moral culture and private character. Charity campaigns in that century, accordingly, sought to effect moral reformation and self-discipline. In exchange for society's help, the poor bore an obligation to better themselves.

Like many of his conservative collaborators, Olasky argues that the issue with modern welfare is not its cost, but its tragic results for those who turn to it for help. His prescription—to encourage moral regeneration through nineteenth-century style discipline—has received broad circulation and support, especially within Congress.

Although the nineteenth century offers important lessons for today in delivering effective charity, even Olasky acknowledges that the circumstances of the late twentieth century are radically different from those of the last century. Modern values and systems, with their emphasis on secularism, compartmentalization, and professional specialization, will not be easily or rapidly cast off.

The Ideology of Welfare

The move to reform today's welfare system draws impetus from more powerful sources than narrow concern over the system's inefficiency or ineffectiveness. In many ways the debate over welfare represents the vortex of clashing arguments over the role of the state in both causing and mending the nation's social ills.

The welfare debate has shaped up as a larger critique of the entire twentieth-century experiment in centralized government, which its most ardent critics believe was animated by a conscious hostility toward local civic institutions and networks. Indeed, much of the animus in conservative circles toward government was generated by the failure of that sector of government that delivers human services.

To conservatives, the negative effects of the welfare state on civic community are not surprising—in many respects, they were foreseen, if not intended by the welfare state's twentieth-century architects. Leading welfare critics at the Hudson Institute, a leading conservative think tank, lay the blame for the collapse of civic community on early-twentieth-century progressives like Herbert Croly, Walter Lippman, and John Dewey.[11] These critics argue that progressives in the early 1900s promoted a vision, not of strong and diverse local communities, but of a "national community," grandiose, artificial, and ultimately destructive of real community.

For progressives, the argument goes, local civic networks and charities conjured up images of corrupt inefficiency presided over by unenlightened nonprofessionals harboring retrograde social attitudes. Bill Schambra, another important conservative voice in the civil society debate, says the approach of progressives toward civic community was disdainful of what they viewed as a vast "chaotic jumble of divergent civic institutions and local loyalties" that the state would proceed "ruthlessly to extirpate or absorb."[12] The progressive goal was to organize a cadre of qualified professionals trained in the most advanced theories at elite policy schools to replace local caregivers who were consistently disparaged as ignorant and untrained.

However grand the intent of these progressive visionaries might have been and however justified their concerns about the inadequacies of local programs were, the progressive movement, critics argue, gave birth to the "governmental assumption," which became the "ubiquitous unchallenged modus operandi of the twentieth century." Under this assumption, only national solutions were adequate to confront local problems. Federal government activism became seen as the social panacea. Federal programs would end poverty; Congress would eliminate gangs through new programs; a federal bureau with a well-funded staff of professionals would revitalize any schools that fell into mediocrity. Guided by these operative beliefs, "enlightened" managers assumed the role of trustees over the provision of social services, badly weakening the old civic order with its private, voluntary, and decentralized approach to collective action.[13]

Because of the powerful role that ideology historically played in creating the welfare state, the civil society debate often becomes an arena for settling older and larger philosophical scores. Liberals and conservatives distrust each other in the argument over the welfare state, and with good reason. Liberals generally suspect conservatives of wanting to eliminate the welfare state altogether. For their part, conservatives cite a century-long fondness for "national community" and governmentalism among progressives as the basis for suspicion of recent interest by liberals in civil society.

Conservatives suspect that President Clinton and his allies have used civil society merely as "a facile rhetorical bridge" over the chasm between those supporters who genuinely yearn to revitalize civil communitarian structures, and those who seek to expand government's reach. Civil society permits him to speak the language of civic renewal, while pursuing the policy of government revival.[14]

Problems with the Debate

The debate on the powerfully destructive effects of welfare programs on families and communities has contributed to a widened and generally welcome interest in reconfiguring the entire American social welfare system. The nonprofit sector, long diminished by doubt and disfavor, has been restored to legitimacy in the policy debate. The old consensus favoring centralized social planning has had to yield to a new consensus centering on the flaws of centralized, professional, impersonal, and undemanding social services.

The realization that intrusive government has weakened neighborhoods and turned citizens into self-interested and idle clients of the state has increasingly been taken seriously, for it is clearly valid. By itself however, the narrow focus on governmental malfeasance has clear limitations. For one, focusing narrowly on welfare reform as the key to civil society can project a vision of society no larger nor more complete than the vision of those who erected the welfare state in the first place. After all, civil society is much more than an alternative administrative delivery system for social services. It is a sector that plays a wider role in the democratic and civic life of all citizens.

Second, placing blame for society's problems solely on government operates on a number of challengeable assumptions. This position assumes that government programs are always the cause, and rarely, if ever, the effect of declining civil society. Blaming wrong-headed politicians and flawed policies for societal regression is a tempting and convenient way to dismiss other more discomforting and complex moral and cultural factors, including middle-class culpability for many social problems. This conviction that welfare is the sole culprit feeds on and reinforces the assumption that moral disorder and civic dysfunction in the United States is largely confined to poor neighborhoods, even though family fragmentation, illegitimacy, incivility, crime, and a host of other social ills are increasingly common in many middle-class enclaves as well.

Ill-conceived policies are not single-handedly capable of producing the scale of general criminality and family abandonment that exists now in virtually every demographic category. Costly and ineffective policies have obviously compounded such social problems as teen pregnancy, adolescent crime, drug abuse, and educational decline—problems that tear deep into the fabric of civil society. But these social ills have grown out of a weakening of the character-forming institutions in civil society as well as a fairly dramatic loosening of standards in the culture.

This assumption that the welfare state is the sole culprit for the dismal condition of society leads logically to another assumption—that the elimination of government will ensure civic renewal. Those who believe that the relationship of civil society to the state works this way often insist that disestablishing the welfare state will automatically yield a renewal of civil society. Destroying the welfare state is often presented to be sufficient in itself to produce social renewal.

Schemes to replace welfare and end dependency have sometimes been guided by the same utopian rhetoric that went into building up the welfare system. The drive to dismantle welfare can operate on the basis of a similar determinism: Change the state and society will reform itself accordingly. If the mistake of the Democratic majority was believing it could create the good society by merely building government up, the danger for the Republican majority may be believing it can recreate the good society by merely tearing government down.[15] Civil society is about a human order larger and richer than the state. Once weakened it cannot be magically restored by simply eliminating government's involvement. New civic capacity must be built.

Volunteerism

An outgrowth of the movement away from government has been a renewed call to volunteerism. Conservatives, like Speaker of the House Newt Gingrich, have heralded volunteerism as the answer to a host of social problems from illiteracy to drug abuse. Not to be outdone, President Clinton's summit (technically it was Colin Powell's) on volunteerism in April 1997 asserted that volunteerism would reduce the number of at-risk children and youth.

Volunteerism has emerged as the new common ground in American politics. Volunteerism is undoubtedly good for civic life, but it is often sold as the answer to poverty. Politicians who support volunteerism regularly cite the statistic that 93 million Americans annually volunteer 20 billion hours of their time—an average of 218 hours per person. Much of that volunteering, however, is not provided in the form of human services, the area of most concern in the welfare reform debate. In fact, only 8.4 percent of those 93 million volunteers work in such human service fields as helping the homeless, while nearly a fourth of volunteer activity consists of such neighborhood activity as baby-sitting and helping out with school fund-raisers. Another large percentage of volunteer activity is in the civic and cultural arenas, helping in museums and theaters and serving on community boards.[16]

This realization has led some, including a few conservatives, to openly express doubt about the capacity of the private volunteer sector to meet many of the problems confronting the disadvantaged. Mike Gerson, aide to one of the leading architects of the conservative approach to replacing the welfare state, Dan Coats, praises voluntary community action but raises doubts about its ultimate potential. Writing on the president's summit on volunteerism in *U.S. News and World Report*, Gerson says, "[T]here are many acknowledged benefits of volunteering. It helps build a sense of community, breaks down barriers between people, and often raises the quality of life." Some types of volunteering, he says, are especially successful, like the outpouring of volunteers to help in areas devastated by natural disasters.[17] He continues, however, by saying that "it is one thing to celebrate volunteers. It is another thing to depend upon them to fill the gaps left by failures and cutbacks in welfare and other government programs."

Gerson publicly acknowledges what many conservatives have been reluctant to even think—that "the volunteer sector is not ready for the responsibilities now being thrust upon it."[18] As important as it is, the volunteer sector has serious limitations that must be taken into account. For one, because the volunteer "market" does a poor job of connecting supply with demand, it often does not deploy volunteers to the front lines of poverty. For another, volunteers often lack either the interest or the necessary training for confronting the hard-to-solve cases.

Volunteerism is often sold as the only solution to poverty's hard cases—those whose needs are such that they cannot be helped through government intervention. Personal engagement is, according to civil society proponents, the key to the success of noninstitutional responses to human need. From this perspective, the solution to the welfare crisis is to expand private programs and dramatically increase personal involvement by volunteers.

Those who speak for the poorest of the poor, however, are skeptical about the adequacy of the volunteer solution. Boston pastor and community activist Eugene Rivers, asks angrily, "If there are really 93 million volunteers in the United States, then why are our cities worse than they have ever been?" Volunteers have not reached Pastor River's neighborhood because people rarely volunteer beyond their private sphere of living, much less across the racial and class lines. This is even true in churches, where no more than 15 percent of volunteering reaches beyond sanctuary walls.[19]

Evidence shows that deeply troubled children usually cannot be rescued by the casual volunteers to whom they are often assigned. Volunteers are not adequate substitutes for parents and they cannot restore broken families. In fact, if adult workers disappear after short stints of volunteering rather than developing a meaningful, long-term relationship with children, they may only end up reinforcing a child's sense of betrayal and distrust. There is no example in history of a society that succeeded in solving its social crisis by assigning mentors and volunteers to needy children on a massive scale.

Nonprofit Organizations

Private charities are often presented as "a great untapped source" and an answer to human need. Probably the most important issue in the debate over replacing the current welfare system concerns the institutional capacity of the nonprofit sector. Estimates differ widely on the state of private charity in the United States, but those directly involved in this field worry, not that the programs are untapped, but that they are overtapped. As charitable time and money have waned,[20] private charities have increasingly turned to the government for help.

Of the Catholic Charities' $1.9 billion budget, for example, $1.2 billion, or 65 percent, now comes from government sources. Many other major charitable organizations depend on the government for similar percentages of their revenue.[21] Overall, today's human service charities receive 40 percent of their money from federal, state, and local government agencies.[22] None of these charities provides income support for poor families—they mainly provide food, shelter, and other forms of in-kind assistance.

Like the distribution of American volunteer activity, private charitable giving may have to be expanded dramatically if it is to fill the gap in social services. Of the $144 billion given to charity in 1995, 44 percent went to religious organizations, 13 percent went to educational organizations, 8 percent went to health organizations, and only 9 percent went to social service organizations.[23]

Spending by functional category tells a similar story. Over 50 percent of spending within the nonprofit sector went to hospitals, another 23 percent went to schools and other educational activity, and only 10 percent went to human service organizations, even though human service organizations make up about 40 percent of total nonprofit organizations.[24]

These statistics do not cast doubt on the effectiveness of private charity in serving the poor, and especially not the vitally important role of religious charity, only their actual capacity under current circumstances. As discussed, the truly effective work being done in the nonprofit sector is being done by religious groups. In fact, research shows religious faith, like no other force, having a positive impact on a host of pathologies like drug abuse, alcoholism, and crime.[25] Even though the numbers of participants remain comparatively small, faith-based programs often show remarkable results, and they will undoubtedly play a large role in the emerging debate.

The debate over private charities and volunteerism raises important questions: How much private sector capacity is presently in place? How long will it take to create additional capacity? Are private groups and individuals capable of treating the "tangle of pathologies" that often mar the lives of the long-term poor? What if, in the haste to reform, these approaches do not produce the expected results?

The most important consideration in this new debate is how to regenerate a vibrant and caring civic sector where it has been weakened, especially in the most blighted neighborhoods where it is needed the most and where this sector has largely disappeared. These issues must be addressed by civil society advocates if their vision of social renewal is to be taken seriously.

Conclusion

In the United States, the social debate often becomes a political debate, generating new ideas, new assumptions, and new directions for society. Civil society has become the end and the means for many welfare reformers, setting in motion a long-term decentralizing trend designed to strengthen local civic capacity.

Already the debate has shown that government displacement is real, that local charities do important and unique work and thus should be supported in official policies, that the poor require personal engagement, and that the traditional role of communities in providing care for their members must be restored.

In a remarkably short period of time, faith-based charities have emerged as not only legitimate nonprofit players, but perhaps the preferred weapon in private sector antipoverty strategies. *The Chronicle of Philanthropy*, the largest and most influential newspaper in the nonprofit world, gives front-page status to a story documenting the sudden rise to prominence of faith- and value-centered charities. Though the story tells of the success of faith-based charities, it also indicates that many difficult issues remain to be resolved. Leading the list of concerns is the problem of potential mission distortion that often arises when the government gets involved in funding.[26]

These experiments in community-based care, though promising, are in many ways untested. Policymakers will have to confront many issues before turning government functions over entirely to local civic associations and faith-based charities. These issues vary from rather simple questions of administration and finance to complex and thorny questions about church-state separation. In a book entitled *Seducing the Samaritan,* Joe Laconte of the Heritage Foundation has raised serious concerns about nonprofits being "co-opted" by the government through public financial support, which could lead to the destruction of their distinctive functions. Issues of local zoning are also surfacing as churches become busy places of weekday social activity and service.[27]

The possible extent of volunteerism and private charity in replacing the welfare state remains especially unclear. John Clark of the Hudson Institute says that the move toward volunteer-based charity "depends very much on the current and potential health of civil society in this country." If the private sector is really in the bad state statistics suggest, "we may be taking a big risk to shift much of the relief provided by the welfare state to voluntary organizations."[28]

The optimistic rhetoric of some conservatives about the boundless potential of the American people to care for their own has also run up against a more realistic view of the human condition. Major leaders like William Bennett and Senator Dan Coats raise such questions about civil society's potential, even as they seek to renew it. They ask the questions that are on many people's minds: How can we revivify social institutions? How can we reverse the civic atrophy that has occurred over the past 30 years? Civil society, they note, "is organic, not mechanical. It can be coaxed and nurtured, not engineered." Public policy must be humble and realistic, because "even if government directly undermined civil society, it cannot directly reconstruct it. Getting government out of our lives will not ipso facto lead to a rebirth of private and civic virtue."[29]

A larger cultural and religious rebirth, far deeper than structural reforms, may be required. One of the most enthusiastic proponents of sweeping welfare reform, the Hudson Institute, interrupts its report praising civil society's potential for replacing big government with a stark word of caution: "Without a genuine and widespread revival of the habits and attitudes that Tocqueville observed on these shores," such reforms will prove insignificant.[30]

Notes

1. Steven Hayward, "The Shocking Success of Welfare Reform," *Policy*

Review: The Journal of American Citizenship (January-February 1998): 6-7.

2. Charles Murray, quoted in Charles Oliver, "Conservatism vs. Capitalism," *Investor's Business Daily*, 22 April 1997, 1(A).

3. Gregg Vanourek, Scott W. Hamilton, and Chester E. Finn, Jr., *Is There Life After Big Government? The Potential of Civil Society* (Indianapolis: The Hudson Institute, Inc., 1996), 3-4.

4. Marvin Olasky, "Addicted to Bureaucracy," *The Wall Street Journal*, 15 August 1995.

5. William J. Bennett and Dan Coats, "Moving Beyond Devolution," *The Wall Street Journal*, 5 September 1995.

6. "The New Mission for Philanthropy," *Policy Review: The Journal of American Citizenship* (September-October 1997): 49.

7. Adam Meyerson, ed., "Statement of Purpose," *Policy Review: The Journal of American Citizenship* (March-April 1996): 2.

8. Peter L. Berger and Richard John Neuhaus, *To Empower People, The Role of Mediating Structures in Public Policy* (Washington, D.C.: American Enterprise Institute for Public Policy Research, 1977).

9. Robert Nisbet, *The Quest for Community* (San Francisco: Institute for Contemporary Studies, 1990).

10. See Michael S. Joyce, "Americans Are Ready for a 'New Citizenship,'" adapted from a speech to the Milwaukee Bar Association (23 June 1993), and Joyce, "The Bradley Project in the 90s: An Overview," from a speech to the Thiensville-Mequon Rotary Club (12 October 1993).

11. Hudson Institute Executive Briefing, "Renewing the Promise of American Life," Report on a Hudson Institute Conference, 7-8 December 1994 (Washington, D.C.: Hudson Institute, Inc., 1995).

12. William A. Schambra, "Toward a Conservative Populism? Some Questions for the Wilderness," prepared for "Populism in the 1990s" (Washington, D.C.: Hubert Humphrey Institute of Public Affairs, University of Minnesota, and The Empowerment Network, 3 March 1994), 5.

13. Schambra, 6-7.

14. Schambra, 6.

15. Don E. Eberly, "Toward Civil Society," *The Wall Street Journal*, 3 February 1995.

16. Michael J. Gerson, "Do Do-Gooders Do Much Good?" *U.S. News and World Report*, 29 April 1997, 27.

17. Gerson, 27.

18. Gerson, 28.

19. Gerson, 27.

20. Laurie Goodstein, "Churches May Not Be Able to Patch Proposed Welfare Cuts," *The Washington Post*, 22 February 1995.

21. William Tucker, "Sweet Charity," *The American Spectator*, February 1995, 38.

22. Jonathan Alter, "Powell's New War," *Newsweek*, 28 April 1997, 33.

23. "On Giving and Volunteering in America: A Summary of the Essential Data" (Washington, D.C.: National Commission on Philanthropy and Civic Renewal, September 1996).

24. "On Giving," 2.

25. Joseph P. Shapiro and Andrea R. Wright, "Can Churches Cure America's Social Ills?" *U.S. News and World Report*, 9 September 1996, 50.

26. Paul Demko, "Faith-Based Charities to the Rescue?" *The Chronicle of Philanthropy*, 11 December 1997, 1.

27. Evan Gahr, "Communities and Churches Clash over Zoning Issues," *Insight*, 16 January 1995, 17.

28. John Clark, "Shifting Engagements: Lessons from the 'Bowling Alone' Debate," *Hudson Briefing Paper* (October 1996), 9.

29. Bennett and Coats.

30. Vanourek, Hamilton, Finn, 14.

Chapter 5

Community Building and Civic Engagement

The characteristic of Americans that Tocqueville admired most was their penchant for forming associations. Americans of "all ages, all stations in life, and all types of dispositions are forever forming associations," he said. Nothing is accomplished in the United States without the formation of associations of an infinite variety. The tendency to join and participate in voluntary associations may be the distinguishing element of our unique democratic heritage, what some have termed American exceptionalism. Nothing, Tocqueville said, deserves more attention.

Through the art of association—what Tocqueville called the first law of democracy—American citizens would prosper without being commanded from above. In the United States, the shaping of democratic habits would not fall to aristocracy, established religion, or rigid class structure. The habits of mind and heart thought necessary for democratic life on the American continent would be nourished instead in the rich soil of civic culture that Tocqueville observed and praised.

It is difficult to fully capture the full extent of Tocqueville's argument. He regarded the formation of associations as the chief means of political socialization, and as such were nothing less than the very life spring of American democracy. Civic associations were thought to be far more important than politics itself because they harmonize, stabilize, and routinize life in democratic society. Tocqueville went so far as to say that if these habits of working together in the affairs of daily life are not maintained, civilization itself would be in peril. Without "the faculty" of doing great enterprises together, society would "fall back into barbarism."

The organizations and initiatives that focus on civic community represent a distinct category in the civil society movement, one that seeks to build communities by involving individuals in public service and volunteer projects. In contrast to the family restorationists and welfare reformers, these advocates make the restoration of America's communities and civic associations their highest priority.

What distinguishes this category of groups from the welfare reformers is that they show little concern for the displacement of civic community by government, the issue raised consistently by most conservatives. As in the case of the Americorp project, which encourages civic responsibility among youth through government-sponsored volunteerism, the government is presented, not as an obstacle, but as a possible source of help. Many adherents of this point of view are quick to cite how Harvard Professor Robert Putnam's analysis of regional governments in Italy showed civic community strengthening government, making it work better, and helping it do more. Government, for this group, is not the problem—in fact, it can become a partner in building civic community.

For civic restorationists, the term *social capital* is largely interchangeable with the concept of civic participation. For them, social "connectedness" through membership and participation are the operative words. As Putnam puts it, "By social capital, I mean features of social life—networks, norms, and trust—that enable participants to act together more effectively to pursue shared objectives."[1]

Civic restorationists also tend to place all human groups that connect and nourish people—from the family to choral societies—on the same moral plane. Although they sometimes voice concerns about children or religion, these primary institutions are rarely recognized as priorities. Instead, their concern is directed to the public purpose of building and sustaining private civic networks.

From Civic Bounty to Bowling Alone

Robust civic engagement has been a distinguishing mark of American history from the beginning of the republic. Scholars have recorded and analyzed an infinite variety of associations, building an entire academic specialty around the study of national, state, and local organizations, from mutual aid societies to fraternities.

American citizens over the past two centuries have prided themselves in their civic accomplishments, enough that most cities diligently compiled and maintained directories of civic groups and membership for posterity.

Recently, data from the nineteenth and early twentieth centuries have been organized and reviewed by such scholars as Robert Putnam and Gerald Gramm. Their findings were astonishing. These two analysts found over 63,000 organizations and civic institutions—an average of 300 civic associations per city—in existence over these years.[2] One third of these associations included fraternal or sororal organizations, one third served other economic, social, or cultural purposes, and a final third included churches and other religious affiliates.[3]

Civic historians also regularly acknowledge that religion played a major role in forming voluntary associations during the eighteenth and early nineteenth centuries. In fact, many of the groups that helped fuel the American Revolution, like the Committees of Correspondence and the Sons of Liberty, were religiously inspired and directly linked to the First Great Awakening. Similarly, the Second Great Awakening led to a proliferation of new churches, missionary and tract societies, benevolence organizations, Sunday schools, and temperance movements. Tocqueville marveled at the power of religion in the United States, calling it the "first political institution" because of its power in shaping social mores and democratic habits.

Voluntary associations often worked for broad social and political reforms. This was especially true during the period between 1830 and 1850, a high watermark in American civic life, when an explosion of social and moral reform movements, including antislavery societies, propelled the nation toward a confrontation over slavery. Historian Stuart Blumin notes that the three decades preceding the Civil War witnessed the rise of formal associations "so numerous, so elaborately organized, so appealing to so many people, so various in purpose, and in many instances so powerful, that this may fairly be called an era of voluntary institutional innovation without parallel in American history."[4]

Scholars call the late nineteenth and early twentieth centuries the golden age of associational life, as civic associations of a different kind flourished—the service club. During this period, such service organizations as Boy Scouts, Girl Scouts, Young Men's Christian Associations (YMCAs), veterans groups, farmers organizations, and industrial unions proliferated. Millions of citizens also joined fraternal organizations like the Masons and the Odd Fellows, as well as service clubs like Rotary, Kiwanis, and Lions, during this time period.

Civic life has followed this cyclical pattern throughout history as new associations arose to meet the unique challenges and circumstances of their times. Whether the issue was fighting a war of independence, tearing down the institution of slavery, reforming vice and moral debauchery, or moderating the disrupting influences of industrialization and urbanization, civic institutions arose largely in response to social and economic conditions.

Though some prominent civic organizations have lasted over a century, despite this ebb and flow of civic life, the great majority followed a life cycle pattern of birth, growth, stagnation, and eventual decline. These natural cycles and regional and local characteristics make a realistic assessment of the nation's present civic circumstances difficult.

Tocqueville himself worried that the civic spirit would wane with time as various factors of modern life altered how Americans viewed citizenship and civic obligation. Tocqueville feared most the age-old vice he called egoism, which drove each person to live apart, "a stranger to the fate of the rest." The retreat of the individual into private life apart from community, Tocqueville predicted, would spawn "a multitude of men, all equal and alike, incessantly endeavoring to procure the petty and paltry pleasures with which they glut their lives."[5]

The United States today is, in many ways, confirming Tocqueville's fears. Much of the current discussion of civil society focuses essentially on a privatized vision of citizenship, which reinforces a public cynicism and indifference to what Tocqueville described as "the fate of the rest." A recent decline in membership among mainline civic associations has been cited as evidence of a decline in civic well-being.

Robert Putnam raised national interest in this issue with his January 1995 essay, "Bowling Alone: Democracy in America at the End of the Twentieth Century." Putnam diagnoses symptoms of a larger problem as he reveals that membership in such basic institutions as bowling leagues has declined. According to Putnam, "the recent decline in civic engagement represents an unprecedented, and serious event." Putnam's civic jeremiad has caused many to wonder if the nation is in a new state of permanent civic decline, and if so, what the impact will be on democratic institutions.

Putnam claims to have discovered a decline in membership in such common social groups as Garden Clubs, Boy Scouts, and the Elks. Using General Social Survey data on civic membership, Putnam found that among men and women at all levels of education, membership in all sorts of groups has declined by one quarter since 1974. Measurements of individual trust in political authorities and social institutions also registered a decline of one third during the same period, although it is not yet clear whether this is a cause or effect of declining civic membership.[6]

Those in the civil society movement whose primary concern is civic restoration direct their energies to the civic arena—on renewing civic structures and spaces where people gather to perform civic duties. Their interest is in restoring those nonprofit organizations and networks that actually serve civic functions, or perform "public work." This does not include what Putnam calls "mailing list organizations" because, though members of these organizations are tied to common symbols and ideologies, they are not "connected" to each other. Nonprofit organizations that exist to perform functions other than connecting people are also not included in the civic arena.[7]

Causes of Civic Stagnation

Individualism

Putnam's work has triggered a vigorous and consequential debate about civic health in the United States. As most acknowledge, declining civic engagement is a puzzling phenomenon with only a few clearly identifiable causes. For one, people are busier and families often need two incomes to make ends meet. Second, women, who have long constituted the primary volunteer pool, now often direct their energies toward career and financial objectives.

Extreme individualism in the United States, such as was described and predicted by Tocqueville, is also frequently cited as perhaps the most dominant causal factor in civic decline. The United States has long been recognized as one of the world's most individualistic societies, but as social historian David Popenoe points out, this individualism has evolved in consequential ways, and to the detriment of social groups.

Popenoe maintains that, for most of American history, the nation has been marked not by a pure form of individualism, but by what could be termed "a communitarian or balanced individualism." This individualism, he says, was

> balanced, or tempered, by a strong belief in the sanctity of accepted social organizations and institutions, such as family, religion, voluntary associations, local communities, and even the nation as a whole. While individualistic in spirit, people's identities were rooted in these social units, and their lives were directed toward the social goals that they represented.[8]

A more recent trend in individualism has been toward a more radical or "expressive" individualism, one "that is largely devoted to 'self-indulgence' or 'self-fulfillment' at the expense of the group."[9] The older form of individualism was tied to social obligation and moral norms, while the new is a wholly private and autonomous form that is unprecedented in the American experience.

In many ways, the civil society debate is responding to a permanent and indigenous characteristic of American life—its restlessness and rootlessness. Americans, says E. J. Dionne, "have always been on the move and in search of new opportunities," happily leaving behind old commitments and relationships. In many ways the old ties that many casually abandon to achieve upward mobility represent limits on personal freedom. Says Dionne, "One person's stable neighborhood is another person's stifling neighborhood."[10]

Economic Changes

If individualism, or "egoism," leads the list of explanations for the loss of American civic life, then changing economic fortunes comes in as a close second. The collapse of a blue-collar manufacturing economy and the rise of the two-paycheck suburban family, caused, in large part, by a massive shift of employment opportunity from the manufacturing sector to a global information economy, is often cited as the most powerful driving force behind other demographic changes affecting civic participation.

Economic strength among the lower one fifth of American workers has clearly eroded, taking a heavy toll on lower income, working class, and poor communities. A leading proponent of this position, William Julius Wilson, has studied a new class of urban poor who appear closed off from adequate employment opportunities. According to Wilson, the absence of good jobs paying decent wages has precipitated the social collapse of many poor communities, causing stores to close, banks to leave, churches to lose parishioners, and civic organizations to cease to function.

Even suburban life is affected by civic deterioration. Today, 55 percent of Americans live in suburbs, up from 20 percent 50 years ago. Suburban life, with its comfortable homes, safe streets, and good schools, in many respects represents the American dream, but attaining that dream has come at a high price to civic life.

The rise of suburbia, says Karl Zinsmeister, is

a fairly radical experiment, and one directly linked to many modern woes. The hurried life, the disappearance of family time, lack of local ties, an exaggerated focus on money, the anonymity of community life, the rise of radical feminism, the decline of civic action, the tyrannical dominance of TV and pop culture over leisure time—all of these problems have been fed, and in some cases instigated by suburbanization.[11]

Suburbanization has clearly changed patterns of social interaction in the United States. The spatial design of neighborhoods not only reflects the values of its residents, it also shapes them. The physically compact urban neighborhood that many suburbanites fled reinforced regular face-to-face contact among residents, whereas suburban neighborhoods often reinforce the modern values of separation, individualism, and private choice. Allen Ehrenhalt describes his blue-collar Chicago neighborhood in the 1950s as a place where adults visited on the front stoops of houses, children mingled and played under the shared parental authority of neighborhood adults, and everyone shared responsibility for safety and civility.

Ehrenhalt also remembers that streets in the urban neighborhood of the 1950s teemed with mothers and children. This has changed drastically with the social revolution that swept women into the paid workforce. Bill Galston of the National Commission on Civic Renewal speaks candidly about the civic effects of changing gender roles. "I cannot help thinking," he says, "that as a matter of history, the term 'social capital' refers in significant measure to the uncompensated work of women outside the domains of both home and market. I find it very difficult to believe that the massive entrance of women into the paid labor force over the past 30 years has been devoid of consequences for informal social networks."[12]

Work and living patterns develop in tandem with changes in a nation's economic life. Whereas the urban core represented the great center of American social and commercial life for much of the twentieth century, thanks to the continued momentum of industrialism, the twenty-first century is quickly becoming the suburban century. Suburban life has a different social texture and rhythm, especially in its civic aspects.

Zinsmeister describes the suburban experiment as having a certain "machine-like artificiality to it. At its core lies the social engineer's confidence that if you don't like society the way it is, you only need to manufacture a new society. Never mind all the social evolution, and individual trials and errors, and intangible little inheritances from history that go into making communities work." "With no past, no inherited standards, no evolved wisdom wormed down into their cores," Zinsmeister adds, "suburbs lack a base on which to build cooperative feelings."[13]

Putnam's own metaphor for the decline of the United States, "bowling alone," may itself unintentionally illustrate how changes in civic life merely reflect the decline of urban industrialism and the rise of the American suburb. True, fewer people bowl in leagues, even though more are bowling than ever. But as Putnam critic Katha Pollitt points out, it would be amazing if this were not true. League bowling could not survive the way of life that brought it about in the first place.

Bowling leagues, says Pollitt, were rooted in a 1950s "working class and lower middle-class life: stable blue collar or office employment (businesses and unions often started and sponsored teams) that fostered group solidarity, a marital ethos that permitted husbands plenty of boys' nights out, and a lack of cultural and entertainment alternatives." "The bowling story," she continues, could be told "as one of happy progress: from a drink-sodden night of spouse avoidance with the same old faces from work to temperate and spontaneous fun with one's intimate friends and relations."[14]

Harvard Professor Theda Skocpol presents a variation on this thesis, with decidedly more class-conscious ingredients. She blames civic decline on shifting allegiances among a burgeoning upper-middle stratum of "highly educated and munificently paid managers and professionals" who have pulled out of local civic associations. Historically, the founders and sustainers of the nation's voluntary associations were the "well-educated and economically better-off citizens." Leadership in the American Legion, for example, provided a stepping-stone for aspiring professionals, and involvement in the PTA privileged homemakers to gain community credentials. Now, she maintains, this upwardly mobile stratum gets ahead by "working long hours and networking with each other through extra-local professional or trade associations, while dealing with politics by sending checks to lobbying groups headquartered in Washington, D.C."[15]

In other words, yesterday's league bowlers are today's corporate managers. Skocpol maintains that this group of "privileged men and women—who spend most of their waking hours in their offices, on jet airplanes, and in front of computer screens"—believe that "civic irresponsibility is the fault of average Americans." How ironic it would be, she says, if

> after pulling out of locally rooted associations, the very business and professional elite who blazed the path toward local civic disengagement were now to turn around and successfully argue that the less privileged Americans they left behind are the ones who must repair the nation's social connectedness, by pulling themselves together from below without much help from government or their privileged fellow citizens.[16]

Skocpol also argues that civic group formation has always been associated with attempts to influence public life and social policy, often working in partnership with government to design and deliver social programs. In other words, the creation of civic organizations and the development of political movements are often closely linked.

Beginning in the 1960s, the mechanisms for this organizing activity changed dramatically. Efforts to organize through locally rooted organizations "gave way to television advertising, polling and focus groups, and orchestration by consultants paid huge sums with money raised from big donors and massing mailings."[17] Diverse, local, and essentially non-professional organizations were supplanted by advocacy groups and lobbies that were as similar in structure and technique as they were dissimilar in politics. In other words, civic life was unavoidably and inevitably altered by the continued advances in economics and technology: upward mobility, computers, polling, and professional specialization.

Peace and Prosperity

Ironically, another culprit in the breakdown of civic life is peace and prosperity. Americans may have wrongly expected that their prosperity would generate more civic generosity and public decency. But this is not the general pattern—it may, in fact, work the other way. The most civic generation that the United States ever produced was not shaped by ease and plenty, but by war and economic depression. According to pollster Daniel Yankelovich, prosperity has a tendency to relax social standards and soften harder virtues like sacrifice and duty.

Without major crises, the nation can easily drift away from civic solidarity. It turns to government agencies, for example, to clean up natural disasters with financial aid and assistance, displacing traditional functions of citizens and communities. There is clear evidence of some government displacement, but few agree on the extent of this displacement and the consequences for many forms of civic participation. The continued spontaneous outpouring of relief efforts in response to floods, hurricanes, and disasters like the Oklahoma City bombing indicates that the civic spirit endures, even in the midst of government intervention.

Putnam believes civic decline has a number of sources, but one leading factor he points to is the passing of the post-World War II "civic generation," whose penchant for civic cooperation was strongly shaped by the crisis of war and the need for national service. Other factors include time and financial pressures, mobility, public cynicism dating back to Vietnam and Watergate, and the movement of women into the labor force.[18]

Putnam claims "directly incriminating evidence has turned up" against one suspect—television. The sheer amount of time Americans spend before the tube (the average is four hours a day), the Harvard professor says, rules out many other activities. Television viewing is also associated with "low social capital," as citizens settle for the "petty and paltry pleasures" Tocqueville warned of, instead of caring for others.

Flaws in the Thesis

Another explanation for declining civic participation has to do with the very natures of current civic structures. Many leading institutions that Americans have joined in the past have gone through dramatic changes in their core missions and beliefs. For example, many argue that the membership decline in mainline Protestant denominations and the migration of parishioners to other evangelical churches were caused by a softening of church teachings and lessening demands on their members. Higher standards and costs for membership often confer a greater sense of belonging, suggesting that the price of admission for many mainline churches has perhaps become too low.

Other civic groups facing declining membership have made the opposite mistake: They have failed to adapt to the changing expectations of their members. Slow at detecting important generational shifts, these organizations have failed to replace older members with younger ones. In other cases, civic institutions have either finished their assigned tasks, saw their agendas superseded by more urgent concerns, or simply no longer inspired heartfelt allegiance in their followers.

The PTA, for example, may have been effective in mediation and problem solving at a time when public schools enjoyed a broad consensus of parental support, but the PTA cannot maintain trust and loyalty when schools become a cultural battleground. In conflict-ridden institutions, many simply leave out of frustration as stakeholders take sides in divisive disputes, and as mediation and service are replaced with polarizing advocacy.

A more complete evaluation of civic engagement would take into account certain countertrends. Putnam's method may be too stagnant to catch dynamic changes in American society. By only focusing on membership patterns of large, centuries-old organizations the analysis may fail to detect the arrival of new civic movements, large or small. Putnam's tracing system may ignore, for example, the Promise Keepers movement that is reaching tens of millions of men, or the 40 percent of Americans in support groups ranging from prayer networks to Alcoholics Anonymous.

A growing number of observers disputes the civic decline thesis outright, claiming that, by any measure, civic participation has not declined at all. To be sure, Americans are still among the most sturdy joiners in the world. Eighty-two percent of us belong to at least one voluntary association. This rate is only exceeded in Iceland, Sweden, and the Netherlands, and the United States is above average in most categories of civic membership.[19]

Robert J. Samuelson, economic writer for the *Washington Post*, writes that "bowling alone is bunk. The idea that there's been a massive retreat from civic life is farfetched." The whole theory is based on the "dubious" assumption that because better educated people who belonged to groups in the past are not joining at the same rate, civic life in general is stagnating.[20]

Doubt has also been cast on the Putnam thesis of civic decline by more recent surveys that indicate continued civic engagement in spite of widespread distrust in many public institutions. A survey by the American Association of Retired Persons has found that 90 percent of Americans belong to at least one group or association, and that Americans on average belong to four associations or clubs. The study also found that many Americans continue to volunteer. Forty-four percent of the respondents had volunteered for a charitable organization during the previous year, and 86 percent said they helped someone in need.[21]

Pollster Everett Ladd, director of the Roper Center for Public Opinion Research, believes there are ways to interpret changes in civic membership more hopefully than Putnam has concluded. Membership in mainstream civic groups like the PTA may merely reflect, for example, the ebb and flow of the school-age population. With school registration increasing again in recent years, PTA membership and attendance at school board meetings have rebounded sharply.[22] Ladd also sees signs of recent increases in volunteerism, private philanthropy, and small groups.

Some groups decline for obvious and entirely natural reasons. Labor union membership declines as technology, self-employment, and home-based enterprises increase; farm groups thin out as farm mechanization spreads; veterans groups decline as aging veterans are not replaced by new survivors of war, and so on.

People's lives and tastes also change over time in ways that affect civic participation but which are essentially harmless. True, Little League participation has dropped, but the ranks of youth soccer clubs have swollen to 2.4 million—20 times the figure two decades ago. Adult bowling leagues may be languishing, but membership in other sporting leagues, like softball, has ballooned (from 19,000 registered teams in 1967 to 261,000 today). Ladies' garden clubs have declined because women are working, but these same women now attend evening book clubs in unprecedented numbers.

Size is another factor in the changing fortunes of major civic institutions. Many of the large civic associations in the United States have succumbed to the same forces of professionalization and bureaucratization that have undermined the effectiveness and legitimacy of public agencies. Management scandals at charities like the United Way remind onlookers just that many major civic groups have become large, administratively cumbersome, and prone to mismanagement.

In many cases, civic America has come to resemble the bureaucratic state it was meant to replace. Civic megastructures are often the kind of distant and impersonal institutions that many would now like to see replaced with local organizations. Princeton Professor of Sociology Robert Wuthnow maintains that Americans tend to eschew large bureaucratic organizations in favor of smaller local ones. Civic participation, he says, "has become more diverse and loosely structured so people can move in and out of issues and organizations."[23] Many of the civic categories experiencing growth are local and highly participatory, like crime watch groups, book clubs, Bible study groups, and mentoring activity.

Distrust of large and distant institutions is especially prevalent among Generation X. While this generation possesses higher levels of distrust than any other category, there are indications that they are far more civic-minded than the generation immediately preceding them. They may also differ from their elders in that they appear far more interested in local projects than in large-scale civic enterprises. But there is little evidence that they lack civic motivation, as their reputation suggests.

The nation's largest annual survey of college students, involving 250,000 freshman at 500 universities, shows that students are apathetic about governmental affairs, but register the highest levels of commitment to volunteerism in decades. About 72 percent of these freshman performed volunteer work over the past year—10 percent more than those in 1989.[24] Though they may not be voting, they certainly are volunteering.

Other surveys show that many more teens would volunteer if asked. A survey conducted by the Gallup organization shows that teens are four times more likely to volunteer when asked than when they are not. Of 51 percent who were asked to volunteer, 93 percent did.[25] This survey suggests that the impulse to volunteer has not weakened; only society's success in conveying the expectation to volunteer as a part of citizenship.

A final factor in civic decline that has received little notice is the trend toward secularization within mainstream civic organizations. Civic renewal tends to run in tandem with renewed spiritual interest. This was certainly the pattern in the nineteenth century. The explosion of voluntary associations in the nineteenth century was inspired largely by an impulse to deepen religious practice and reform moral habits. Spiritual awakenings, temperance movements, private charity campaigns, and children's aid societies were formed to instill virtue and self-restraint. These awakenings, in turn, inspired Sunday School movements, the YMCA, and vigorous character education programs in the public schools.

As in earlier periods, Americans again appear to be engaged in a widespread search for a deeper spiritual dimension in their lives, both in private and in public life. Many Americans long to reconnect themselves, their institutions, and their culture to a moral and religious core. If existing civic institutions fail to meet these expectations and to provide this connection, new civic arrangements will rise to take the place of older institutions.

Today, many new groups appear to be forming with the purpose of firming up character and moral fortitude in society. The remarkable success of the Promise Keepers movement may be explained in part by the inability of the more secular YMCA to meet today's deeper need for spiritual and moral uplift. Other groups and movements like the teen abstinence campaign True Love Waits have attracted millions of members, as they sidestep the "value-neutral" approach to human sexuality promoted by secular groups. Habitat for Humanity, another recently formed charity with a strong orientation toward religious faith, has also seen dramatic growth.

The United States may be in the early stages of a new phase of civic reform and replacement. This should not be surprising. If structural transformations can shake business, government, and education, there is no reason to expect civic institutions to remain unphased by those wider trends. Institutions, whatever their nature, wax and wane. Says Richard Stengle, "The principal flaw in the civic-decline argument is that it misses a new and different direction in American life. There hasn't been a disappearance of civic activism in America so much as a reinvention of it. It is not dissolving, but evolving."[26]

Institutional Players

The movement to renew civic America has benefited from significant intellectual ferment and institutional support. Only several of the major institutional players can be identified here, and some of them do not fit neatly into this category, but each seeks to strengthen the nation's communities and civic networks and to recapture a wider appreciation of the importance of the voluntary sector.

The National Commission on Civic Renewal, cochaired by Bill Bennett and retired Senator Sam Nunn, is probably the most ambitious of these projects. This commission was established to tackle the entire sweep of topics that concern the civil society movement, including the decline of trust, the health of social institutions, and the status of civic participation. The aims of the commission are both practical and empirical, partly descriptive of current American civic life and partly prescriptive for the individuals and institutions that serve as civic "agents of change."

According to Director Bill Galston, the commission hopes "to get the facts straight" and to tell the story "of our civil and civic condition in a manner that is consistent with the best available evidence." The commission has set out to collect data and assemble evidence of new "promising initiatives now under way in communities across the country" so it can recommend "additional steps that potential agents of change in the public private, and voluntary sectors could take to address the civil and civic ills identified by the commission."[27] Like other civic renewal initiatives, the National Commission on Civic Renewal does not primarily take aim at government and its flaws, but at the need to expand the civic sector, sometimes working in partnership with government.

Another organization advancing civic renewal, the Communitarian Network, a Washington, D.C.-based organization, was established by Amitai Etzioni to promote communitarian ideas in scholarly research, public policy, and community organization. The communitarian movement does not fit neatly into this analysis, but its central claim is that human problems cannot be solved through autonomous individuals operating alone in the market or the procedural state. Man is a social creature, according to the communitarians, requiring an ethical community in order to flourish.

While the communitarians are concerned, as their name suggests, about the status and place of community in society and democracy, their interests and intellectual contributions reach far beyond general topics of community to issues of morality, political philosophy, and finding balance in our political culture between rights and responsibilities. Etzioni is the movement's most prolific writer, contributing numerous books and articles to the civil society movement, and producing his own journal. He is the leading and original theoretician for a new national, and increasingly international, communitarian movement.

John McKnight of the Center for Urban Affairs at Northwestern University has also made significant theoretical and practical contributions to the civic renewal movement. In his book *Building Communities from the*

Inside Out, McKnight offers distressed communities strategies calling for "asset-based community development." Effective community building must be organized, he says, around the assets already important in neighborhoods, even if they have been significantly diminished. The wrong approach, he says, but the one most frequently followed by government and private groups, is to focus on a community's needs, deficiencies, and problems. Instead, McKnight says, to renew civic life, one must inventory a community's strengths, then build on and replicate them.[28] This is also the approach taken by the National Center on Neighborhood Enterprise, mentioned earlier.

Another major player, the Points of Light Foundation, is a national organization promoting volunteer service. It has developed a nationwide project, Connect America, that seeks to build a movement around shared values and common ground. The project was designed to confront the fragmentation of communities and the isolation of individuals within communities. Connect America sponsors events to inspire greater community dialogue and collaboration around organized volunteer projects.[29]

The Points of Light Foundation was a leading sponsor of the President's Summit for America's Future, held in Philadelphia on April 27, 1997. The summit's purpose was to call on Americans to volunteer and to ask major institutions, especially businesses, to redouble efforts to direct private sector resources to troubled communities. The summit attracted all the living former presidents, except for the ailing former President Ronald Reagan, who was represented by his wife. A press release announced that the summit hoped to bring the United States "to a new level of commitment to volunteer service, especially targeting the nation's young people."[30] The project's general chairman, retired General Colin Powell, stressed that volunteerism was "no replacement for government help." "We're partners," he declared.[31] The summit also attracted a high degree of skepticism, largely because of its ambitious goals.

The Alliance for National Renewal is a coalition of over 170 organizations led by the century-old National Civic League. The alliance uses examples of communities solving problems from within to replicate their positive innovations in other communities with similar problems. The league offers such services to communities as strategic planning, training in collaborate leadership, assistance in "asset mapping" to focus on a community's strengths instead of on its needs and "visioning," or rediscovering shared values. The National Civic League is best known for its Civic Index, an evaluative tool that helps communities assess the size and strength of their "civic infrastructure." The index is designed to measure a host of civic indicators including citizen participation, community leadership, government performance, civic education, and intergroup relations.[32]

More publications and projects than can be documented here have organized around the mission of promoting renewed citizenship. The Civic Practices Network supplies on-line communications service for the civic renewal movement. It attempts to electronically network civic innovators around the stories, tools, and best practices of community empowerment activists. The National Issues Forum sponsors forums for citizen conversation over difficult political problems, seeking "a different kind of talk, another way to act." Communities of the Future, led by Rick Smyre, attempts to organize communities around new technologies that enable citizens to participate more fully in the life of the community, and to confront the challenges posed by technological trends.

A relatively new magazine, *Who Cares*, serves a readership of 50,000 civic entrepreneurs and volunteer coordinators, providing them with methods for promoting positive social change along with information on how to effectively manage nonprofits. Linking the United States to the international civil society movement is Civicus, an international alliance that attempts to bring together those engaged in efforts to strengthen citizenship and civil society around the globe through publications and annual conferences.

Major philanthropies have also stepped up their involvement in civic improvement, in some cases providing resources and in other cases developing their own programming. The Pew Charitable Trust has also launched the Pew Partnership for Civic Change, which has spearheaded a number of projects including a Community of the Future Network that replaces "old paradigms" for community problem solving. The network helps communities understand future trends affecting their well-being and develops a process for community dialogue, leadership development, and broad public education.[33] The Pew Charitable Trust was also the principle financial backer of the congressional summit on civility in Hershey, the presidential summit on volunteerism in Philadelphia, and the National Commission on Civic Renewal.

Another philanthropy, the Johnson Foundation of Racine, Wisconsin, has developed civic programming and a magazine, *The Wingspread Journal*, which is devoted to "reweaving our social fabric" through stronger communities. Through conferences, projects, and publishing, the foundation promotes community empowerment, civility, and service.[34] One entire edition, in fact, was dedicated to rediscovering the successes of earlier social movements. Similarly, the Kettering Foundation develops partnerships to promote civic renewal and publishes a journal dedicated to improving civic and democratic life.

Conclusion

These disparate movements to recover civic life and restore community have contributed greatly to awareness of civil society and its problems in the United States. They have done much to educate Americans on the importance of civic institutions and volunteer action and marshal a response through public debate and new initiatives.

The greatest weakness of these institutions, however, is in their limited premise that a nation's social health and capital are entirely functions of civic membership and volunteer activity. These groups generally give little attention to core questions concerning the deeper sources of individual civic character and have little to say about the moral determinants of social action. Civic restorationists admonish citizens to join, collaborate, and partner, but rarely address how individuals gain the capacity for these types of interactions. They frequently assume that people are naturally disposed to empathize and act upon an innate social concern. To the absence of these characteristics among citizens, civic restorationists usually offer a vague structural explanation, disregarding private moral conscience, psychological maturity, or personal competence.

The notions of community advanced by these organizations tend to be secular and abstract. Rarely do they seriously evaluate the deeper foundations for community formation. Little interest is shown by this school of thought, for example, for the ultimate foundation of all community, the family. In this important way, the civic restorationists differ from other leading civil society factions. Bill Galston, who regularly admonishes his colleagues that "we must examine the consequences of changing family structure," is one notable exception to the rule. He cites a mounting body of evidence suggesting that children of broken families "are less secure than other children and find it more difficult as young adults to trust either their peers or social and political institutions."[35]

Few in the civic recovery movement seem to have thought about how difficult it is to create competent and caring citizens out of fragmented families and collapsed moral values. Their indifference to these core questions has caused Galston to ask, "What changes are we prepared to make to strengthen civil society?" He notes that his own modest proposals to strengthen marriage and family "have received a decidedly mixed response." "Of all the requirements I have discussed for strengthening civil society, only cleaning up television and securing public spaces enjoy anything approaching a consensus."[36]

Galston is skeptical about the gap between stated public wants and private willingness to act decisively to fulfill those needs. "[I]n the end, the least tangible cause of civic decline—cultural change—may prove to be the most important." "Our dominate norms are choice at the level of individual conduct and entitlement in the construction of social policy." Civil society, Galston concludes, "rests on the very different norm of reciprocity: honoring mutual obligations, doing one's fair share, discharging the responsibilities that sustain a system of rights." Are we prepared, he asks doubtfully, "to accept restraints on choice and entitlement to create a stronger society that can endure?"[37]

The civic restorationists have made an important contribution to revitalizing citizenship in the United States. However, if those pursuing civic recovery continue to exclude the fundamental moral and cultural conditions that have eroded civil society, their labors may fall short of producing widespread and lasting results.

Notes

1. Robert D. Putnam, "The Strange Disappearance of Civic America," *The American Prospect* (Winter 1996): 34.

2. Gerald Gramm and Robert D. Putnam, "Association Building in America, 1850-1920," paper presented at the 1996 meeting of the Social Science History Association, New Orleans, La., 7.

3. Gramm and Putnam, 7.

4. Stuart Blumin, *The Emergence of the Middle Class: Social Experience in the American City, 1760-1900* (Cambridge: Cambridge University Press, 1989), 192.

5. Alexis de Tocqueville, *Democracy in America* (Garden City, N.Y.: Doubleday Anchor Books, 1996), 692.

6. Putnam, 35.

7. Putnam, 34.

8. David Popenoe, "The American Family Crisis," *National Forum*, no. 3 (Summer 1995): 17.

9. Popenoe, 17.

10. E. J. Dionne, "Why Civil Society? Why Now?" *The Brookings Review*, Fall 1997, 6.

11. Karl Zinsmeister, "Are Today's Suburbs Really Family Friendly?" *The American Enterprise*, November-December 1996, 36.

12. William A. Galston, "Won't You Be My Neighbor," *The American Prospect* (May-June 1996): 16.

13. Zinsmeister, 39.

14. Katha Pollitt, "For Whom the Ball Rolls," *The Nation*, 15 April 1996, 9.

15. Theda Skocpol, "Unravelling from Above," *The American Prospect*, (March-April 1996): 20.

16. Skocpol, 22.

17. Skocpol, 26.

18. Skocpol, 36.

19. World Values Survey, 1990-1991.

20. Robert J. Samuelson, "Bowling Alone Is Bunk," *The Washington Post*, 10 April 1996.

21. Debra E. Blum, "Americans Aren't Bowling Alone," *The Chronicle of Philanthropy*, 15 January 1998.

22. "People, Opinion, and Polls," *The Public Perspective*," June-July 1996, 6.

23. Richard Stengel, "Bowling Together," *Time*, 22 July 1996, 36.

24. Rene Sanches, "Survey of College Freshmen Finds Rise in Volunteerism," *The Washington Post*, 13 January 1997.

25. Beth Ashley, "More Teens Would Volunteer if Asked," *USA Today*, 35.

26. Ashley, 35.

27. Bill Galston, private letter to author, 13 January 1997.

28. John P. Kretzman and John L. McKnight, *Building Communities from the Inside Out* (Evanston, Ill.: Center for Urban Affairs and Policy Research, Neighborhood Innovations Network, Northwestern University, 1993), 1.

29. *Connect America*, pamphlet (Washington, D.C.: Points of Light Foundation, March 1996).

30. From summit press release, President's Summit for America's Future, 24 January 1997.

31. Margaret Carlson, "The General's Next Campaign," *Time*, 17 March 1997.

32. *The Civic Index*, pamphlet (National Civic League).

33. See *Creating Change in American Communities*, pamphlet (Charlottesville: Pew Partnership for Civic Change, Summer 1994), and Bruce Adams, *Building Healthy Communities*, from the Leadership Collaboration Series (Charlottesville: Pew Partnership for Civic Change, Winter 1995).

34. The Johnson Foundation, Inc., *The Wingspread Journal* 17, no. 3 (Autumn 1995).

35. Galston, 17.

36. Galston, 17.

37. Galston, 17.

Chapter 6

Renewing the Public Realm: Public Space and Democratic Deliberation

Another important wing of the civil society movement is taking aim at the impoverished state of the nation's public life and debate. Thanks to this movement, Americans are caught up in a public debate about their own public debate. The indicators of discontent over the quality of public life in the United States are many. Concern over declining trust and confidence in public institutions has heightened to the point that some worry about the continued success of democracy itself. A 1991 Kettering Foundation report issued the grave warning that "the legitimacy of our political institutions is more at issue than our leaders imagine." "Politics is like leprosy," the report said, "people don't want to be around it."[1]

There is broad agreement that the state of American democracy is not good. The link between citizen participation and decision making, indispensable to preserving democratic legitimacy and vitality, is badly weakened. In the United States, the sacred connection between elections and governmental action is becoming increasingly tenuous. The role of the citizen is mostly one of following, not forming major government decisions.

That portion of public life presided over by elected politicians has, from time to time, become particularly degraded. Much of the incivility that has surfaced in political debate, from the Congress to local school boards and city councils, is a result of the loss of trust among individuals and in institutions. Contemporary politics, with its transparently calculated and canned approach to issues, has contributed to the erosion of trust and confidence in our political culture.

Little about politics today fortifies public spirited citizenship. Politics reinforces a vision of society inhabited by unencumbered private individuals, pampered with promises, fortified with multiplying legal rights, and awash in consumer choices, yet paradoxically more subject than citizen.[2] Political debates that once engaged public reflection on the higher ends of life and the requirements of a just and good society are now seen as empty, evasive, or irrelevant.

The desire of the democratic renewal movement is not simply to connect individual Americans to civic purposes—it is to strengthen democratic values, renew democratic institutions, and draw Americans into the pursuit of public purposes as fully developed citizens. Leaders in this movement can be heard attacking the litany of problems confronting modern American democracy, including gridlock, public cynicism, negative journalism, manipulation of the political process by professional bureaucrats, declining voter participation, uncivil debate, special interest power, and more.

In confronting these problems, the movement attempts to recover the "public realm" where citizens can meet to engage in public activity. American society has dramatically expanded the range of choices available to private individuals in recent decades, leaving the space in society where citizens can come together to discuss their common values and lives in a shrunken state.

Democratic values, according to this movement, must be cultivated through cooperative activity in the public sphere. Richard C. Harwood, a leading voice for the recovery of public life, sees "a profound disconnect between citizens and the very institutions intended to help them understand and deal with the dilemmas they face." The problem, he says, "is that public institutions have become separated from the public realm—the very arena they were created to serve."[3]

It is not just government that suffers from this disconnect, according to Harwood, but the many intermediary institutions that should serve public purposes and contribute to improved government in a democratic society. He includes in this category "newspapers, foundations, corporations, nonprofit groups, and even the smallest neighborhood association."[4]

According to the democratic renewal wing of the civil society movement, we have lost the attitudes and behaviors that are conducive to informed public debate. Too frequently, those who control public debate "dumb down" issues on the assumption that uninformed and unmotivated citizens can then comprehend them and respond. The antidote to democracy's many diseases, according to the reformers, is a newly empowered, educated, and involved citizenship that demands more both of itself and its representatives. It doesn't merely demand to have its way; it demands that democracy work for everyone.

Projects and Institutional Players

The popular and academic literature on the problems of democracy is too voluminous to consider here, and space permits attention to only a few of the organizations and public leaders who are seeking to give new birth to democratic citizenship.

One leading initiative is the American Civic Forum, led by Harry Boyte of the University of Minnesota. The forum has issued a call for renewed citizenship entitled the Civic Declaration. Coordinated by Boyte, political scientist Benjamin Barber, and Will Marshall of the Progressive Policy Institute, the declaration attracted signatories from across the political spectrum. The forum's "Call for a New Citizenship" seeks

> a return to government of and by as well as for the people, a democracy whose politics is our common public work: where citizens are as prudent in deliberation as we expect our representatives to be; where public problem solving takes the place of private complaint; where all give life to liberty, and rights are complimented by the responsibilities that make them real.

A "citizen democracy," the declaration reads, "turns blame of others into self-reliance" and transforms "passive clients and consumers into active agents of change in our communities."[5]

Like other segments of the civil society movement, this group also describes civil society as "a vibrant array of voluntary associations," and seeks to strengthen civic activism and innovation, but for the purpose of bettering democratic life. Their desire is to see institutions that mediate on behalf of the individual (the civil servant, the press, civic enterprises, charitable organizations, and community organizers) rediscover the "civic dimension" of their work to help recover a fuller and more complete form of citizenship.[6]

Public Conversation

The nation's founders had in mind a system of government in which opinions and passions would be refined and enlarged through public debate and practical compromise. Divided government was created, in effect, to bring divided people together around workable solutions. John Adams described this process of expanded public participation combined with institutional checks and balances as "the ripening of public judgment."

Many have concluded that few opportunities exist anymore for ordinary citizens to participate in forming sound public judgment on pressing issues. Some have stepped forward to offer new arrangements and forms of deliberation so that individuals with diverse backgrounds and opinions can actually meet face-to-face, deliberate, agree or disagree, but at least develop a common regard for each other and better understand their differences.

This deliberative process has suffered many setbacks, but it is widely assumed that the increased domination of politics by technology and professionals has played a role in marginalizing the citizen. Computer-driven politics is geared, more and more, to drive poorly informed voters toward one or another partisan position, as quickly as possible, often by whatever negative means are necessary. Such methods of public debate as talk radio and public opinion polls often fall short of cultivating citizenship, producing outlets for venting hastily formed opinions but not opportunities for participation and education.

Technology can certainly serve to widen citizen participation and increase citizens' knowledge of public matters. But the concern is that the sheer speed of action in today's media-driven politics eliminates opportunities for unhurried and respectful discussions in relaxed settings. Jean Elshtain, author of *Democracy on Trial*, worries that this technology is skewing democracy itself. Technology, she says, has brought us to the brink of a politics based on instant plebiscite. Who needs debate with one's fellow citizens when opinion can be instantly captured and acted upon?[7]

Even attempts to reconnect individuals to public deliberation often fail because those attempts refuse to take seriously the need for an informed and involved citizenship, says Richard Harwood. According to Harwood, "We dump information on people to 'educate' them, but instead it leaves them overwhelmed and confused. We implore citizens to get involved through public relations campaigns as if slick TV ads are enough to create a sense of common purpose and motivation."[8] Harwood maintains that if professionals want to engender a more thoughtful public, "people need time to learn from one another. People must have room for ambivalence—time and space to test ideas, explore and listen—so they can sort out what they believe."[9]

The presumption behind the public conversation agenda is that there are few easy answers or convenient solutions to the nation's vexing problems, whether they are local development conflicts or national policy disputes over affirmative action, welfare, or health care. If public action is to enjoy broad support among citizens, the people themselves need more time and opportunity to find paths for action on public problems.[10]

Several groups have advanced projects to encourage broad public deliberation over American values and policies. A National Conversation on American Pluralism and Identity, initiated by the National Endowment for the Humanities, was one such attempt to foster conversations among citizens of all ethnic and racial backgrounds on the values they hold in common as Americans. The initiative was created by Endowment Chairman Sheldon Hackney "to promote the examination of what unites us as a country, what we share as common American values in a nation comprised of so many divergent groups and beliefs."[11]

Another example was the more recent attempt by President Clinton to preside over a national conversation about the nation's racial divisions. The effort generated wide skepticism centering on questions of whether any national politician is capable of guiding honest discussion of anything, but especially on a topic so charged or disingenuous as the discussion of race. Like the Hackney project, the racial conversation appeared to many to be superficial. Rather than involving a conversation with real people, it came across as the contrived exchange between public elites.

A more localized effort sponsored by the Kettering Foundation and Public Agenda is the National Issues Forum, which seeks more meaningful public debate through hundreds of cooperating community groups. The forum describes its purpose as deepening public judgment, rather than advancing private interests, and helping people to make hard choices among competing alternatives. The Kettering Foundation also publishes a journal, *Kettering Review*, which is dedicated to "improving the quality of public life in the American democracy." The journal, always substantive and intellectually serious, focuses heavily on assisting individuals to learn how to deliberate in a democracy.[12]

Public Journalism

The democratic renewal movement has also targeted for improvement the role of journalism in bringing citizens directly and actively into public discussion of politics and public policy. It seeks to improve public deliberation and reconnect journalists with the real lives and issues in the communities they serve. A Kettering Foundation report describes the public's "anger and dismay with a press that emphasizes the negative, polarized conflicts and trivial pursuits, rather than the strengths and stories that show ways to solve our common problems."[13]

The Pew Center for Civic Journalism focuses on media-based strategies for encouraging broader citizen involvement in public life by creating partnerships that involve local newspapers and radio and TV stations. Pew Trust President Rebecca Rimel sees civic journalism as "a way to get the public reconnected, reinvigorated, recommitted to democratic values."[14]

The Knight Foundation funds a clearinghouse called the Project on Public Life and the Press, offering information on the theory and practical applications of civic journalism. The desire of the project's backers is to move beyond conflict, prevent cynicism, raise public understanding of emerging issues, and make sure information is made available on differing approaches and attitudes toward public problems. This project also emphasizes the importance of journalists belonging to, and preferably living in, the communities they cover and serve.

Problems and Limitations

The widespread search for connection, civility, and citizenship serves as a reminder of the gaping hole in our democratic life. It reflects a desire to see greater respect for public space, and a greater willingness on the part of political antagonists to engage their political opponents with elevating speech. Much of the work described above deserves credit for diagnosing and seeking to treat our many democratic deficiencies.

The call to citizenship advanced by the Civic Forum deserves special commendation primarily because it places some of the blame at the feet of citizens themselves for demanding too much of politicians and too little of themselves. These projects, however, have a long way to go, and in many ways may simply be treating symptoms of a far deeper discontent and disorder.

Just how high-minded and public-spirited the media is capable of becoming, outside of a small group of reformers, remains doubtful. Attempts to cleanse democracy of its impurities are likely to fall prey to the very jaded attitudes civic journalists seek to confront. The civic journalist faces internal pressures having to do with the prosecutorial aspects of journalism itself.

Similarly, many of the attempts at improving public debate and deliberation have not taken the difficulty of the challenge seriously enough. For example, Hackney's national conversation never generated a following among serious people. What the so-called conversation project did generate was widespread ridicule, even from many who would like to see it succeed. One conversation of 200 "citizens" in Philadelphia broke into a discussion that compared the current decline in some workers' wages to slavery, leaving the panelists little to resort to except evasive tactics. Another heated debate arose centering on whether race, class, or gender consciousness was the greatest imperative in implementing urgently needed social change. Some felt diversity could not be achieved in the conversation without applying a quota system to guarantee that all ethnic identities and points of view were represented.[15]

Democracy is rooted in a basic moral system that enables us to debate ideas in the context of shared principles, respecting each person as an individual rather than a member of a politically privileged group. What Hackney may have failed to comprehend is that many people from within his own progressive ranks are not capable of democratic debate because they have lost touch with democracy itself.

To be both authentic and civil, public argument must occur within the context of a shared commitment to basic democratic and moral ends. Only when "we hold these truths" in common can we as citizens argue meaningfully about how those normative principles should be applied. The best public debate involves arguments over the most effective means for advancing common ends. When the public lacks a general agreement over what is just, right, and good, there is only one way to proceed: not with either evasion or needless polarization, but with frank discussion that admits to the differences and which relies on respectful persuasion, not on subtle tactics of imposition or manipulation. While coming to superficial agreement is tempting, coming "to disagreement," as John Courtney Murray put it, is very difficult.

Extreme multiculturalists think and behave in ways that make a real conversation virtually impossible. Hackney insisted that his conversation would be a failure "if it doesn't include everyone," but his notion of inclusiveness was actually based upon a narrow ideological conformity that denied the possibility of real dialogue over honest and legitimate differences. Consequently, a true dialogue never happened.

Hackney wasn't interested in debating legitimate ideological differences or searching for common ground. When confronted with certain core social issues, Hackney either changed the subject or offered his own controversial views, in a manner inconsistent with the requirements of constructive dialogue. For example, in a discussion with columnist George Will, Hackney acknowledged that the nation's deepest problems reflect confusion over values. Yet when the subject of the family came up as a central moral concern, according to Will, "Hackney the moralist becomes a materialist," ascribing the problem to economic factors and to the economic policies of two Republican administrations.[17] These are hardly tactics that are conducive to conversation building.

Those who preside over public debate carry a burden to avoid needless polarization, but also to move people toward a deeper understanding of public problems as well as a clearer understanding of our differences. Civility cannot become an excuse for evasion. A public that is cynical toward an unruly political class will become even more jaded if civility becomes simply the latest ploy for politicians to improve their self-image or for public debate to lack authenticity.

If mean-spirited public debate is unhealthy for democracy, so is a civility that is synonymous with fuzziness and fudging. The two irreducible requirements of civil and informed public debate are: (1) acknowledging that democracy is enriched by competing ideologies and political perspectives and that competition over ideas therefore must be conducted honestly and openly, and (2) possessing a genuine respect for the rights and dignity of one's opponents as human beings.

Notes

1. Dave Matthews, foreword to *Citizens and Politics: A View from Main Street America*, by The Harwood Group (New York: Kettering Foundation, June 1991), iv.

2. Don E. Eberly, introduction to *Building a Community of Citizens*, ed. Don E. Eberly (Lanham, Md.: University Press of America, 1994), xxxvii.

3. Richard C. Harwood, "The Public Realm: Where America Must Address Its Concerns," *The Harwood Group Series*, vol. 1, issue 1 (January 1996), 2.

4. Harwood, "The Public Realm," 2.

5. *Civic Declaration: A Call for a New Citizenship*, A New Citizenship Project of the American Civic Forum (Dayton, Ohio: Kettering Foundation, 9 December 1994), 6.

6. *Civic Declaration*, 6.

7. John Leo, "The Unmaking of Civic Culture," *U.S. News and World Report*, 13 February 1995, 24.

8. Richard C. Harwood, "Get Back to Basics to Tap Americans' Civic Capacities," *The Harwood Letter*, (1 June 1994), 2.

9. Harwood, "The Public Realm," 10.

10. Harwood, "The Public Realm," 3.

11. George Will, "Sheldon Hackney's Conversation," *Newsweek*, 18 April 1994, 66.

12. Robert J. Kensington, editor's letter, *Kettering Review* (Fall 1995), 4-5.

13. *Civic Declaration*, 10.

14. Alicia Shephard, "Buying Press Coverage: How Pew's Civic Journalism Project Put Newspapers, Radio, and Television Stations on the Payroll," *Foundation Watch* 1, no. 7 (1 August 1996), 4.

15. Warren, "What Does It Mean to Be an American?".

16. Will, 66.

17. Will, 66.

Chapter 7

Cultural Cleanup: Manners and Re-Moralization

Much of the current debate over civil society is animated by a desire to clean up American society and culture. Culture undoubtedly has increasingly come to play a dominant role in the health of our society. At its deepest level, culture embodies the basic ideas, attitudes, beliefs, and habits by which individuals define and order their lives. Culture is shaped in such numerous fields as philosophy, art, education, science, and government, and it is reflected in daily life through speech, myths, rites, rituals, and beliefs.

The institutions of civil society cannot possibly remain unaffected by the kind of cultural influences that dominate the United States today. Profound cultural shifts have occurred over the past 30 years as many gatekeepers of popular culture seem to have concluded that their job is to debase, not elevate and ennoble. At the level of mass culture, the entertainment industry floods American homes with programming of mind-numbing banality, trivializing life and desensitizing Americans to their deepening cultural disorder.

The proliferation of moral relativism and cultural coarseness can have grave consequences for every aspect of public life. Many observers believe that the nation's cultural elite have undertaken a determined effort to free individuals from the bonds of social conventions and moral restraint. Journalist Paul Greenberg says that while many debate whether the United States is a modern or postmodern, industrial or postindustrial society, he must conclude that this nation is becoming "post-civilized." Whereas, before only art was dehumanized, now, he says, there is a "dehumanization of culture in general."[1]

Charles Krauthammer argues that the single greatest shaper of wants and values "is not government, but culture." Mass culture, a fairly recent phenomenon, has been "vastly under appreciated" as an engine of social breakdown. "Never before in history have the purveyors of a degraded, almost totally uncensored, culture had direct, unmediated access to the minds of a society's young. An adolescent plugged into a Walkman playing 'gangsta rap' represents a revolutionary social phenomenon: youthful consciousness almost literally hardwired to the most extreme and corrupting cultural influences."[2]

No longer a matter of purely partisan interest, the cheapening of culture and human worth is raising alarms in nearly every corner of society. From Pope John Paul II to Holocaust survivor Elie Wiesel comes a common message: A society that celebrates debauchery and treats human beings in utilitarian fashion as objects of material and sexual gratification is a society in the process of disintegration.

Many civil society advocates believe that a movement for societal renewal must, above all, confront cultural corruption. For these cultural observers, the central issue isn't government. It isn't economics. It isn't even civil society. It is the culture.

Social Capital as Moral Capital

For this group, social capital is essentially moral capital. "The solution to the trials of our time depends upon replenishing America's moral capital," says Bill Bennett, the dominant voice in the movement.[3] According to this school, the erosion of social capital and the collapse of social institutions have been caused by the rise of a form of untrammeled freedom that disregards moral authority.

Leaders and institutions in this movement believe that the loss of community, the erosion of trust in authority, the increased abuse of power, and a host of other phenomena began when society was severed from its moral and religious underpinnings. The decline of civility is thus a function of a culture that no longer nourishes the soul but instead feeds human appetites and passions. Christopher Beem, director of the Council on Civil Society, doubts that, absent the recovery of moral ideals, civil society can live up to its billing. "It's the absence of commonly held values, not the decline of community groups, that should concern us."[4]

Of all the contributors to the civil society debate, the cultural recovery advocates have the least confidence that social problems caused by cultural disorder can be solved through public policy reforms, or recharging our civic life. Campaigns to boost civic life centering on gentle appeals for participation and civility are far too superficial to cope with the coarsening of culture. Moreover, the explosion of such crippling social pathologies as drugs, crime, and illegitimacy are not seen as responsive to civic initiatives aimed merely at reconnecting people. What is needed is a recovery of moral order.

The cultural revivalist school is also distinguished in that it is the least reluctant among civil society advocates to embrace religion as a source of cultural renewal. Says Bill Bennett, a leading advocate of this view, "The real crisis of our time is spiritual acedia . . . an aversion to and negation of spiritual things," which accounts for the breakdown of American culture.[5]

Many acknowledge that culture must be linked once more to the nation's religious heritage if it is to be revived. The loss of transcendence produces results for every sphere of human activity, from law, to politics, to economics, to society. Without transcendent moral principles, morality is contingent upon personal choice and the social contract becomes grounded, not in ethics, but on extreme rights-based individualism. Lacking grounding in moral principle, the law becomes arbitrary, intrusive, and burdened down with conflicting and irreconcilable demands.

The solution for the culturalists is the recovery of those institutions that gird up moral capacities: churches and synagogues, religious schools and faith-based charities. Like perhaps no other influence, spiritual transformation through strong families and moral communities turns self-absorbed individuals into morally fit citizens. Observing the growing confidence that many have in spiritually based projects, columnist William Raspberry observes, "Show me a program that helps people to change their lives and I'll show you a program with a strong element of the spiritual."[6]

Re-Moralization

Culture is difficult to reform because it is not merely about social and cultural institutions—it is about the basic ideas, assumptions, and moral precepts that are embedded in those institutions.

A focus on culture implies that the work of renewing civil society involves re-moralizing and reordering society—not through the coercive realm of government but in culture and society itself. In fact, culturalists frequently worry about the enthusiasm of some who believe vice can be eradicated through legal or political means. A proper understanding of the Western tradition would counsel realism and caution, not confidence, in this pursuit. Government should not harm social institutions or moral traditions, and in reality, it often harms both. But cultural problems require cultural solutions.

Public leaders and academics from across a broad spectrum of opinion have sounded a call to virtue. Leading academics in this field include such neoconservatives as James Q. Wilson, author of *The Moral Sense*,[7] and Gertrude Himmelfarb, author of *The De-Moralization of Society*;[8] communitarian Amitai Etzioni, author of *The Moral Dimension*,[9] and liberal Stephen Carter, author of *Culture of Disbelief* and *Integrity*. We act with integrity, Carter says, when we discern through moral reflection what is right and wrong, and then behave consistently on that basis.[10]

Gertrude Himmelfarb has little confidence that civil society is the answer to the nation's cultural problems because civil society itself "has been infected by some of the same viruses that produced these problems" in the first place.[11] According to Himmelfarb, many of the experiments and theories that spawned social pathologies are "still being promoted by some of the most influential institutions in our civil society—universities, philanthropies, foundations, learned societies." Himmelfarb is thus skeptical about the possibilities of devolving much of society's governance outward toward the institutions of civil society.[12]

Cultural Disconnect

Though this critique of the nation's cultural elite is often associated with intellectuals and spokesmen on the political right, the same arguments have emanated from other quarters as well. The late Christopher Lasch, who authored *The Revolt of the Elites and the Betrayal of Democracy*, describes an "aristocracy of brains"—a broad group that ranges from lawyers to journalists to investment brokers—that worships their own technological expertise, science, and rationality, disdaining the traditional habits of people linked to community, family, religion, and country. This elite, according to Lasch, is "in revolt" against "middle America," which it views as "technologically backward, politically reactionary, repressive in its sexual morality, middlebrow in its tastes, smug and complacent, dull and dowdy." The new aristocracy, he says, are at home "only in transit." These onlookers without any real ties to their nation have "essentially a tourist view of the world—not a perspective likely to encourage a passionate devotion to democracy."[13]

Communitarian Robert Bellah describes a cultural transformation of American life so complete that ordinary people now speak in a different "voice" from the institutional leaders around them.[14] Though not closely aligned, these writers all lament the loss of moral consensus within our political institutions and throughout many of the institutions of civil society.

University of Virginia sociologist James Davison Hunter, author of *Culture Wars*, argues that Americans are now locked in a heated contest over "different systems of moral understanding." Conflicts go beyond single divisive issues to deeper moral and philosophical concepts. The United States "is in the midst of a culture war that has had and will continue to have reverberations not only within public policy but within the lives of ordinary Americans everywhere."[15]

The views held by many in the institutional elite are frequently described as "progressive," meaning secular, rationalistic, and antitraditional. The "progressive" cultural coalition described by Hunter does not look favorably upon re-moralization, with its commitment to recovering enduring moral precepts. Progressives frequently focus on alternative notions like diversity, inclusion, and tolerance, which are usually advocated as a means of guarding against moral judgments.

Himmelfarb prefers the term "moral pathology," a term directly linked, she adds, to "the language of theology" because it is more descriptive of the social phenomena that concern us than terms like social pathology.[16] She believes that a revival of virtue must precede or at least accompany the recovery of social reforms, and that the humanitarian goals of progressives are not attainable without "moral reformation."[17]

This critique of culture shows a society where adults refuse to accept the requirements, morally or intellectually, of adulthood. For example, men's movement guru Robert Bly describes "a sibling society" that sought liberation from repressive paternalism by giving way freely to impulse, thereby regressing back to childhood. "People don't bother to grow up," which leaves Americans like "fish swimming in a tank of half-adults."[18] Bly describes a society in which adults no longer advance higher ideals and many adults are comfortable emulating adolescents, paying deference to the always shifting attitudes and trends of the youth culture.

A culture dominated by adolescent thinking essentially centers on the self. In this culture, the individual is guided by a youthful spirit of creation and cultivation in a world of unlimited imagination and few rules, rather than following the natural developmental process toward the demands of adulthood. This is the society of unimpeded freedom imagined by Rousseau in his famous line, "Man is born free, but he is everywhere in chains." Rousseau's society is supposed to be a "happy sanctuary," free of responsibilities, disappointments, or limits. Life is lived naturally and childlike, with each person seeking to living in accordance with his native or natural impulses, no matter how base.

Moving beyond adolescence requires making judgments about one's own conduct as well as the conduct of others, seeking to improve one's character and accepting natural limits. Rochelle Gurstein, author of *The Repeal of Reticence*, illustrates the difficulty of making these judgments in a society that has judged such activity to be wrong when she writes, to ask adults in society, especially those in cultural authority to "occasionally rise above a puerile, sniggering adolescent level, is evidence of snobbery or, worse yet, of attempting to inculcate middle-class or 'highbrow' values in others." To raise objections to free expression or individual choice, "no matter how graphically violent, sexually explicit, perverse or morbid—is to invite the epithet 'puritan.'"[19]

Gurstein argues that modern expressive liberalism has broken down because it can "no longer discriminate between the essential circulation of ideas, which is the cornerstone of liberal democracy, and the commercial exploitation of news, entertainment, and sex as commodities." Likewise, this modern form of liberalism, "can no longer distinguish between the expression of unorthodox ideas in the pursuit of truth, which is the lifeblood of art, and the desire to publicize anything that springs to mind in the name of artistic genius."[20]

In other words, the restraint and appropriate inhibitions necessary to preserve the good society have become intolerable to the cultural avant-garde. Any common notion of the true, the beautiful, or the good has been lost. In fact, according to Gurstein, it is no longer possible to converse in an older language of love and beauty. Such discussion, she says, is seen as "evasive, sentimental, platitudinous, or naïve." To be bound by a restricted view of the good is to be inauthentic and not truly free.

The impulse toward liberation is neither neutral nor benign in its effects on civil society. When culture no longer orders lives through a broadly accepted notion of the good, society is pushed toward nihilism. When art and entertainment aim mostly to emancipate the individual from constraints, society increasingly becomes conditioned to resist conventional moral and cultural tastes.

Conventional moral norms, indeed the very idea of a norm, imply certain boundaries in the public realm where our common life is developed. Cultural nihilism necessarily destroys these boundaries between the private and the public. In the name of openness, it exposes, often in great detail, those functions of body and mind that were once universally considered too private and secret, if not shameful, to expose. Privacy, which once served as a protective container for matters considered personal, has instead become aligned with a movement to publicly legitimate private choices.

We have witnessed the defeat of what Gurstein calls "the party of reticence" in the twentieth century. With that defeat, our "faculties of taste and judgment—along with the sense of the sacred and the shameful—have all become utterly vacant." Without faculties of taste and judgment, "it is now clear that disputes about the character of our common world can only be trivial, if not altogether meaningless."[21]

Civility and Manners

Much of the concern over declining civility voiced by civil society advocates centers on a generalized worry that ideas of acceptable behavior have changed. People may enjoy their newfound freedom to conduct themselves as they will, but they now worry about a decline in respect.

Pollster George Gallup, who has long tracked American attitudes about values, has "a sinking feeling" when he looks over current surveys. A recent Gallup poll showed a large majority of Americans see around them a world of despair. "There is a harsh and mean edge to society," Gallup says, noting that the United States has become "a society in which the very notion of a good person is often ridiculed," where "retribution is the operative word."[22]

A survey by *U.S. News and World Report* and Bozell Worldwide indicates that many people believe that the behavior of Americans has worsened.

> A vast majority of Americans feel their country has reached an ill-mannered watershed. Nine out of 10 Americans think incivility is a serious problem, and nearly half think it is extremely serious. Seventy-eight percent say the problem has worsened in the past 10 years. Their concern goes beyond rudeness as a personal irritant. They see in it portends of social disintegration. Respondents see in incivility evidence of a profound social breakdown. More than 90 percent of those polled believe it contributes to the increase of violence in the country; 85 percent believe it divides the national community, and the same number see it eroding healthy values like respect for others.[23]

The move to embrace civility is an attempt to recover rules of social behavior—essentially manners. It is an attempt to link freedom to reestablished social rules and restraints. Manners has a unique history as a tool for shaping social conduct. In 1530 the philosopher Erasmus wrote in his etiquette book, *de Civiltate*, that a young person's training should consist of four important areas: religion, study, duty, and manners. Over 450 years later, manners are making a comeback with the support of scholars as well as neighborhood advocates who see them as the route to social harmony.

John Moulton, a noted English judge, speaking on the subject of "law and manners" divided human action into three domains. The domain of law essentially compels people to obey, while the domain of free choice grants the individual unconstrained freedom. Between these two domains lies a third domain that is neither regulated by the law nor free from constraint. This "domain of obedience to the unenforceable" was what Moulton termed manners. Manners were about proper behavior, of course, but they also entailed moral duty and social responsibility. They involved "doing right where there is no one to make you do it but yourself."[24]

A breakdown in cultural norms practically ensures that the state, as the only remaining arbiter of conflict, will be expanded. Whereas the rules for determining what is right and true were once set by custom, morality, and religion, social and moral rules are now regularly decided through politics. As manners lapse and the law becomes the only arbiter of moral conduct, individuals make their decisions less and less according to private conscience or a public moral consensus and more on the basis of the political process.

Under the legalistic regime citizens are at the same time more prone to resort to law than voluntary conflict resolution in sorting out their differences and they are dismayed by the overreach of the law. They are also prone by this law-based system of conduct to assume that whatever behavior the law does not formally forbid, the right of individual privacy and freedom presumes to make right. What is excluded from the equation are ethical reasons and voluntary social constraints.

Social regulations are softer, gentler, and more flexible. Social regulation leaves room for nonadherence and requires no costly governmental controls. The state's rules are absolute and binding—enforceable through arrest and imprisonment. Thus, when conflicts arise in a society governed by pervasive law rather than social constraints, these conflicts—whether on highways, school playgrounds, or in malls—quickly escalate and must often be resolved by external authorities.

Periodically throughout American history, society has realized the importance of "the unenforceable" social rules and turned to renewal movements to revive them. For example, books and manuals for the application of manners to every aspect of life flourished in nineteenth-century America. One bibliography assembled during this period counted

236 separate titles on manners.[25] Today's manners movement has arisen in very much the same fashion. Manners are offered as a corrective to the excesses of a generation that spent its youth determined to wipe out anything that smacked of stifling conformity.

To be sure, the society of the 1940s in which today's "baby boomers" were raised may have erred on the side of conformity. Writing in the fall of 1996 in the *Wilson Quarterly*, James Morris describes films from the postwar era that show Americans in public places, like baseball games, almost as though "they're under the sway of an alien force. The women wear blouses and skirts or dresses or, more formal still, suits—and hats, hats, hats. The men are suited too, and hatted row after row to the horizon with brimmed felt jobs, deftly creased." Rules were set by people in communities, not the halls of Congress: "[T]he kids you were told not to play with, the people who could not be invited to dinner, the topics that could never be discussed, the Sears-sized catalogue of actions that were 'shameful' and 'unforgivable' and 'unmentionable.'"

If the 1950s were stifling, as most would agree, Morris says the present age is its radical opposite. "In this age of 'whatever,' Americans are becoming slaves to the new tyranny of nonchalance." For 30 years, every facet of the culture has steadily coarsened. Movies, music, television, newspapers and magazines dwell routinely on topics that, according to Morris, were "once too hot for whispers."

Morris doubts Americans will exchange the present for a past considered "speciously safe, ignorant and restricted." Manners depend on acknowledging authority, but authority is hard to come by in "a vigorous, strutting democracy." No one, Morris adds, "wants to make a judgment, to impose a standard, to act from authority and call conduct unacceptable." Until standards of intelligence and behavior are defined and defended once again, "we had better be prepared to live with deterioration."[26]

This doubt has not prevented many from trying to revive manners as an antidote for a culture's excesses. In fact, a growing interest in manners is reflected in the popularity of books on the subject and a widening network of civility advocates. These contemporary authors carefully avoid appearing stiff and Victorian, and instead link manners to a widely expressed desire for greater social harmony and mutual respect. Modern-day manners philosopher Judith Martin, who has written extensively on the subject, says manners are defined as that "part of our fundamental beliefs or wants that include such notions as communal harmony, dignity of the person, a need for cultural coherence, and an aesthetic sense."[27] Etiquette is the set of rules that emerges from these fundamental beliefs.

While some think manners are confined mostly to table etiquette, Martin sees manners fulfilling a "regulative" function, similar to that of the law. Where manners function properly, the conscience is informed and behavior is constrained without having to resort to police or the courts. Martin says that manners work to "soften personal antagonisms, and thus to avert conflicts," so that the law may be restricted to "serious violations of morality."[28] Social rules bring respect and harmony to daily situations. Without a solid foundation of restraint on individual behavior from within through unwritten laws reinforced by the community, civilization unravels.

University of Texas Associate Professor of Government J. Budziszewski is among those who bemoans the coarsening of society and links it to a loss of manners. From college students to radio talk show hosts, Budziszewski sees Americans saying and doing as they please, regardless of their harmful effects on others. He believes practicing courtesy will not only take the edge off some of society's coarseness, it will begin to fundamentally change people. Though courtesy is a "mask" of the unpleasant things one might feel, Budziszewski says this type of mask is not hypocritical, as many are quick to conclude, because it has a high purpose. "Masks, of course, can be used to deceive, but in courtesy that is not the aim."[29] It is to guard against the wanton disrespect of human beings.

As C. S. Lewis, Gilbert Meilaender, and a host of other social critics have explained, masks are worn partly in hopes that our true faces will gradually grow to fit them, and partly to set a good example in the meantime. "If you please," "thank you," and "the pleasure is mine" may be mere formulae, says Budziszewski, but "they rehearse the humility, gratitude, and charity that I know I ought to feel and cannot yet." Courtesy, he says, finds its place in a world where people "would like to be better than they are."[30]

The applications of this "rehearsed" politeness are many. Sensing that courtesy might strengthen the city's tourism industry, New York City civic leaders launched a campaign to encourage its citizens to be nicer to the 25 million visitors who visit the city each year. "Instead of Making a Wise Crack, Smile" the campaign encourages, and "Turn your Back on Tourists and They'll Turn Their Backs on New York."[31] Thanks to the program, cabbies get a new supply of air fresheners, while cops, airport personnel, and subway workers get sensitivity training.

Similarly, corporate America is coming to realize that manners can affect their bottom line, and are turning to business etiquette training companies for help. Letitia Baldrige, former chief of staff to First Lady Jacqueline Kennedy and protocol expert, says this was not always the case.

In the early 1980s, when Baldrige first offered training to chief executive officers (CEOs) she was told that things were just fine and "if anything needed to be said it should be done in secret or shareholders would hoot them out of office."[32]

Although manners may be what one etiquette trainer calls the new status symbol—"pricier than a Rolex, more portable than a Day-Timer, and shinier than handmade shoes"—they have lost considerable ground with schoolchildren.[33] Teachers see children coming to school with few social skills and little respect for authority. To bring back civility, many schools are joining the character education movement with the renewal of good manners as their goal.

Various organizations such as the National Parents Association in Indiana, and Distinctions, directed by Sheryl Eberly in Pennsylvania, provide manners curricula to equip schools to do the job. Eberly's curriculum, entitled "Good Manners Open Doors," provides lessons and activities to teach respect. Eberly, a former White House aide, takes inspiration for her curriculum from George Washington's first rule in a list of 110 *Rules of Civility and Decent Behaviour in Company and Conversation*, that declares, "Every Action Done in Company, ought to be with Some Sign of Respect, to those that are Present."[34]

Shame and Respectability

Few partisans in public debate seem to appreciate how the expansive role of government in the United States has been shaped by a changing morality. Without the aid of morality, as discussed, law is paralyzed as it tries in vain to deal with the infinite conflicts that occur in daily human interaction. In contemporary society, the law is weighed down by burdens and conflicts that ought to be mediated in the realm of civil society, by social constraints, not government. "It's hard to remember now," says Bill Bennett, but "there was once a time when personal or marital failure, subliminal desires and perverse taste were accompanied by guilt and embarrassment."[35]

If personal lives are to be recovered from the arbitrary rule of law, and governed instead by mores and manners, shame is one tool available to society to impose social constraints on behavior. A front-page *Newsweek* story heralds "The Return of Shame" with a subtitle that reads, "Intolerance has gotten a bad rap in recent years, but there should be a way to condemn behavior that's socially destructive."[36] We need to "restore a sense of shame in our society," states Colin Powell. "Those who cultivate moral confusion for profit should understand this," said 1996 GOP presidential nominee Bob

Dole, referring to a debased entertainment industry. In one political speech he threatened to "name their names and shame them as they deserve to be shamed." A panel at Renaissance Weekend, attended and popularized by President and Mrs. Clinton, is called, "About Shame: Morals, Manners and Today's Pop Culture."[37]

Harvard Professor Harvey Mansfield maintains that improving public decorum requires that we simply think differently about it. Public appearances and the need for respectability have been forgotten. "Why do we allow what we used to forbid," he asks, whether it is trash, graffiti, or street beggars? "Because, I think, we have ceased to believe in the value of respectability."[38]

Respectability may have been discarded in recent decades simply because it requires deference to community over personal expression, and thus requires a degree of hypocrisy. The expectations of others must be taken into account, not just personal and individual feelings. In the 1960s, the notion of respectability was overthrown by the opposite idea. Rather than yielding to the expectations of others, the individual was encouraged to follow the dictates of his or her inner self.

Television

The debate within the civil society movement over the need to clean up culture frequently focuses heavily on the role of television and its worsening content in coarsening the wider society's character. Television's pervasive role as a shaper of attitudes and behavior represents an unprecedented development in human civilization. Until recently, society made a concerted effort to protect innocent children from premature exposure to negative influences, making such efforts dramatically easier to uphold. It wasn't left entirely to the individual.

That has all changed with the rise of the entertainment and media culture in which the mentality of the market and consumer choice reign supreme. Entertainment and information technology erodes the power of parents to preside exclusively over their children's moral instruction. Educator John Silber says:

> [P]rior to television and to the breakup of the family, parents typically tried to preserve and extend the ceremonies of innocence in the lives of their children by shielding them from the sordid dimensions of human life, from filthy language, premature exposure to sex, and mindless and indiscriminate violence.[39]

The deplorable condition of television programming is now so widely recognized that it requires little further description.

Television, as a technological device, is not necessarily the issue. In fact, television, along with other forms of information technologies, will continue to play a large and vital educational and commercial role in the information society. This is inevitable, irreversible, and in some ways, socially beneficial.

Nevertheless, television plays an increasingly powerful role in shaping civil society, often for the worse. Television's harmful influence is seemingly limitless. It consumes far too much time, stifles the imagination, and encourages a passive posture toward the world. Above all, television deadens social sensibilities. Even if youths do not imitate the violent acts they have witnessed, as some insist, the deluge of television violence, says college educator Silber, "infects their sensibilities." "Revulsion and abhorrence, our natural reactions to violence, are suppressed,"[40] and we become reconciled to violence "as though it were a normal part of life, as indeed it has become."[41]

Recent studies confirm what parents and educators like Silber have long suspected: Television violence poses serious risks to children. Media researcher Dale Kunkel found that 61 percent of shows now contain violent programming, raising child aggression demonstrably.[42]

There is little doubt that television programming has changed and that it significantly influences behavior. Prime-time programming portrays nearly four times as much sex as it did two decades ago, according to a Kaiser Foundation study. A majority of programs during the family hour of television viewing talk about sex and depict sexually related behavior. The rise of prurient content on television has also been accompanied by a decrease in religious content over the past five years.[43]

According to surveys, children themselves believe television encourages them to experiment with sex too soon, and treat their parents badly and lie. In a survey of 750 respondents between 10 and 16 years old, 76 percent percent said television too often depicts sex before marriage, 62 percent said sex on TV influences their peers to have sex too early, and two thirds said television encourages them to disrespect their parents.[44]

Television, by most accounts, is the most powerful source of socialization in society. Silber describes it as the most "important educational institution in the United States."[45] It has replaced other formative institutions like church, family, and schools, "thoroughly eroding the sense of individual obedience to the unenforceable on which manners and morals and ultimately the law depend."[46]

The real issue, then, is this displacement of core social institutions with an omnipresent entertainment and information media conglomerate. Henry Johnson, in writing about character development, warns that the United States is becoming "a society created by the media."[47] Television, in becoming the chief conveyor of culture, has altered understanding of the public sphere and how public problems are viewed and discussed. For this reason, no strategy to restore moral character to American life will likely succeed without heightening a sense of responsibility in the national entertainment industry and providing parents with better safeguards over what their children see.

The invasiveness of today's information technology has opened the door for vice to flow as freely and widely as virtue. The crudest forms of vice were once contained and confined to the back alleys of society. "Every society has had its red-light districts," says columnist Arianna Huffington, "but until very recently, going there involved danger, stigmatization, and often legal sanction. Now the red-light districts can invade our homes and our children's minds."[48]

Any discussion of television provokes arguments over whether entertainment shapes or mirrors culture. Whatever one concludes on this issue, producers and consumers alike bear a certain measure of the blame. So long as there is a ready market of culturally corrupt, self-absorbed citizens, amoral advertisers will likely continue to appeal to them. *U.S. News and World Report* columnist John Leo writes that "advertisers are focusing more and more on the emerging market of people who do what they want to do, that is, people who yearn to be completely free of all restraint, expectations, and responsibilities." Themes such as "relax, no rules here" and "peel off inhibitions, find your own road" appeal to "the classic infantile wish for an infinite self, free of all restraint."[49]

Clearly, one major reason for television's continuing degeneration is the market. Only recently in American history, however, did the market come to exert more power than the moral scruples of those whose responsibility is to preside over programming. The country may not get the behavior it deserves, says James Morris, "but it does get the behavior it countenances. If violent movies drew no audiences, they could implode and vanish." What makes this difficult today is that the "floodgates that once kept popular culture in check—including presumptive self-censorship on the part of its purveyors, and a much narrower pre-TV access to markets—no longer function; they're rusty with disuse and stuck in an open position."[50]

Television programmers now have both the technological means and the moral license to pollute the cultural environment. Bill Bennett accuses television executives of "practicing philosophy without reflection," broadly damaging society. The "summum bonum" of life for the television philosophers is "self-indulgence, self-aggrandizement, instant gratification; the good life is synonymous with license and freedom from all inhibitions; other people are to be used as a means to an end; and self-fulfillment is achieved by breaking rules."[51]

Parents, who wish to remain the guardians of their children, have no choice but to maintain constant vigilance over television viewing, something parents find difficult to exercise for obvious reasons. Polls show that many kids watch television alone, and 68 percent of parents with young children can only be with their kids for half of the time that those kids spend in front of the TV.[52] While some look to recently devised television rating systems to solve the problem, many more, sensing danger, are simply unplugging their television sets altogether.[53]

Conclusion and Prospects

Assessing prospects for the recovery of moral values and the restoration of culture is difficult. Culture, after all, is basically about ideas, attitudes, and values that take root in our lives and institutions. These culturally imbedded ideas exert a most basic form of influence over our lives, and are the most difficult to alter.

Few observers of cultural developments today dare to predict the paths American culture will follow, but they do recognize the stakes for civil society. Boston University Professor Thomas Lickona describes "a growing sense that we stand at a cultural crossroads." "Either we reverse the current trends," Lickona says, "or we continue the slide and go down the tubes."[54]

On the positive side of the ledger, many signs point to a greater willingness among Americans to come to terms with the excesses of recent decades. The baby boom generation, so self-conscious over its alleged role in the deterioration of social values, is ready to replace the "do-your-own-thing" ethic of the 1960s and 1970s with greater personal discipline and social stability.[55]

If best-selling books are any indication of the culture's path, Americans may soon be discarding the fads of self-indulgence and self-esteem for greater self-control. Case Western Reserve University Professor Roy Baumeister reflects these changing sentiments this way, "If we could cross out self-esteem and put in self-control, kids would be better off and society in general would be much better off." Simply liking yourself is not enough, says Baumeister, citing studies that show a weak link between good feelings and improved behavior.[56]

Once concerned mostly about subjective feelings, people today are focused on objective behavior. A majority of Americans worry about declining civility, but they also want to see changes in rates of out-of-wedlock childbearing, teen sexual activity, family decline, and children's exposure to violence and sex.[57] Culturalists cite this data, hoping to show that Americans are ready to right a lot of cultural wrongs.

A closer look at American attitudes, however, suggests that the American mind is riddled with deep contradictions, ambivalence, and resignation about what can or should be done to correct moral wrongs. For one, few are personally prepared to accept personal culpability for social decline, a necessary precursor to widespread social reform. A *Los Angeles Times* poll suggested that, while 57 percent felt that "too many people have lifestyles and beliefs that are harmful to themselves and society," only 11 percent of Americans believe their own moral behavior has contributed to the nation's problems. In the United States, 96 percent believe they are doing an excellent or good job of teaching their children about morals and values.[58]

If few people blame themselves for social breakdown, they are not likely to embrace interventions curbing their own freedom. Concern over culture does not translate automatically into a mandate to moderate it. Americans are deeply ambivalent about attempts to establish greater social control through public action. The same *Los Angeles Times* poll asked people to identify which annoyed them more: government intrusion into citizens' private lives or government failure to confront challenges to traditional values. A comfortable majority found government intrusion to be the greater source of irritation.[59]

Many are simply fatalistic about changing people's behavior. For example, on the issue of drugs, 49 percent of baby boom parents experimented with drugs in their youth, and are not convinced that it was a serious mistake or that their own children can resist the temptation. Two-thirds of these parents expect their own kids to do the same and are not deeply troubled by it. "What is infuriating," says former Health and Human Services Secretary Joseph Califano, a key antidrug leader, is "the resignation of so many parents."[60]

Many parents are not convinced that their children can be protected from cultural values. Americans have starkly negative views of popular culture, and by a large margin blame television more than any other factor for teenage sex and violence, according to a recent *New York Times* survey. But by as large a margin, people do not believe that current proposals to protect children will make any difference.[61]

Similarly, evidence suggests that knowledge of a problem does not necessarily lead to a change in individual behavior. On a range of destructive personal behaviors, from unprotected sex to drugs, mere awareness of danger does not alter lifestyles. In their work to slow the AIDS epidemic, for example, government officials have discovered that knowledge alone does not change behavior.[62]

For these reasons, the move toward cultural recovery is both difficult to predict and daunting to accomplish, not withstanding some of the more encouraging recent developments. Many, if not most, culturalists are pessimistic, at least about short-term prospects. Francis Fukuyama argues that the social capital of shared moral values has been depleted and "may take centuries to replenish, if it can be replenished at all."[63]

Charles Krauthammer cautions that, absent a broad spiritual reawakening, the arrest of social decay and the revitalization of civil society become far more difficult and uncertain propositions. This raises a final concern about what may happen next if deeply rooted change is not achieved. Krauthammer warns that if moral renewal does not occur within and throughout civil society, "it must then depend upon the more coercive and less reliable agency of politics—a politics crucially incapable of articulating cultural with structural reform."[64]

The cultural reform movement is not an organized movement. It lacks many of the ingredients that other segments of the civil society movement possess, above all, a plentiful supply of thoughtful and skillful leaders. Many who could speak up and organize around cultural renewal simply refuse to do so. For example, many liberal intellectual and public figures privately lament our current cultural condition and occasionally write about it for public consideration. But few offer concrete solutions, apparently out of fear of weakening First Amendment protections or inviting the charge of reaction, nostalgia, or intolerance.

Politicians find cultural territory deeply problematic and, except for William Bennett, have largely steered clear of it. Politicians often abandon the subject because they are not certain about solutions to cultural deterioration and lack the necessary philosophical understanding and rhetorical skills to effectively use their "bully pulpit." Nevertheless, as Amitai Etzioni states, the country is yearning for a figure "who will eloquently speak about social values even when there is little that the government can or should do about them."[65]

Whether this nation will receive that kind of leadership remains to be seen. Basic divisions over philosophical concepts and moral precepts run deep, and many are repelled from confronting so difficult a challenge.

Notes

1. Paul Greenberg, "Culture of Death," *The Weekly Standard*, 9 October 1995, 16.

2. Charles Krauthammer, "A Social Conservative Credo," *The Public Interest*, Fall 1995, 17.

3. William J. Bennett, foreword to *Restoring the Good Society*, by Don E. Eberly (Grand Rapids, Mich.: Hourglass Books, 1994), 11-12.

4. Christopher Beem, "Civic Virtue and Civil Society," *Los Angeles Times*, 27 May 1996.

5. William J. Bennett, Redeeming Our Time," *Imprimis,* 24, no. 11 (Hillsdale, Mich.: Hillsdale College, November 1995), 4.

6. William Raspberry, "The Moral Center," *Washington Post*, 8 February 1995.

7. James Q. Wilson, *The Moral Sense* (New York: The Free Press, 1993).

8. Gertrude Himmelfarb, *The De-Moralization of Society: From Victorian Virtues to Modern Values* (New York: Alfred A. Knopf, Inc., 1994).

9. Amitai Etzioni, *The Moral Dimension* (New York: The Free Press, 1988).

10. Alan Wolfe, "Looking Good," a review of *Integrity*, by Stephen L. Carter, *The New Republic*, 18 March 1996, 34.

11. Gertrude Himmelfarb, "Re-Moralizing America," *The Wall Street Journal*, 7 February 1995.

12. Joseph Shattan, "The De-Moralization of Society: From Victorian Values to Modern Values," a review of *The De-Moralization of Society*, by Gertrude Himmelfarb, in *The American Spectator*, June 1995, 61.

13. Daniel J. Silver, "The Revolt of the Elites and the Betrayal of Democracy," a review of the book by the same name, by Christopher Lasch, *The American Spectator*, May 1995, 72.

14. See Robert N. Bellah et al., *Habits of the Heart: Individualism and Commitment in American Life* (New York: Harper and Row, 1985).

15. James Davison Hunter, *Culture Wars: The Struggle to Define America* (New York: Basic Books, 1991), 34.

16. Himmelfarb, "Re-Moralizing America."

17. David Bromwich, "Victoria's Secret," a review of *The De-Moralization of Society: From Victorian Virtues to Modern Values*," by Gertrude Himmelfarb, *The New Republic*, 15 May 1995, 28-34.

18. Margaret Gramatky Alter, "A Nation of Peter Pans," *Books and Culture*, January-February 1997, 24.

19. Rochelle Gurstein, *The Repeal of Reticence* (New York: Hill and Wang, 1996), 5.

20. Gurstein, 5.

21. Gurstein, 7.

22. Don E. Eberly, "Civil Society: The Paradox of American Progress," *Essays on Civil Society* 1, no. 2 (January 1996), 2.

23. John Marks, "The American Uncivil Wars," *U.S. News and World Report*, 22 April 1996, 67-68.

24. John Silber, "The Media and Our Children: Who is Responsible," *Windgate Journal*, from Boston University commencement address (May 1995), 11-13.

25. James Morris, "Democracy Beguiled," *Wilson Quarterly*, August-September, 1996, 24.

26. Morris, 27.

27. Judith Martin and Gunther S. Stent, "I Think; Therefore I Thank: A Philosophy of Etiquette," *The American Scholar*, 59, (Spring 1990): 243-244.

28. Martin and Stent, 245.

29. J. Budziszewski, "The Moral Case for Manners," *National Review*, February 20, 1995, 62.

30. Budziszewski, 64.

31. Anthony Falola, "A Rude Awakening in New York," *Washington Post*, 2 June 1995.

32. Robert McGarvey and Scott Smith, "Etiquette 101," *Training* (September 1993): 52.

33. Marks, 72.

34. George Washington, *Rules of Civility and Decent Behaviour in Company and Conversation* (Mount Vernon, Va.: The Mount Vernon Ladies Association, 1989), 21.

35. Bill Bennett, quoted in Susan Crabtree, "Trash TV Pulls America Down the Tubes," *Insight*, 4 December 1995, 8.

36. Jonathan Alter and Pat Wingert, "The Return of Shame," *Newsweek*, 6 February 1995.

37. Henry Allen, "Shame," *Washington Post*, 9 April 1996.

38. Harvey Mansfield, "Bring Back Respectability," *The American Enterprise*, November-December, 1996, 67.

39. From a May 1995 commencement address by John Silber, Boston University.

40. Silber, "The Media and our Children," 12.

41. Silber, "The Media and our Children," 12.

42. "TV Violence Can Pose Risk to Children," *Knight-Ridder News Service*, 27 March 1997.

43. "TV Less Moral, Religious Now, Viewers Say," *Associated Press*, 21 March 1997.

44. "TV Encourages Bad Behavior, Kids Say," *Associated Press*, 27 February 1995.

45. Silber, "The Media and our Children," 12.

46. Silber, "The Media and our Children," 12.

47. Henry C. Johnson, "Society, Culture and Character Development," in ed. K.

K. Ryan and G. F. McLean *Character Development in Schools and Beyond*, (New York: Praeger, 1987), 59.

48. Arianna Huffington, "Internet Evils Beyond the Decency Limits," *Washington Times*, 16 March 1996.

49. John Leo, "Decadence, the Corporate Way," *U.S. News and World Report*, 4 September 1995, 31.

50. Morris, 28.

51. William J. Bennett, "Television's Destructive Power," *Washington Post*, 29 February 1996.

52. Richard Morin, "Confronting Sex and Violence on Television," *Washington Post*, 23 December 1996, 38.

53. Knight-Ridder News Service, "How and Why Some Are Turning Off TV," *Lancaster (PA) New Era*, 10 February 1996.

54. Melissa Healy, "Moral Crisis," *Los Angeles Times*, 2 June 1996, 12.

55. Ann Symonds, "'Me Generation' Parents Should Grow Up," *The Wall Street Journal*, 30 October 1995.

56. Ulysses Torassa, "Self-Control, Not Self-Esteem, May Become the Primary Goal of the '90s," *Lancaster (PA) New Era*, 27 November 1995.

57. Gary L. Bauer, "Polls to Pols: Restore the Nation's Moral Compass," *Insight*, 18 December 1995, 22.

58. Healy, 12.

59. Healy, 12.

60. Associated Press, "Many Baby Boomers Don't See Drugs as a Crisis, Study Finds," *Lancaster (PA) New Era*, 9 September 1996.

61. Elizabeth Kolbert, *New York Times News Service*, 21 August 1995.

62. Jeff McGaw, "High-Risk Behavior Not Deterred by Knowledge," *Harrisburg Patriot-News*, 1 December 1995.

63. Richard Grenier, "The High Cost of Low Trust in America," *Insight*, 6 November 1995, 24.

64. Charles Krauthammer, "A Social Conservative Credo," *The Public Interest*, Fall 1995, 22.

65. Amitai Etzioni, "The Politics of Morality," *The Wall Street Journal*, 13 November 1995.

Chapter 8

Recovering Individual Character and Ethics

One of the most dynamic movements to strengthen civil society in the United States is a rapidly growing attempt to recover character in schools and community groups. More and more groups and projects tie the recovery of civil society to the renewal of personal character. They are distinguished from other strands of the civil society movement by their conviction that the central job of civil society is to impart character to young and old alike, especially in the schools. Though still small, the character movement is making substantial inroads in public education and related civic programming.

The nation's founders believed character was central to citizenship and indispensable to maintaining a healthy, free, and civil society. Character was at the core of what G. K. Chesterton described as the nation's "creed." The nation's constitutional framers understood and expected that the less individuals practiced self-regulation the more costly and meddlesome government controls would expand into the private realm.

For most of the nation's history, it was taken for granted that citizens and leaders would embrace and maintain character. The founders simply assumed that such character-shaping institutions as families and houses of worship would remain central to the lives of Americans, and civic institutions would strive confidently to moralize the young. The founders' generation shaped public institutions, like the public school system, around the development of character.

In recent decades, however, the work of fostering character has fallen on hard times. The institutions that once played this role have been weakened, and the position of character as a preeminent concern has yielded instead to competing appeals to individual self-esteem and self-fulfillment. Philosophical and cultural influences have also steadily undermined society's consensus over moral values and weakened society's character-shaping institutions.

The Collapse of Character

Many of the nation's costliest and most consequential social problems originate in the erosion of personal character. The signs of this erosion can be found everywhere, but especially among the young. Author and character education expert Tom Lickona has surveyed the ethical condition of youth and has identified the following ten trends that are entirely contrary to the requirements of democratic character: rising youth violence; increasing dishonesty (lying, cheating, and stealing); growing disrespect for authority; peer cruelty; a resurgence of bigotry on school campuses, from preschool to higher education; a decline in the work ethic; sexual precocity; a growing self-centeredness and declining civic responsibility; an increase in self-destructive behavior; and ethical illiteracy.[1]

Lickona's ten troubling trends are substantiated through extensive social data and scientific surveys. The fact, for example, that the United States leads developed nations in its rates of juvenile crime, teen pregnancy, and drug abuse, and that its high school students must cope with assaults and weapons possession, suggests a wide collapse of character.[2]

This collapse has many explanations, from changing patterns of work, family, and social life, to the rise of a highly materialistic society—what Daniel Yankelovich calls "the affluence factor"[3]—to moral relativism. Philosophical influences have also played an important role. For instance, logical positivism, a belief system that separates values from objective facts, has relegated values to the subjective realm of preferences, feelings, and tastes. The result, says Tom Lickona, is that morality has been "relativized and privatized—made to seem a matter of personal 'value judgment,' not a subject for public debate and transmission."[4]

As noted earlier, the civil society debate unavoidably makes reference to some conception of "the good"—the concept of citizenship, for example, centers on well defined positive character traits. However, the prevalence of relativism in recent years caused many educators to fear that moral instruction was nothing less than unwarranted indoctrination. For the relativist, the right answer to ethical questions can only be determined by the individual making his own decision based upon the circumstances of a particular situation.

In losing a consensus on the centrality of character, the capacity to judge good behavior from bad has also weakened. According to ethics professor Jean Elshtain, judging the conduct and content of others' character, an exercise long thought necessary for society, is now considered to be "in bad odor." It is equated "with being punitive or with insensitivity," or with various "phobias" or "isms."[5] When issues of moral principle and character are made private and subjective, society has a harder time developing and preserving a common moral story, and the very notion of "a good person" loses its meaning.

The most compelling explanation for the decline of character is the loss of influence by those institutions in society that have traditionally been responsible for inculcating character, such as parents, schools, churches, and public authorities, as discussed earlier. These shapers of the young have seen their authority eroded by more powerful cultural influences such as the entertainment industry.

The Character Recovery Movement: Finding Common Ground

Like other social reform movements, interest in character seems to follow a cyclical pattern in American history. As character declines, new groups emerge, seeking to focus fresh attention on the urgency of renewing character and the importance of building public consensus around moral norms.

Evidence suggests that such a movement is again emerging. The first task of a character movement is to develop a new framework to make the discussion of values palatable to a large majority of citizens. The values debate throughout much of the 1970s and 1980s was often presented as a choice between extremes—secularism or sectarianism, relativism or absolutism. But framing the debate this way allowed for little common ground across cultural and religious boundaries.

As an alternative to such fragmented and unproductive debate, the character movement offers new assumptions and a new approach designed to establish common ground. One group that exemplifies this new approach is the Character Counts Coalition. Avoiding polarization and gridlock, the coalition has attracted support from across the political spectrum. The organization's stated objective is to replace situational ethics and moral relativism by advancing character in "a common language."[6] This goal is achieved by promoting the six "pillars" of character: trustworthiness, respect, responsibility, fairness, caring, and citizenship.

Many wonder whether a society as pluralistic as the United States can construct and impart a system of values without favoring one religion or culture over another. The character recovery movement asserts, in response, that ethnic and religious diversity can only exist as long as common ground is found in society. By emphasizing demonstrable external displays of virtue —like honor, duty, sacrifice, and trustworthiness—character programs try to avoid the twin traps of either the values balkanization or the soft situational ethics of the recent past.

Members of this new movement emphasize that the quest for character is not to be confused with solving vexing moral dilemmas or staking out positions on issues of social policy. Character advocates focus instead on teaching the basic principles of character and virtue for individual application, on which there is broad agreement. Rather than speaking to matters of social controversy, those in the character recovery movement encourage individuals to cultivate personal integrity and moral character, based on the view that acquiring civilized moral habits must precede any discussion of social dilemmas or moral controversies.

Pollster George Gallup found that "surprisingly high" numbers of Americans agree key moral qualities should be imparted to youth. Sixty-nine percent believe community agreement can be found on core values and principles and even larger majorities agree on what those values should consist of. Over 90 percent of citizens agree that honesty, democratic ideas, the golden rule, and acceptance of those with different political and social views should be taught, while nearly three quarters agree on teaching children sexual abstinence outside of marriage.[7]

Habituation

The return to character is guided by a clear understanding of how character is caught and inculcated through character-shaping institutions. Unlike the vague and often divisive "values" debate, character education is guided by a formula of "knowing the good, desiring the good, and doing the good."[8] In other words, character has cognitive, affective, and behavioral dimensions. The cognitive side of character training provides knowledge of right and wrong. The emotional side includes the capacity to empathize with others and the behavioral side acts on cognition and empathy to do what is right. Doing the good, then, requires learning the habits of sound character through practice.

Character education represents a return to the classical notion of moral education in two ways. First, it holds that moral virtues are universal in nature and can be found in successful civilizations throughout the world from the beginning of time, and are not the product of a particular culture or country. Second, it applies the Aristotelian notion that good character comes through practice—through the repetition of good and heroic deeds. Character is not compartmentalized, therefore, in some private category; it has social origins and ramifications. It is not so much taught as it is "caught" in the routines of ordinary life in civil society.

According to character advocates, sound character is acquired through the development of sound habits, or through "habituation," to use James Q. Wilson's familiar term. Family habituation, in particular, according to Wilson, is "the chief method by which every society induces its members to exercise a modicum of self-control and to assign a reasonable value to the preference of others."[9] Moral conduct occurs when "right actions are regularly, promptly, and consistently followed by approval and rewards and when wrong actions are regularly, promptly, and consistently followed by disapproval."[10]

It is at this point that individual character and the institutions that shape character become interdependent. In a free and democratic society, the individual and society influence each other. Character development is not just an individual process, nor is it simply a function of pedagogy. Strategies for renewing character must focus on multiple sectors, and especially on character's primary source—family. Developmental research conclusively shows that empathy, the ability to assume another person's point of view, develops mainly in the first years of life under the care of competent parents.[11]

Just as civil society depends upon individuals who are strong in character, individual character finds its source in strong community institutions that establish and assert social norms. The root of the Greek word for ethics, *ethikos*, means an ethos, rooted in community and transmitted through customs.

Restoring character requires rebuilding character-shaping institutions, not just engaging in moral admonition. Character is not simply something to be taught through moral instruction; it must be taught as our young are raised among moral exemplars. Parents, pastors, and pedagogues display and impart character in the daily connections and activities of life.

The movement to restore values demands a sociology of character. The problem with many efforts to guide moral reform, according to communitarian Amitai Etzioni, is that they are "asociological"—they address moral life simply as a matter of individual development. In the process, says Etzioni, "many Americans disregard the crucial role of the community in reinforcing the individual's moral commitments."[12] Individuals are powerfully affected by "the approbation and censure" of others, especially those with whom they have close relations, such as family and neighbors. A society that wishes to preserve character, then, will encourage these voices in the community to speak in "unison and with clarity," to strengthen individual judgments about right and wrong.[13]

Applications

Character is once again being promoted in a variety of contexts, including sports, entertainment, public discourse, charity, and official conduct. In Colorado, one of the oldest United Way agencies in the United States is undertaking a year-long character project to recover rules of civic conduct in public space. The mayor of Dallas has organized the business and civic community to develop a citywide strategy to recover character.[14] Dozens of major universities are restoring programs in ethics that were abandoned years ago. The Jefferson Center for Character Education, directed by David Brooks, trains law enforcement officers and consults with cities and social agencies to find out where to apply character education in confronting gangs, violence, and vandalism.[15]

No single institution bears exclusive responsibility for imparting character. However, next to parents, schools may play the most vital role. Several states have moved in recent years to explore or adopt character education programs. In Georgia, the state Board of Education adopted a rule requiring all local school districts to provide education in values like citizenship, responsibility, and respect for others. The state leaves the details to local communities, but recommends resources and strategies for implementation.[16] New Hampshire has established a program of values training for teachers. In Michigan, the state Education Board is debating a statement of principles that focuses on character and the duties of citizenship. Hundreds of local school districts are developing character programs with the assistance of several national character organizations.

The Character Counts Coalition, mentioned above, a project of the Josephson Institute of Ethics, plays a central role in promulgating information and assistance. The coalition provides a range of services to interested parents, schools, and civic organizations, including guidance on developing community support for character education programs. The coalition's advisory board includes top public figures from Marian Wright Edelman to Bill Bennett, with the American Red Cross, Boys and Girls Clubs of America, 4-H, the YMCA of America, and other leading civic organizations as charter members. Character Counts is now working through an alliance of over 160 nonprofit organizations to take the character message to youth.

Several major groups are developing character education programming and curricula. The Jefferson Center for Character Education in California has developed a comprehensive program for public schools that has been implemented in all 430 elementary schools in the Los Angeles school district. The Character Education Partnership also promotes "civic virtue and moral character," predominantly in America's schools. The partnership organizes forums, media campaigns, and national awards, and offers a clearinghouse to promote its "Eleven Principles of Character Education."[17] Also working in schools and with businesses is the Institute for Global Ethics, which has developed a character curriculum.

The most experienced voice in character education is Joseph Gauld. After years of frustration as a professional educator, in 1962, Gauld founded the Hyde School in Bath, Maine, upon the principle that learning begins with the development of character and a sense of purpose. Cultivation of character, Gauld believes, is not possible unless it is a part of the child's entire environment, especially the family.[18] The school relies heavily on peer pressure and well developed norms to enforce its core principles of courage, concern, curiosity, and leadership. Gauld's success has not only been a model for many public schools, he has recently founded his own public school in Maine.

Conclusion

The growing movement to recover character in the nation's schools and communities is one of the more dynamic features of the nation's newfound interest in civil society. Because of its many practical applications, it may also prove to be the most durable. By transcending existing divisions over moral values and finding a new synthesis focusing on personal character, this movement has attracted thousands of new recruits to the effort to improve personal character and civic virtue.

Notes

1. Thomas Lickona, "The Return of Character Education," *Educational Leadership* (November 1993): 9.

2. Don E. Eberly, "The Quest for America's Character," in *The Content of America's Character*, ed. Don E. Eberly (Lanham, Md.: Madison Books, 1995), 7.

3. Daniel Yankelovich, "How Changes in the Economy Are Reshaping American Values," in *Values and Public Policy* (Washington, D.C.: Brookings Institute, 1994), 18-19.

4. Lickona, 6.

5. Jean Bethke Elshtain, "Judge Not," *First Things*, October 1994, 37.

6. Josephson Institute of Ethics, press announcement, 8 October 1993.

7. Princeton Religion Research Center, newsletter 15 (1994), 1.

8. Lickona, 9.

9. James Q. Wilson, "Culture, Incentives, and the Underclass," *Values and Public Policy* (Washington, D.C.: Brookings Institute, 1994), 62.

10. James Q. Wilson, "Public Policy and Personal Character," in *Thinking about America: The United States in the 1990s*, ed. A. Anderson and D. L. Bark (Palo Alto, Calif.: Hoover Institution, 1988), 493.

11. "The Moral Child," *U.S. News and World Report*, 3 June 1996, 54.

12. Amitai Etzioni, "Restoring Our Moral Voice," *The Public Interest*, Summer 1994, 109.

13. Etzioni, 110.

14. Mark Potok and Andrea Stone, "Values Get a Chance at a Comeback," *USA Today*, 3 February 1995.

15. See B. David Brooks, "Strengthening Character through Community-Based Organizations," in *The Content of America's Character*, ed. Don E. Eberly (Lanham, Md.: Madison Books, 1995), 225-238.

16. Charles E. Greenawalt, II, "Character Education among the States," in *The Content of America's Character*, ed. Don E. Eberly (Lanham, Md.: Madison Books, 1995), 202.

17. See Thomas Lickona, Eric Schaps, and Catherine Lewis, *Eleven Principles of Effective Character Education* (Alexandria, Va: The Character Education Partnership), and Renee Stovsky, "Character Matters," *St. Louis Post-Dispatch*, 27 August 1995.

18. Joseph Gauld, "Character Development: A School's Primary Task," *The Wall Street Journal*, 1 April 1992.

Chapter 9

Toward a New Public Philosophy: Common Ground and the Common Good

James Davison Hunter, director of the Post-Modernity Project at the University of Virginia, asks, "Does democracy require a coherent public philosophy, or is it enough to establish a viable consensus on democratic procedures?"[1] This is the central question civil society theorists and practitioners wrestle with as they attempt to connect social values and institutions with the life of democratic politics. How are the nation's prospects as a democracy affected by the state of thinking that pervades culture and society?

Many conclude that the philosophy that has guided modern American parties and political movements, from left to right, is stagnant and deeply inadequate to the challenges of these times. Though attempts by many current projects to strengthen democratic structures and practice and to enhance citizen ownership of the public process are noteworthy and significant, explanations for the decline in citizenship and public-spiritedness go far beyond the structural factors and surface excesses of modern politics.

Explanations for the weakening of American democracy must include the philosophical content of modern democracy itself. Democracy may not possess the means of its own preservation. After all, the structures of democracy are an empty vessel into which Americans pour the contents of their minds and hearts. As Abraham Lincoln observed, a country consists of its people, its laws, and its territory, but only its territory is assured of durability. In democracy, little is assured, and only those things that are valued by the people remain durable.

The public philosophy wing of the civil society movement argues that if a society based upon character and community is to be rebuilt, the nation must recover a public philosophy adequate to the task. The current dominant public philosophy is seen as a flawed and unsustainable form of liberal individualism whose focus on unbounded individual interests and rights is unable to provide an enduring foundation for democracy. American democratic capitalism rests upon a supply of virtue, which it has been steadily spending down without attempting to sustain or replenish. As Kenneth Anderson put it, liberalism "exists by scavenging off of older, traditional forms of social life." Because liberalism does nothing to conserve these traditional sources of democratic order, he adds, they can "disappear in a historical flash."[2]

Liberty depends upon a capacity and willingness to place voluntary constraints upon passions and vice. Yet public life in the United States gets little help from either our sensate culture, with its emphasis on self-emancipation and impulse gratification, nor by politics itself, which with rare exceptions gives scant attention to the republican virtues once thought to be so central to American success.

A revitalized public philosophy centers on the need to cultivate character and virtue among citizens by moderating the current preoccupation with rights, and by promoting responsibility and social obligation.

The search is on within the civil society movement for a new public philosophy capable of curbing the fragmenting influence of extreme individualism and promoting the common good. Many in the civil society movement believe that current political assumptions and ideologies contribute to the impoverishment of public life. Civil society advocates are among the first to raise concerns about the fragility of American democracy.

Democracy's Fragility

American democracy is frequently referred to as an experiment. The continued use of the term *experiment* after two centuries of practical success implies persistent doubts over democracy's basic durability. Those who supplied the philosophical foundations of American democracy recognized that the republican system of government was fragile. Because public well-being flows from the wellspring of private virtue, as Madison put it, it is "chimerical" to assume the republic can endure without a rich supply of virtue.

In democracies, responsibility is always left to individual citizens to maintain communities that are safe, civil, and humane, and thus liberal democracy cannot survive without a large endowment of human capital and individual competence. From the beginning, the American experiment presupposed the existence of individuals with democratic habits and dispositions.

The path to freedom, as Michael Novak has described it, was thought to be "a narrow road." Democracy, predicated as it was upon individual freedom, was only suitable for those prepared to undertake the rigors of self-governance. Citizens could not possibly hope to be entrusted with the governance of the larger society if they were incapable of self-governance. Thus, free democratic societies require far more virtue than other social systems.

Much of the analysis of democratic disorder in the United States centers on alleged procedural flaws, which are undoubtedly serious. But an emphasis on procedure too easily ignores society's deeper failure to cultivate and maintain positive democratic habits. In public conversation, the language of the technical and procedural aspects of governing, like lawmaking, elections, appropriations, and fiscal projections, is the reining dialect. Only rarely is there serious or sustained talk about the importance of democratic character or competence to the well-being of society.

Democratic character, however, must be cultivated, and it flows not merely from formal constitutions and congressional acts, but from the vital, character-shaping institutions in civil society. According to Harvard Professor Mary Ann Glendon, "governments must have an adequate supply of citizens who are skilled in the arts of self-government." These arts consist of "deliberation, compromise, consensus-building, civility, and reason-giving."[3]

Free people need written constitutions and representative institutions, of course, but they also need an unwritten social bond that makes the work of deliberation and compromise in democracy possible. Countries moving successfully toward democracy, like the recently liberated nations of eastern Europe, recognize the need to rebuild the social institutions that supply these democratic habits and skills. Because the institutions of civil society in many of these fledgling democracies have been badly weakened, a range of social viruses, from pervasive public corruption and crime to private greed and distrust among citizens, frequently hampers democratic development.

For civil society to be strong, citizens must have confidence in their institutions and in each other. Trust, the essential glue of democracy, binds isolated individuals together in common pursuits. The replacement of the traditional handshake in the context of civil society with bureaucratic regulations, contracts, and litigation, represents a major departure from the nation's older tradition of trustful association.

As discussed earlier, this distrust has many causes, some of which are endemic to the modern bureaucratic state. The work of democracy is too frequently delegated upwards from citizens to interest groups, specialists and power brokers, who earn their livelihood by gaining clout for competing factions and interests. Distrust also finds some of its origins in the uprooting effects of modernity itself. Robert Nisbet described modern people as "uprooted, alone, without secure status, cut off from community or any system of clear moral purpose." Because of the fragmenting effects of modern life, people are "estranged from others, from work, from place, from self."[4]

Declining satisfaction with the democratic process is also rooted in the many contradictions that exist within the public mind itself. For example, many resent the intrusive and costly nature of government, yet are attracted to the great advances in human health, safety, and environmental protection that government intervention helps make possible. In other words, Americans may be unprepared to live with the trade-offs that now confront them, which for example, forces government to protect against risks while also simultaneously guaranteeing the rewards of unencumbered risk taking. Whatever government does or doesn't do under these circumstances, it fails to meet public expectations.

Another influence that frustrates progress toward a common public philosophy is the fact that public debate frequently centers not on the broad concerns, hopes, and values of Americans, but on mundane issues of programs, appropriations, and the technical workings of government. Politics no longer molds and shapes private aspirations into a vision for the common good.

The Market versus the State

Much of public debate has focused on either the state or the market. Each of these emphases produce what Bill Galston calls a "politics of nostalgia, whether practiced by those who wish to hold on to The New Deal or those pushing as an alternative an "ideologically-driven laissez faire." Neither, he says, will solve our problems. The answer lies with a return to "civic localism."[5]

The entire public debate grinds forward along a sterile and predictable grid of either governmentalism or market incentivism, based on the idea that lives and communities will be bettered by simply getting government policies right or by liberating the marketplace. Each argument draws on liberal individualism, one emphasizing the empowering possibilities of the state through rights and entitlements, the other exalting the unlimited possibilities of the market through expanded personal freedom to create wealth and consume goods.

Governmentalism assumes that the human condition can be altered through the enlightened application of scientific solutions by credentialed specialists. American institutions, and especially the central government, have been subjected to a creeping twentieth-century culture of managerialism that treats amateurs as though they are inept and citizens as out of place for wanting a role in their own government. Much of government programming since the rise of the New Deal has been influenced by the principles of scientific management as espoused by Frederick Taylor, emphasizing efficiency, specialization, and com-partmentalization. The particular needs of individuals and the particular characteristics of communities are often ignored.

Michael Joyce explains how the policy sciences have led to the false belief that every problem of society can be solved through technical expertise. According to Joyce:

When the government applies its resources of science, management and money to projects that can be accomplished with science, management and money, it is successful. When it applies science, management and money to the problems of the human condition, it is not so successful.[6]

Joyce compares the impressive accomplishments of scientific management displayed in such projects as the interstate road system, the lunar landing, or missile defense systems to the monumental failure of the policy sciences in healing race relations, rehabilitating criminals, or halting drug use and child abuse. In the latter examples, Joyce says, experts either do not know what to do or should never have been given the problems in the first place. Curbing problems like teen pregnancy should be assigned to civil society. The search for moral wisdom and truth, he says, is an activity "that only civil society can contemplate."[7] What is unique about civil society is that it is often seen as a haven or refuge for such things as finding moral or spiritual meaning. This is not the kind of activity that should be delegated to the state.

Similarly, economic liberalism essentially seeks to subject more and more spheres of life to the instrumental logic of the market. Those who hold this position believe that if the state is curtailed and individuals are left to their own devices, society will move spontaneously and rationally toward self-organization and harmony. Economic liberalism insists on little else than that the market must be freed, whether in snack foods, automobiles, pornography, human cloning, or the ownership of the national parks.

This triumph of the logic of the market is a relatively new phenomenon. Adam Smith treated economic transactions in the context of human associations, an approach that was better grounded in ethical and humanitarian considerations than today's market utilitarianism. Economic life was linked to the Protestant work ethic or a notion of "enlightened" self-interest that attempted to subordinate self-interest to moral purpose. The nation's biblical and civic republican traditions have held that because man is fallible, the pursuit of private interest alone quickly becomes corrupting.

In considering the state of contemporary public philosophy, some attention must be given to the dominant role economic theory has come to play in the social sciences and public policymaking. The supremacy of economics and an economic rationale for every human activity have deeply affected public life. Economics seeks to quantify things, often on the assumption that if something can be quantified, we assume it can be predicted and even controlled. Chiseled over the entrance to the Social Science Building at the University of Chicago, which gave the United States so many Nobel Laureates in economics, is a statement that captures this mindset: "When you cannot measure it, when you cannot express it in numbers, your knowledge is of a meager and unsatisfactory kind."

Francis Fukuyama maintains that this approach offers a very limited picture of how society works, and a worse portrait of how it should work. Often, the most important things in society cannot be captured in numbers or predicted by economic formulae. To understand the true functioning of democratic society, factors like religion, tradition, honor, and loyalty must be taken into account. By supplying the necessary trust for communal life, these "arational" factors in turn enhance rational economic interaction.[8]

Self-interest alone can even fall short of preserving prosperity, much less engendering a stable democracy. Even Peter Drucker, the world-renowned business consultant and advocate of capitalism, has become critical of modern economic thinking. "We are learning fast that the belief that a free market is all it takes to have a functioning society—or even a functioning economy—is pure delusion."[9]

Markets, says Alan Wolfe, "flourish in a moral order defined by non-economic ties of trust and solidarity; markets are necessary for modernity, but they tend to destroy what makes them work." Similarly, "the liberal theory of the state was neither purely liberal, for its originators relied on preexisting moral ties to temper the bleakness of the social contract, nor purely statist, because it assumed a strong society."[10]

In essence, the entire debate has focused on only two instruments for social and democratic progress—the state and the marketplace—both placed in service of autonomous individuals. The "liberalism" of the left and right both rely on either the market or the state to organize "codes of moral obligation," says Wolfe.[11] Ironically, civil society, which the founders believed democracy depended upon for success, is completely ignored.

Michael Sandel, a leading theoretician in an emerging movement to revitalize the nation's public philosophy, strongly criticizes the dominant liberal paradigm, for viewing citizens merely as "freely choosing, independent selves, unencumbered by moral or civic ties antecedent to choice."[11] Under the liberal vision of society that Sandel critiques, "government should not affirm, through its policies or laws, any particular conception of the good life; instead it should provide a neutral framework of rights within which people can choose their own values and ends."[12]

Government cannot and must not, under this conception, affirm any particular definition of virtue or the good, but rather must remain entirely neutral over the ends citizens may choose to pursue. Briefly stated, Sandel says, our current public philosophy "affirms a voluntarist (or consumerist) conception of freedom"—we are free "in so far as we are able to choose our own ends, unencumbered by attachments or duties that we have not chosen."[13] This belief contrasts starkly with the republican view that certain habits and qualities of character are a necessary condition for maintaining democratic freedoms.

Individualism

To most observers of American culture, individualism is one of society's most dominant and enduring features. American individualism is usually recognized as a source of strength, for in its best form it contributes to an ethic of self-reliance, entrepreneurial initiative, and even civic enterprise. American individualism, however, has changed over time, in ways that are often detrimental to civil society.

Historically, American individualism was tempered by the gentling influence of community life rooted and grounded in places of worship, in neighborhoods, and in voluntary associations. Contemporary American individualism often assumes an entirely different form. Casting aside traditional restraints, it has embraced an ideal of absolute autonomy for the individual, leaving community institutions with little vitality or voice and almost no authority over the individual.

Yesteryear's individualism understood that the individual was governed by moral constraints and social obligations that transcended the self. Individualism was held in check by a Protestant religion that demanded the public good be valued along with the rights of individuals. According to Barry Shain, "The notion that the self could be the grounding of its own being" was viewed by Protestants as "a devilish temptation, exhibiting the sins of self-worship and pridefulness."[14]

Tocqueville understood the critical difference between a well-moderated individualism and the more extreme form that he worried would emerge in the United States. Well-regulated individualism was based upon self-interest "rightly understood," alive to the interests of others. Tocqueville believed individualism was good and necessary, but it had to be held in check by other influences. Rather than harnessing individualism to serve constructive purposes, society has instead mostly succumbed to it. Today's unenlightened individualism has turned many spheres of human activity into a battleground for personal advancement at the expense of cooperative endeavor.

Today's individualism presents the self as the only sovereign: autonomous, empowered, and dangerously detached from transcendent morality or social restraints. Michael Sandel speaks of an earlier conception of the individual as "the situated self," where the individual was bounded in a web of social relations and activities, in contrast to the current view of the individual as the "unbounded self."[15]

The Politically Organized Society

In many ways, the civil society movement cuts against the grain of contemporary culture, pursuing what was once unabashedly called the common good. By elevating civil society, one implies respect for social forms and arrangements—the little platoons of family, fraternal association, and religious belief—that are important sources of moral meaning and action. As discussed earlier, many in today's elite have repudiated these human associations as retrograde and oppressive.

The individualism mirrored in American public culture reflects an image of atomized individuals in retreat from the very idea of society. The portrait of the modern and postmodern American is often one of isolated and self-absorbed individuals pursuing private interests and governed by an ideology of me-ism. The result is distrust and fear as communities lose their cohesion and order and the democratic process yields to the tribal politics of resentment and retaliation. Worst of all, and paradoxically for the individualist, individuals feel powerless to change the situation. The kind of individualism we now have can produce huge problems for collective action, whether in politics, community, or culture.

Many from across the political spectrum see profound threats to democracy in this isolation of the individual. Liberal scholar John Gardner states starkly, "Without the continuity of shared values that community provides, freedom cannot survive. Undifferentiated masses never have and never will preserve freedom against usurping powers."[16]

One result of such isolation is the rise of a politically organized society in which the pursuit of happiness is advanced through power, interest group privilege, and litigation. In a politically organized society, citizens essentially agitate against each other, each striving for minor gains at the others' expense, creating what Richard Harwood describes as a permanent form of "civic dissonance." A society where individuals organize to use the state against each other is a society where the individual and the state advance, but civil society, a place of peaceful, consensual, and voluntary action, rapidly retreats.

Defenders of individualism, including both economic and moral libertarians, typically present the autonomous individual as the one true bulwark against the intrusive state. Closer examination, however, presents the opposite possibility. Unbounded individualism can be seen as the cause of the state's rapid advancement. As voluntary associations wither under the influence of atomized but politically empowered individuals, the state moves in to take up the slack, exacerbating the problem of social disintegration.

This transference of power from associations to the state has profound consequences for law, politics, economics, and society. As the state expands and individual restraint wanes, public life is reduced to what Michael Sandel calls "proceduralism," leaving the public realm little purpose except to maximize private opportunity. If politics is to recover its civic voice, according to Sandel, "it must once more ask questions society has forgotten how to ask," questions about ends beyond rational self-interest and economic and political advantage seeking.

Proceduralism places an impossible burden on the state. In a well-ordered society, the state serves a subordinate role to other sectors of society, and is thought ill-suited to carry the full load of mediating every dispute. In the good society, politics is peripheral, not the central means for advancing individual happiness.

The state consumes but does little to resupply the social glue generated by voluntary cooperative endeavor, the trademark of civil society. In fact, the state frequently hinders and displaces efforts toward this voluntary cooperation, resulting in a vicious cycle of state expansion and societal enervation. As Bill Schambra observes, "[W]hen government moves aggressively into the civic realm to take up the slack where mediating structures may be faltering, their authority is thereby only further undermined."[17]

When the law is forced to compensate for the absence of social restraint and manners, it becomes the catalyst for a rights-based individualism and degenerates into an arbitrary tool of the politically organized. If only the law and politics arbitrate human affairs, even the most basic and intimate human relations become political, and the spirit of consensual problem solving is replaced with the raw assertion of power. Life in democratic society becomes a zero-sum struggle of all against all. A right conferred upon one group becomes an obligation imposed on another. The pursuit of the good and just society is reduced to a dehumanizing struggle over rules. Democracy's "habits of the heart" degenerate into cold proceduralism, and its institutions become exhausted from overload.

Today, democracy is widely thought to be losing its internal cohesion, its spiritual dynamism, and its universal appeal. Jean Elshtain, author of *Democracy on Trial*, states that "our democracy is faltering," it is succumbing to "exhaustion, cynicism, opportunism." She admits she has joined the "ranks of the nervous."

Elshtain speaks directly to the problem of modern public philosophy and its inadequacy in setting forth common political values that sustain democracy over time. Democracy feeds on the qualities of citizenship that are nourished through the institutions of civil society. The democratic social covenant, Elshtain maintains, rests on the assumption that "one's fellow citizens are people of good will who yearn for the opportunity to work together, rather than to continue to glare at one another across racial, class and ideological divides."[18]

Elshtain and others identify several troubling developments resulting from the rise of the private self and the collapse of the public good. When civic space declines, a politics of displacement emerges to fill the gap. This "complete collapse of a distinction between public and private [is] anathema to democratic thinking," says Elshtain. The politics of displacement follows two trajectories.

> In the first, everything private—from one's sexual practice to blaming one's parents for one's lack of self-esteem—becomes grist for the public mill. In the second, everything public—from the grounds on which politicians are judged, to health politics, to gun regulations—is privatized and played out in a psychodrama on a grand scale.[19]

The public arena becomes a place where "me and my fleeting angers, resentments, sentiments, and impulses," unmediated by local institutions, become important public business. Not only is society politicized, the "personal is political." Nothing personal remains exempt from "political definition, direction, and manipulation."[20] When distinctions between the public and the private collapse and there are no "clearly established institutions to focus dissent and concern," the center does not hold, and private identities take over.[21]

A related and equally troubling trend is the rise of "identity politics" following the embrace of what Elshtain calls "politicized ontology." This phenomenon requires persons to be judged "not by what they do or say but by what they ARE." Racial or sexual identity becomes "the sole ground of politics, the sole determinant of political good and evil." Those who disagree with my politics are regarded as "enemies of my identity."[22]

Arthur Schlesinger, Jr., worries that assimilating citizens into a common framework of values, or "a unifying American identity," is growing more difficult because of identity politics. "[T]he militants of ethnicity" now view the main objective of society not as assimilation, but "the protection, strengthening, celebration, and perpetuation of ethnic origins and identities." This separatism only "nourishes prejudices, magnifies differences, and stirs antagonisms."[23]

The solution to these problems is recovering the individual person in civil society; not the individual captured in identity politics or ethnic tribalism, but tied once again to the intermediary institutions of family and community. This understanding of the citizen—not as tribesman, client, or consumer, but as a builder of the commonwealth—can close the gap between the individual and the state.

Beyond Politicized Society to Civil Society

Democracy is a thing of the heart. The widest possible distribution of the democratic franchise, by itself, does little to guarantee that people will feel enfranchised. Democracy is not simply about procedures, parties, politicians, and ballot participation, as discussed. These procedural features only assure that the political system will be generally responsive to the people's wants and aspirations. Democracy must consist of unchanging substantive qualities.

Democracy's survival depends on the presence of a democratic disposition, habit, and outlook among the members of society, which must be carefully nourished, generation by generation. Tocqueville captured the loss of common democratic values when he wrote, "Without ideas in common, there is no common action. There may still exist human beings, but not a social entity. In order for society to exist and, even more, to prosper, it is necessary that the spirits of all citizens be held together by certain leading ideas."[24]

The job before us, then, is to revive the spiritual and moral dimensions of democracy. Sandel calls for the replacement of rights-based individualism with the "classical republican tradition" where private interests are "subordinated to the public good and in which community life takes precedence over individual pursuits."[25]

The classical republican tradition offers a vision of the individual, not merely in competition with others through the market nor in conflict with others via the state, but in cooperation through civil society. The central concern of civic republicanism as a public philosophy is renewing a substantive and vigorous democracy by expanding the role of the mediating institutions of civil society.

Through the civil society movement a rich but long neglected feature of Western moral and political thought is revisited. The concept of civil society is rooted largely, though certainly not exclusively, in the Christian natural law tradition. The emphasis within this tradition, which is to view civil society as a realm independent of the state, was critical to developing a philosophy of limited government and ordered liberty. Government remains limited to the extent that nongovernmental institutions play a vital offsetting role.

Conclusion and Outlook

If our current public philosophy is impoverished, as many believe, then the question becomes: If man was made for civil society, and civil society is to be the centerpiece of a new public philosophy, what must be done to revitalize it? How can old civic forms and institutions be replaced with new ones that more directly respond to today's need for connection? How can the excesses of the sensate culture be moderated? How can social and technological change be harnessed to strengthen voluntary human association? And how should this effort be organized?

Public policy certainly plays a role, though limited for the reasons discussed above. Devolution of power to state, local, and community-based institutions can continue to move decision-making authority downward and outward to citizens. Government support and resources can be directed toward "protecting, reinforcing and nurturing the varied groups" of society, as Nisbet put it.

Just as policy will play a part, so will dynamic new social movements. James Q. Wilson and others have traced various social reform movements that arose in American history to uplift moral standards. These movements had a common desire to instill character, by once again treating the individual as capable of and responsible for exercising self-control. Social ills were confronted by recovering "a self-activating, self-regulating, all-purpose inner control."

The institutions that effectively socialize people are private and local, according to Wilson, which means that Americans should

> identify, evaluate, and encourage those local, private efforts that seem to do the best job at reducing drug abuse, inducing people to marry, persuading parents, especially fathers, to take responsibility for their children, and exercising informal social controls over neighborhood streets.[26]

These private efforts include the fatherhood movement, the marriage movement, the character movement, the teen abstinence movement, and many of the public reform movements discussed in previous chapters.

The most urgent work of all may be pursuing moral and cultural reformation. Civil society is, after all, a moral and social order that transcends each person, and requires yielding some cherished personal autonomy in order to restore the legitimacy of community institutions. As Bill Schambra puts it, the problems of society "are above all moral and cultural phenomena," which in a free society necessarily involve "questions of right and wrong personal behavior, of decent and indecent individual behavior, in short, the questions that are so troubling to us today."[27]

Modernity and the public philosophies it has spawned have placed the sovereign, autonomous self at the center of all things, making decisions of right and wrong strictly contingent upon human choice. Ethical relativists convinced the nation for a time that education, technology, and professional expertise alone could preserve social order and harmony without the aid of morality.

Needless to say, experience has proven this utopian vision deficient, and more and more people know it. The challenge that lies before Americans approaching a new century is not merely one of reforming or reconfiguring the administrative systems of government, nor of revving up the economy or carrying technology and science to new heights. The central challenge for Americans is to build a civil and humane society.

There is much to cheer in current talk about community and civil society. But the difficulty of the challenge makes the outcome highly uncertain. Czech Vaclav Havel, the well-known poet-turned-politician, foresees profound change ahead in the new millennium—"a new 'post-modern phase' where everything is possible and almost nothing is certain."[28]

Nothing short of a new spiritual vision of global dimensions, says Havel, will save human civilization. Strengthening families, neighborhoods, and civic associations will not be possible without first recognizing that these institutions are essential to a civil and humane society, and having the courage and moral strength necessary to restore them. The truth is, we must look beyond man—beyond what Havel calls an "arrogant anthropocentrism" that has dogged this century—and find moral wisdom in truth that transcends our existence.

The struggle under way in the United States is literally to revive the lost soul of a nation, to effect broad-based moral, civic, and democratic renewal. A fresh embrace of a moral order centered upon transcendent reality, the basic moral worth of people, and the inherently moral nature of human community must undergird the movement toward civil society.

This work must be inspired by hope. Few people knew more about society's tendencies than Tocqueville himself. He wrote with an awareness of the impending storm that is now upon us, and predicted the unraveling of communities, the rise of atomized individualism, and our absorption in a culture of "paltry pleasures." Yet, he was an optimist. He believed Americans were capable of assessing their condition and mustering the resources to confront it.

Notes

1. "Democracy on Trial," *Echoes* 3 (Winter 1997), 1.

2. Kenneth Anderson, "Heartless World Revisited: Christopher Lasch's Parting Polemic against the New Class," *The Good Society*, 6, no. 1, 36.

3. Mary Ann Glendon, "Introduction: Forgotten Questions," in *Seedbeds of Virtue: Sources of Competence, Character and Citizenship in American Society*, ed. Mary Ann Glendon and David Blankenhorn (Lanham, Md.: Madison Books, 1995), 4.

4. This is an extrapolation of the thesis developed by Jacques Ellul in *The Technological Society*, trans. John Wilkinson (New York: Alfred A. Knopf, 1965).

5. William Galston, "Is Democracy in Unique Peril?" *Echoes* 1 (Winter 1997), 24.

6. Michael Joyce, "Toward One Another: Reclaiming Civil Community," *The Wingspread Journal* 18 (Autumn 1996), 9.

7. Joyce, 18.

8. Christopher Power, "When Selfishness Doesn't Pay Off," *Business Week*, 11 September 1995, 18.

9. Peter Schwartz and Kevin Kelley, "An Interview with Peter Drucker," *Wired*, August 1996, 184.

10. Alan Wolfe, *Whose Keeper? Social Science and Moral Obligation* (Berkeley: University of California Press, 1989), 19.

11. Wolfe, 20.

12. Michael J. Sandel, "America's Search for a New Public Philosophy," *The Atlantic Monthly,* March 1996, 70.

13. Sandel, 58.

14. Michael J. Sandel, "The Politics of Public Identity," *Echoes* 1 (Winter 1997), 6.

15. Jean Bethke Elshtain, "Protestant Communalism," *Crisis*, October 1995, 41.

16. George F. Will, "The Politics of Soulcraft," *Newsweek*, 13 May 1996, 82.

17. John W. Gardner, "Building Community," *Independent Sector*, September 1991, 5.

18. William A. Schambra, "Toward a Conservative Populism? Some Questions for the Wilderness," prepared for "Populism in the 1990s" (Washington, D.C.: Hubert Humphrey Institute of Public Affairs, University of Minnesota, and The Empowerment Network, 3 March 1994), 9.

19. Jean Bethke Elshtain, quoted by Don E. Eberly, in *Civil Society: The Paradox of American Progress* (Harrisburg, Pa.: The Civil Society Project, 1996), 3.

20. Elshtain, quoted by Eberly, 38.

21. Elshtain, quoted by Eberly, 43.

22. Elshtain, quoted by Eberly, 40.

23. Elshtain, quoted by Eberly, 53.

24. Arthur M. Schlesinger, Jr., *The Disuniting of America: Reflections on a Multicultural Society* (New York: W. W. Norton and Company, 1992), 17.

25. Alexis de Tocqueville, *Democracy in America*, vol. 2., trans. George Lawrence (New York: Anchor, 1969), 433-444.

26. Michael J. Sandel, quoted from John O'Sullivan, *The Loss of Virtue: Moral Confusion and Social Disorder in Britain and America* (New York: National Review Books, 1992), 86.

27. James Q. Wilson, "Culture, Incentives, and the Underclass," in *Values and Public Policy* (Washington, D.C.: Brookings Institution, 1994), 74.

28. Schambra, 8.

29. *Newsweek*, 18 July 1994.

Part Three

Civil Society:
Its Promise and Limitations

Chapter 10

Civitas Limited: The Limitations of Civil Society

Several important things can be said about the movement to recover civic community in the United States. First, it reflects and seeks to satisfy a powerful human desire for civic community. As Robert Nisbet, author of the classic *Quest for Community*, says, modern people are "uprooted, alone, without secure status, cut off from community or any system of clear moral purpose."[1] The yearning that Americans have in their hearts for community is rooted in the natural human desire for affiliation, certitude, and membership. The civil society movement would not be taking shape were this not true.

Second, we are reminded through this movement that civil society is the proper place to act upon the widely felt desire for connection and belonging. Only voluntary associations and local communities, not politicized appeals to national community, can legitimately seek to satisfy this longing. Civil society is often described as a place of belonging, a "haven," a "refuge," and a "moral home."

The modern state, says Nisbet, cannot meet deep-seated needs "for recognition, fellowship, security and membership."[2] True, those who find their identity with localities, also consider themselves members of a national state and the human race. But individuals do not find their moral bearing or place of belonging in a secularized, undifferentiated mass society. A person in a mass of depersonalized humanity is not truly a member of a community. Life in a homogenous, universal community is not scaled to the individual and is thus disorienting and unmanageable. As the late liberal scholar and civic advocate John Gardner writes, "Undifferentiated masses never have and never will preserve freedom against usurping powers."[3]

Third, the movement to revive the civil society sector represents a welcome reversal of the long-held prejudice that this "third sector" is antiquated and irrelevant. As Richard Cornuelle says, "For half a century, the third sector was in limbo, the victim of an unexamined supposition that in an industrial society, organized social action outside the state was technologically obsolete."[4] The very fact that the civil society sector has returned to contend with the state and market sectors is healthy for our democratic order. A two-sector society consisting of only the market and the state is well on its way to becoming a one-sector society consisting only of the state.

Finally, the movement is valuable as a source of social regeneration. Civil society is already having positive social effects, as it restores character, private charity and civility, and many other positive social qualities. Much can be accomplished through the civil society movement, but as promising as it seems, there is much about the current civil society debate that falls short.

Problems with the Current Debate

The debate carries with it several questionable assumptions, starting with the widespread belief that the nation's social problems are mostly confined to the civic realm, and the corollary belief that the nation's moral and social ills will be solved if only Americans became more civic-minded.

The problems with these assumptions must be candidly confronted. For one, other forces beyond our neglect of communities and civic associations weaken civil society. Restoring civil society may not be the single most important challenge before us. Society's real challenge is both more urgent and more difficult. We must restore the moral consensus and the shared cultural story that shapes civil society and makes the nation's modern, pluralistic, democratic system possible. The task before us requires more than a simple recovery of civitas; it requires a recovery of the moral and philosophical foundations of the American order.

We must also be candid about the difficulties we face in confronting our present civic conditions, some of which are rooted in the inherent contradictions of the American people. For example, while Americans desire stronger communities and a more ordered and balanced society, not all are willing to make the sacrifices necessary to accomplish this. As discussed, few seem willing to reduce individual autonomy or limit private choices.

The second major problem with the debate is that it reflects a misunderstanding of the foundations of civil society. There might have been a time in history prior to industrialization and modernization when civil society represented a largely independent social order possessing substantial powers of its own for moral regeneration, but civil society was never entirely self-derived or self-sustaining as many assume, and certainly not in the modern and postmodern world. The health of civil society depends on sources beyond itself.

There is no evidence that civil society possesses unique immunities to the cultural and social viruses that have afflicted it as well as other sectors of society, or that antibodies can easily be organized once the body is worn down.

Civil society's infirmity is caused by more than neglect. It has been weakened from within and without by pathogenic forces, and can only be repaired by simultaneously confronting these viral intrusions. Civic associations wither under the influence of excessive individualism, corrosive consumerism, governmental overreach, and the changing patterns of work and life that accompany modern society. No small factor in the demise of local communities has been the rise of what Harvard Law Professor Mary Ann Glendon calls "rights talk" and victim consciousness that turns every public forum into a platform for airing private grievances.

For decades local communities have suffered a thousand different slights by society's progressive elite who viewed morally authoritative local communities as stubborn obstacles to social progress, as they defined it. Nisbet described this attack on local community as "the single most decisive influence upon Western social organization." This is "a process of almost permanent revolution against the social groups and authorities which lie between the individual and the state."[5]

Many praise local communities today for the same reasons that others have long criticized them. Civic communities are simultaneously appreciated and scorned as bastions of autonomy and local solidarity against the buffeting powers of social planners and the encroachments of bureaucracy, regulation, and litigation.

Local institutions and affiliations have also been roundly disparaged for promoting narrow parochial attitudes over broad pluralistic purposes. For as long as they have existed, local communities have been thought to lack tolerance and inclusiveness, two of the few remaining moral certitudes in our universe of moral relativism. These forces, combined with many more, have pounded away and eroded the beach of civil society. Isolated individuals are left, storm-battered and alone, at the mercy of an increasingly intrusive and centralized state.

For much of U.S. history, local communities stiffly resisted the homogenizing centralizing forces of political and cultural power. Today, the victory of those forces over civil society seems nearly complete. But the real picture is more complex. To suggest that intruding forces have single-handedly ruined local webs of affiliation gives only a partial account of the problem. The quaint story of localism that many Americans fondly recite is one that fewer and fewer choose to live out. Americans are instead seduced by attractions far more powerful and appealing than the seemingly suffocating bonds of local affiliation.

The habits and values of community life have been surrendered, even willfully abandoned, in exchange for the newly favored values of privacy, autonomy, and separation. The United States is the most transient society on earth, in part because many people prefer to escape rather than cultivate local roots. American cities are populated with citizens who have fled what they considered dreary, unenlightened, controlling rural enclaves for the freedom and anonymity of the city.

The modern suburbs in which half of Americans now live were explicitly designed around privacy and separation instead of neighborly proximity. The village shop has been replaced by the modern mega-mall; the local diner with its familiar ways and friendly touch has been traded in for plastic, franchised restaurants on every corner. These changes are made possible by the conscious choices of thousands of individuals every day to be consumers rather than citizens. Changes are made, partly because of attractive prices and quality, and partly because the new choices carry fewer social contacts and obligations.

The ties of affection and loyalty on which local communities thrive have steadily been directed instead to market consumerism. In the market, the principle of private choice governs every transaction, whether the commodity is food or entertainment, even family or church.

Though troubled by seedy popular culture's domination of their lives, few Americans do their part to close its floodgates. The social insurance state thrives in spite of widespread taxpayer resistance, because the alternative to socialized care for the elderly and infirm, namely caring for them in our own homes, requires too great a sacrifice for most. As much as Americans might bemoan the mass homogenizing institutions of culture, bureaucracy, and the consumer market, these institutions have their appeal.

Put another way, civil society does not exist in a moral vacuum. Like never before, civil society is shaped and reshaped in a milieu of cultural values and beliefs, whose dominant ethos for decades has been the pursuit of happiness through a narrowly defined self-interest. This self-absorption arises in part from the socially fragmenting forces of modernity, which include science, technology, bureaucracy, and mass communications, each of which offers vast benefits that few would readily relinquish. Civil society and the "gentling influence" of its communities, churches, and local institutions must also compete for space with the "atomizing social dynamism" of a capitalist economy that is now inescapably global in its scope.[6] Finally, civil society operates on the basis of a legal, constitutional order, which in turn relies on some prior understanding of social justice and moral truth.

Recovering Civil Society

The civil society debate has raised expectations for a renewed sense of community and civic commitment. The call to volunteer and to join is fine as far as it goes, but it is doubtful whether the quest for community can be satisfied in its current formulation. Large numbers of Americans are not likely to become more other-regarding simply because politicians and well-paid civic executives publicly admonish us to do so.

Neither is it realistic to think that civic life and voluntary associations will be revived through economic reforms or government downsizing, which frequently occupy our public debate. Even if civic associations came to enjoy some measure of renaissance in response to these new inducements and fresh attention, civic recovery may still be dramatically oversold as a means of renewing the whole of the United States.

The call to civic participation by itself does not carry much compelling moral force. The most vital civic associations may do little by themselves, for example, to recover cultural coherence or social harmony. Appeals to the civic spirit divorced from other changes in the culture may not go very far toward saving families, improving parenting, restoring civility and safety to the streets, or softening the harsh, mean edge to society.

In fact, unaided by moral recovery, the movement toward civic renewal does not go to the heart of the problem. In the past, many of the mass movements seeking to renew moral norms operated on the basis of an existing moral consensus, which is badly weakened today if it has not vanished completely.

Civil society can perhaps only be restored by recovering the moral foundations for our civic existence and by cultivating the moral capacity of individuals. The very term civil society implies the existence of moral ends that transcend individuals and communities. People will reconnect with their neighbors when they are animated by a clear moral and spiritual obligation to do so.

Republican Character

The civil society debate must include a new conversation about the moral foundations of citizenship in a free society, or what has been called republican character. The call to civic participation is inherently linked to a deeper set of issues that are essentially moral and ethical. These issues concern our basic understanding of the human person and his or her place in the world, our moral and civic obligation toward others, and our conception of freedom and social authority.

In other words, at its deepest level, the call to civil society is really about the central question raised long ago by Aristotle: How—on what basis, and by what means—"ought we to order our lives together?" The debate about civil society is inseparably linked to questions of moral truth and "oughtness."

Many among the academic and public elite who have eagerly volunteered for the civil society debate shrink from this challenge. Because of this aversion to matters of morality, much of the civil society debate is cast in the morally evasive language of the social scientist. This language reflects a desire to collect and analyze statistical data, not articulate moral purpose. The very conversation that might have borne fresh honesty about moral principles has instead been co-opted by the social science intelligentsia. Scholars, peddling a sterile and spiritually vacuous intellectualism, only deepen the hunger for a more substantive social renewal—a hunger that provided impetus for the movement in the first place.

This hesitation to engage deeper matters of public life is not shared by most American citizens, who appear to be well ahead of the "knowledge class" that dominates this debate. As citizens view it, the debate must be about more than simply joining associations. In fact, most Americans strain to understand what the fuss about declining civic participation is really all about. For most of us, there is no lack of civic opportunity. In fact, more recent analysis has shown that the gloom and doom assumptions about declining civic engagement are largely unjustified. Perhaps the social experts had the issue wrong all along, in part because their tools of social science are not able to discern or treat moral and spiritual longings.

Declining Social Ethics and the Loss of Dignity

What polls do indicate, again and again, is a consistent worry about a persistent social crisis. The public is reasonably confident about the economy, international affairs, and even recent improvements in governmental performance. It is the social crisis, consisting of the erosion of moral standards and the collapse of social institutions, that concerns them most. This concern centers on the measurable decline of durable institutions like the family and on things that are harder to measure like civility and manners. Many Americans report that their society is coarser, their culture cruder, the public debate angrier, and the treatment of individuals less respectful.

There is a sense that quality, excellence, and core virtues have waned and too many Americans have become shortsighted and selfish through their obsession with rights and entitlements. Ordinary citizens intuitively understand that this deeper corruption, and not merely a lack of civic participation, is driving us toward isolation and distrust. Many in the general public wonder whether Americans are still bound together by any moral agreement of even the most elementary kind, and if not, what can be done to recover a common understanding.

The crisis is not so much about the state of our local civic life, as much as it is about the state of our nation's moral health. Quite simply, the weakening of a service ethic and community loyalty are symptoms of the rise of a wholly utilitarian value system. These values center on pleasure and individual preference, and now pervade every major sector of society.

We see it in the collapse of the ethical standards of many professions and in the decline of such virtues as honesty, fidelity, and generosity. Although the term *virtue* has made something of a comeback recently, much of the language embodying concepts of personal and public virtue has been eradicated. Traditionalist scholar John Howard has documented the vocabulary of virtue that has recently been rendered obsolete on American soil. Modesty, decency, probity, rectitude, honor, politeness, magnanimity, and propriety are words that—along with opposites like shame and disgrace—have disappeared, he says, from current use.[7]

The language of the latter twentieth century, by contrast, increasingly treats personal and civic virtue as purely private concerns. The language of modern life is the dialect of the quantifiable, the rational, the scientific, and the technical—language of calculation and control but not language of values and meaning. It is a dialect well-suited to the designers and managers of the paradigm of the present age.

What happens to the society that has been severed from its underpinnings, where life has become fragmented and devoid of meaning and where citizens have lost a shared basis for a common life together? The result is a loss of community, a declining social order, an erosion of trust in authority, and an increased assertion of human passion through power rather than reasoned judgment. Civic decline is a symptom of a disappearing humanitarianism grounded in a moral vision of life.

What concerns people, in other words, is not merely the collapse of community, but the steady dehumanization and depersonalization of society. When morality becomes completely contingent upon human choice, the basis for preserving core values and for asserting the inestimable work of each person is weakened. The result is a loss of human dignity. We follow a path from humanism to inhumanity, from social progress to social regress.

We see the loss of human dignity everywhere among our poor. The term *poverty* is no longer adequate to portray the tragedies lived out each day by many of America's poor. Most of today's children are not materially poorer than a generation ago, but their impoverishment is often more all-encompassing. It affects the body, the mind, and the soul. For many poor children, life is a struggle for survival in neighborhoods and dysfunctional families hollowed out by the oppressive presence of violence and drugs. Their loss is far deeper than simple economics; they are robbed of elementary human dignity and subjected to the most desperate forms of alienation and hopelessness. Poverty in America is about more than a struggle for daily sustenance. It is a struggle to hold on to one's personhood.

We see the loss of human dignity in the persistent problems of violence and crime. Nothing is more destructive of civic trust and cooperative endeavor than the fear and withdrawal generated by crime. It drives the poor to despair, the middle class to anger and distrust, and the rich to gated communities. Though rates of serious crime and violence have recently leveled off, crime still occurs at historically high and morally unacceptable levels. A country that rests on its modest accomplishments while its children scramble to evade assaults, its elderly cower behind barred windows, and its prisons bulge with the largest incarcerated population on earth is a society in a deep state of denial.

We see the loss of human dignity in our treatment of children. Fewer and fewer American homes offer children security and a place to grow up in unhurried happiness and innocence. Too many of the world's pressures, from materialism to cultural hedonism, are intruding upon home life. The sanctity of the home is now invaded by programming that was once confined to the back alleys of society. For the first time in human history, technology enables our children to have unmediated access to the most corrupting and antisocial subject matter available.

We see the loss of human dignity in many adults' refusals to take responsibility for providing moral guidance, discipline, and boundaries for the young. The result is both a loss of childhood and the postponement of adulthood, leaving more and more adults in a perpetual state of adolescent narcissism. Indeed, as has been stated before, adults today often adopt the fashions, attitudes, and behaviors of youth, rather than reforming the younger generation. Adulthood is being postponed and in some cases abandoned altogether in favor of an adolescent culture of play, pleasure, and life without rules.

We see the loss of human dignity in America's casual attitudes about new family forms. There is today a widespread assumption that the effects of "alternative arrangements" are trivial to children; that family breakup is either inconsequential to society or its fallout is within society's capacity to manage. Many of the civil society advocates who have suddenly rediscovered the little platoons of civic community resist the conclusion that healthy neighborhoods—or the "village"—depend upon the family, as the most essential and original form of human community.

This was not true of Tocqueville, whose name is invoked constantly by civic renewal activists. Tocqueville believed that marriage and the family served powerfully positive social functions. The French analyst saw the family as the incubator of civic values and democratic skills, the irreplaceable cornerstone of a healthy civil society. The family was a source of trust and was perhaps society's chief buffer against excessive individualism. A society that denies so many of its children the basic birthright of a stable, two-parent family can only expect more angry, socially dysfunctional, and distrustful citizens.

We see the loss of human dignity in the sordid state of public life. In the United States, the state is forced to accommodate vastly different understandings of the good, and private preference has replaced objective standards of judgment. A functional society regulates behavior through gentler, noncoercive means like widely accepted standards of personal responsibility. When individuals and their social institutions lose their capacity to voluntarily regulate vice, disputes spill over into the state—the only remaining venue for conflict resolution.

We see the loss of human dignity in the domination of materialism and materialist philosophies that reduce human life to chance and rob the natural world of its mystery and moral meaning. The pursuit of human progress through materialistic principles of rationality and efficiency has reinforced the conceit that society can function without transcendent appeals to spiritual and moral truth. Our search for happiness in affluence has produced boredom, frustration, and apathy among many.

We see the loss of human dignity with the invasion of the "money world," where the market replaces custom, tradition, and the ties of family and community. The market has been an engine of remarkable individual opportunity and social progress, but when the calculation of self-interest and the quest for individual fulfillment overshadow any sense of moral duty toward family and community, society suffers.

We see the loss of human dignity in the woeful state of our nation's educational system. After decades of trendy fashion and faddish reforms, we see only minor and isolated gains at best, and little to cheer. Large numbers of the nation's children are still not up to the task of facing economic competition abroad or fulfilling the duties of citizenship at home.

The educational crisis is at its core philosophical, not structural. An ethically grounded approach to education would draw on the wisdom of the ages. It would confidently transmit a free society's highest ideals. It would impart the knowledge necessary for democratic participation. It would recognize, as education has recognized since Aristotle, that the ultimate end of learning is to instill virtue and character.

When schools seek to enlighten the mind without elevating human character, when they attempt to develop the intellect in a vacuum of moral confusion that denies the worth of duty, sacrifice, and excellence of achievement, they can only fail. Educational decline is the nation's assured fate as long as society requires schools to function as therapeutic social agencies and educators are forced to double as cops, caseworkers, and day-care providers.

We see the loss of human dignity in the balkanization of the United States, where each person's uniquely sacred qualities give way to a faceless group identity in order to validate class oppression theories. The resulting ethnic separatism "nourishes prejudices, magnifies differences, and stirs antagonism," according to Arthur Schlesinger, Jr.[8]

Conclusion

The weakening of civil society, in short, is traceable to cultural and philosophical movements that have dominated the twentieth century. The result is today's earthbound, secular, utilitarian value system. The framers of our democratic order would never have considered this value system sufficient to sustain a republican system of government that depends upon the maintenance of virtue. A country in which there is no transcendent foundation for law, politics, economics, and society is a disordered and potentially dangerous place. This kind of society faces moral depletion, spiritual fatigue, and cynicism. If utilitiarianism, not religious and ethical values, guide conduct, then might makes right.

· Writing in the 1940s, Harvard Professor of Sociology P. A. Sorokin identified as the central self-contradiction of this century the culture's simultaneous glorification and debasement of man. This, he said, was inevitable because American life had become rooted in a "sensate" culture that replaced a belief in universal moral principles with the idea that value only lies in those things that could be perceived with the senses.

The impact of this cultural replacement has been felt across the whole of modern society. Its debilitating effects are not limited to a particular sector, as many civil society advocates suggest. Sorokin described widespread social maladjustment that simultaneously affected almost the whole of Western culture and society in all of its main sectors. It is a crisis, he said, in art and science, in philosophy and religion, in law and morals, in manners and mores; in all the forms of social, political, and economic organization. In short, he said, "it is a crisis involving almost the whole way of life, thought, and conduct of western society."[9] The answer, he said, was to replace the dying forms in each sector with a new superior culture and society.

If the social recession gripping the United States is not solely due to weakened communities, neither is it primarily a child of the economy. Although it contains important economic dimensions, our social troubles have advanced in spite of economic prosperity and to some extent even because of the material abundance of our times. Nor is the U. S. social crisis primarily a child of politics or flawed governmental policies, although it is certainly mirrored in public debate and governmental gridlock. What government does more of, less of, or simply does differently appears to have little bearing by itself on our mostly costly and consequential social problems.

Our social recession is primarily the child of our cultural and moral values, which have contributed to the weakening of the institutions of civil society. The most tragic long-term consequence of this social recession is the decay of those institutions and ways of living that make our free society possible. A continued social recession in the twenty-first century cannot fail to jeopardize the survival of the American experiment in ordered liberty.

Notes

1. Robert Nisbet, *The Sociological Tradition* (New York: Basic Books, 1966), 265.

2. Robert G. Perrin, "Robert Nisbet and the Modern State," *Modern Age*, 39, no. 1 (Winter 1997), 40.

3. John W. Gardner, *Building Community* (Washington D.C.: Independent Sector, 1991), 16.

4. Richard Cornuelle, *Reclaiming the American Dream: The Role of Private Individuals and Voluntary Associations* (New Brunswick: Transaction Publishers, 1993), xx.

5. Robert Nisbet, *The Question for Community* (New York: Transaction Publishers, 1953), 87.

6. Cornuelle, xvi.

7. John Howard, "A Sure Compass" (Rockford Institute, 1992), 6.

8. Arthur M. Schlesinger, Jr., *The Disuniting of America: Reflections on a Multicultural Society* (New York: W. W. Norton and Company, 1992), 17.

9. P. A. Sorokin, *The Crisis of Our Age* (New York: E. P. Dutton, 1943), 17.

Chapter 11

The Fragility of Civil Society

If civil society does not exist in a moral vacuum, as discussed in chapter 10, neither can it be renewed in isolation from other major factors that operate upon it. The culture, the state, and all of its political and legal functions, along with the economic market, are powerful moral actors that continuously shape the health and vitality of civil society.

In the last chapter we examined how utilitarian ethics have permeated much of civil society, eroding the foundations of human dignity. This chapter explores the impact of the culture, the market, and the state on the functioning of civil society.

Culture

One of the most prevalent moral actors in society, and perhaps the most powerful, is the culture. Like never before, the nation's social attitudes and social agenda are being set by the centers of cultural influence. The institutions of culture, perhaps more than any other, increasingly shape the American character and determine national destiny.

Civic advocates, educators, and community leaders rarely discuss the cultural foundations of our democratic society. Democracy was constructed upon cultural as well as constitutional foundations. It was taken for granted by the founders that individual Americans would attend to their communities, respond to need as civic duty required, marry and raise children responsibly, and preserve character-shaping institutions.

Harvard Professor Mary Ann Glendon states it this way:

> If history teaches us anything, it is that democracy cannot be taken for granted. There are social and cultural conditions that are more or less

favorable to liberty, equality, and self-government; and those conditions involve the character and competence of citizens.[1]

The irony is that our recent bid for restored community comes amidst a culture whose dominant impulse has been to emancipate the individual from the constraints of community. It should not be surprising that the authority of those institutions that bind us together in common purpose—our families, churches, and voluntary associations—have all lost ground to a culture that celebrates individual emancipation.

Those who see value in more social authority and less individualism often have the charge of nostalgia leveled against them. True, today's individualism is partly a response to a social narrative that was too restrictive not long ago, yet, as Robert Bellah put it, "in our desperate effort to free ourselves from the constrictions of the past, we have jettisoned too much, forgotten a history that we cannot abandon."[2] According to Bellah, the concept of soul, tied to history, community, and God, has been replaced by a "radically unencumbered and improvisational self."[3]

Appeals to civic duty in today's world must be issued against the backdrop of an ideology of autonomous individualism that is animated by the conviction that there are no moral principles or ends independent of the individual self. The ethos of emancipation affects our attitudes toward sexuality, marriage, child-rearing, and, of course, civic duty.

The concept of freedom is altered in modern culture from its original meaning. Freedom, says Robert Bellah, is perhaps "the most deeply held American value," yet freedom, he adds, means different things today than it did at the founding of this nation. The earlier notion of freedom, shaped largely by what Bellah calls the republican and biblical (meaning early Protestant) strands of influence, was freedom to do what was right, just, and good. This notion of bounded or ordered freedom was held by most of the founders, but it was steadily replaced by a "natural freedom"—a license to do whatever one wants, whether good or evil.[4] Freedom becomes a virtual end in itself, lacking democratic, moral, or civic content.

This licentious freedom not only relaxes a nation's moral code; it can also erode a sense of civic duty and community belonging. The idea of boundless freedom, according to Bellah, means "being left alone by others, not having other people's values, or styles of life forced upon one, being free of arbitrary authority in work, family, and political life." Bellah continues, "If the entire social world is made up of individuals, each endowed with the right to be free of others' demands, it becomes hard to forge bonds of attachment to, or cooperation with, other people, since such bonds would imply obligations that necessarily impinge on one's freedom."[5]

It may be next to impossible to reconstruct community in a culture of emancipation and unlimited freedom. The call to community, the search for civil society, and the hunger for common ground, which are heard and seen all about us, must be understood in the context of this paradox: Though we want community, we insist that the boundaries of community be lined with well-illuminated "exit" signs. In a culture of the liberated, sovereign self, individuals enter into associations with others on the most tenuous of bases. Every relationship must be negotiated and renegotiated at every turn. The desire to connect and serve is easily trumped by the more powerful impulse to revert back to "rights talk" when things do not go one's way.

These attitudes that profoundly affect our capacity to form community are shaped predominantly by the popular culture. It is hard to imagine building a civil and humane society without confronting the forces of dehumanization all about us in the culture. It is also hard to imagine advancing the idea of "otherness" or the idea that we are "our brother's keeper" when our cultural life is characterized by a compulsive skepticism, cynicism, and distrust. It is impossible to preserve civic virtue when the very idea of a good person is ridiculed.

The full dimensions of what we call culture can hardly be captured in a short description. Differentiating culture from the economic, legal, political, or strictly religious realms is difficult in itself. Moreover, culture is also not interchangeable with such notions as the nation, the state, or civil society. At its most abstract level, culture consists of the ideas, values, attitudes, and myths by which we order our lives and which are reflected broadly in the works of our minds and hands. Culture is our souls' writ large; it mirrors what we value and love.

These attitudes and beliefs are continually shaped by powerful cultural institutions, at both the elite and the popular levels. The culture has institutions of its own at both levels, but the culture can also be said to include attitudes and beliefs that are broadly imbedded in all other institutions. Popular culture includes entertainment, film and television, popular books and magazines, theater, and the vast arena of technological communications.

The Loss of a Common Framework

The very term *culture* implies something held in common—as Webster puts it, "an integrated pattern of human behavior that includes thought, speech, action and artifacts." The purpose of culture is really to regulate and order our lives through informal and noncoercive means—through social regulations like manners and moral norms. The culture, in contrast to the state, governs "lightly." Its job is to establish boundaries around the individual; to grant or deny permission in accordance with broadly understood and accepted moral standards in society. Civic duty, for example, is a cultural norm.

The framers of our social order believed there was a direct linkage between these informal social regulations and the health of democracy. The more effective our social controls, the less external control would be needed in the form of governmental restrictions. A healthy culture lessens the burden that otherwise falls upon democratic institutions to carry.

If the job of culture is to bind us together around common ideas and values, it is failing in this role. American society is fast becoming morally norm-less, which is to say that it is steadily ceasing to be a society at all. We have broadened the range of behaviors that are deemed acceptable perhaps more than any previous society. The current trajectory of the culture is to eradicate the few remaining obstacles to maximum personal freedom. There are very few personal acts that anyone can still publicly assert to be morally wrong. Only the most elementary taboos remain—child or spousal abuse, incest, genocide, and bigotry.

When we talk of cultural failure it is usually in reference to the loss of this norm-setting function. Cultural decay involves the loss of what Bill Bennett calls the cultural guardrails, and the phenomenon Patrick Moynihan describes as "defining deviance down." This decay explains entirely the sexual preoccupation of popular culture and the trendy deconstructionism of higher culture. Cultural decay is manifested in the jaded nature of American society. We have lost our capacity for shock, even over the most debased behavior or the violent misogynistic ranting of rappers. Today, intolerance is thought a greater evil than judging a person's character, however defective.

Recent years have seen banal, course, and prurient cultural programming steadily replacing that which is ennobling and elevating in human culture. When senseless acts of violence and degradation become the standard fare of popular culture, people are slowly conditioned to accept a cheapened view of humanity and of human possibilities. All of these things, and more, that daily bombard our senses are surface ripples produced by deeper currents far below the surface of our culture.

Many of our cultural checks, namely, tradition, authority, and religion, have been either completely eliminated or have lost their binding force on the individual. At a deeper and more important level, cultural decay is about the collapse of cultural authority, whereby, as British sociologist Os Guinness puts it, the "beliefs, ideals and values that once defined America have lost their compelling and their restraining power."[6] The United States is witnessing the disappearance of a coherent and widely shared cultural narrative that binds citizens together in a common enterprise.

Our nation is in the midst of a process of cultural disestablishment, in which the ideals and symbols that once animated our collective consciousness are disintegrating, without a viable candidate for replacement waiting in the wings. When society is severed from its original underpinnings of faith and culture, citizens lose the basis for a common life together and society fragments. The new American culture, rather than requiring self-restraint and social obligation as the price of freedom, demands nothing of the individual and everything for him.

What emerges is a picture of the individual radically ungrounded in anything except the self and severed from such sources of moral meaning as family, religion, custom, and even place. Robert Bellah puts it this way: "In the absence of any objectifiable criteria of right and wrong, good or evil, the self and its feelings become our only moral guide."[7] The individual carries the full burden of knowing his own wants and desires. George Panichas describes the idea of self that we see prized today as "the sensate, external self, the self that is a servant, even a prisoner of the temporal world."[8]

Ironically, modern philosophy and psychotherapy's notion of the unencumbered self with freedom to enjoy all of life through psychological perceptions and feelings carries with it enormous psychological burdens. According to Robert Bellah, the American understanding of the autonomy of the self places the entire burden of "one's own deepest self-definition," not on tradition or community, but rather "on one's own individual choice." Most of us, he says, imagine an "autonomous self existing independently, entirely outside any tradition and community."[9]

Postmodern Culture

Our culture is becoming increasingly postmodern as its own foundation in universal rationality is abandoned; which is to say the culture is becoming more and more antimodern and incoherent. Although many early modernists rejected revealed religion and even natural law as the grounds for public order, they still held to such universal transcendent norms as justice, beauty, truth, freedom, and equality. They simply based their understanding of them on the foundation of reason. Modernity, not surprisingly, has even shaken the foundations of reason and the social order based upon reason.

Unaided reason, it seems, is highly precarious. The central idea of the modern enlightenment-based society—that rational and objective knowledge is possible—is yielding to the belief that every observer's perception of truth is socially constructed. In the absence of a body of universal, objectively discoverable truths, the very idea of truth is extinguished.

Thus in the new culture, each person gets to write his own rules based essentially on feelings and perception. There are no universal principles, only personal opinions and desires. There are no proven or privileged values, only personal tastes. There is no concept of justice, only private interests and personal rights. There is no concept of the common good, only self-advancing individuals.

This "culture" is a culture that ultimately leads to man's degradation. Culture, in order to be culture, cannot be man-made. It is rooted in ideas, myths, stories, and religious beliefs that transcend man. This means that today's culture is premised upon a self-contradiction: A culture that elevates individual autonomy and boundlessly glorifies the human personality, unrefined by faith or reason, is a culture that ultimately degrades man.

Technology

If the moral substance of culture has been altered, the institutions that transmit cultural values have faced even more dramatic change. A culture without defining characteristics and boundaries is no culture at all. The business of maintaining coherent cultural boundaries became dramatically harder with the emergence of an uprooting mass consumerism and a market-dominated society. Holding a culture in common has recently been made even more difficult by an unprecedented subordination of all modes of living, thinking, and communicating to some form of new information technology.

Culture and society have practically become subsidiaries of the technological structure that presides over our modern modes of communicating and living. No longer do the rhythms of daily life in face-to-face communities establish our social habits—chat rooms in cyberspace fill the void. The individual is no longer bound in any meaningful way to the moral instruction of his parents, pastors, or pedagogues. He or she receives his information and values independently from an infinite variety of sources, whether legitimate and authoritative or not, unmediated by moral mentors. The morally authoritative institutions that previously carried out mediating functions are simply rendered impotent.

Whereas culture was once contained and community bounded, today we have what could be called the "surfing sovereign," each man, woman, and child with his or her own web site, mouse-clicking his way along the cosmos of unlimited ideas, ideologies, religions, and lifestyles, designing a worldview out of the crazy quilt patches of cyberspace. In most cities, every taste, interest, and ideology has its own website. Television is not far behind and will soon be technologically merged with the computer.

There can be little doubt that technology has powerful liberating effects. In education, commerce, and culture, these are often employed for the good. In some ways, technology can lead to stronger communities. It can be employed to strengthen groups and associations, and technological advancements can lead to less transience and rootlessness in society, as people are able to keep in touch across large distances.

Previous social transformations, such as the industrial revolution, required the person to move geographically to profit from progress. With the so-called third wave technological transformation, the world literally moves in on the person, without him having to leave his seat, much less his geographic location.

But while technology may reduce mobility, it also promises to make man an omniscient observer and vicarious participant in the whole expanse of human experience. The question then arises whether an individual can ever again possess allegiance to a particular community when a whole world consciousness continuously crowds in on him. Community is not virtual; it is real. It involves face-to-face relationships in real institutions like churches, fraternal associations, and volunteer groups. The virtual community does not care for the poor, it does not raise children, and it may not create generous citizens. These task are accomplished by real communities.

The challenge of restoring a common culture, with proper boundaries and controls, has been rendered dramatically more difficult, if not obsolete, by new technologies. Many ask: At what level in society, and by what means, can common culture, even at the most local levels, be restored?

The cultural air we breathe carries a concept of reality in which there are no fixed reference points. Whatever values and opinions we hold today face fresh new permutations tomorrow. This is what futurists mean when they announce that "technology will destroy culture"—not merely a particular culture, but the very possibility of culture.

Technology collapses boundaries. It eliminates the distance of time and space between vice and virtue, which have always been in conflict but never before thrived within milliseconds of each other. The red-light district was far less socially menacing when it was located in a remote place, where it was hard to get to, where it was easy to be detected, and where conditions were unpleasantly seedy. Now, it basically exists at the command of a mouse or remote control, all in the comfort and anonymity of our own homes. Censorship, if it were ever the answer, becomes progressively less viable in this environment. The presumption of self-censorship that once existed among the purveyors of popular culture is gone and the technological means for effective censorship have largely vanished.

The personally empowering but socially disabling nature of modern technology has received extensive discussion in some academic quarters, but like the substantive content of culture it has been given scant attention in the popular debate over civil society and culture. Local institutions, indeed institutions generally, have been sapped of strength and vitality by the content as well as the structural forms of modern culture.

Politics, Law, and the State

Another powerful moral factor affecting civil society involves the vast realm of politics, law, and the state. Here, the interaction of civil society and the state could not be more apparent. Clearly, the state and its multitudinous functions have a direct impact on civil society.

It is not surprising that when a nation's culture is dominated by utilitarian values, its politics and government are as well. The political realm both influences and is influenced by the many "pre-political institutions" of civil society and culture that foster character and positive democratic habits. These habits and competencies are essential to the health of democracy.

Without a functioning culture to maintain the proper conditions for human flourishing, the social can easily evolve into a custodial democracy, mildly authoritarian, in which human transactions are supervised by the state. When social institutions collapse, the nation unavoidably turns to the state. The courts and social service agencies are forced to serve as caretakers for fragile families and poorly socialized individuals. Large numbers of individuals, whether antisocial members of the underclass or dysfunctional children of the middle class, are for all practical purposes parented and supervised today by state agencies.

The supervisory state, which runs largely on the basis of a mechanistic and materialistic view of man, further erodes the independence and dignity of the human person. The provision of social assistance to tens of millions of Americans is often accompanied by the subtle message that the individual is trapped in conditions that require the permanent help of advocates, interest groups, and public workers.

Whether governmental paternalism is mostly the effect or mostly the cause of declining civil society, it is obvious that these sectors interact. A weakness in one greatly compounds a weakness in the other. A degraded culture, for example, not only weakens democratic institutions, it also weakens the capacity of citizens for trust and collaboration. The utilitarianism that now dominates the culture essentially encourages each person to "do what is right in his own eyes," and to seek the help of lawyers and lobbyists in doing so. The fact that citizens have vastly different notions of what is good and right means that society is no longer organized around shared values. The result is dissonance and conflict among the people.

Also exerting a powerful influence over the functioning of civil society is the law. Accompanying the march toward politicization has been the rights revolution, which most observers generally agree has gone too far. The politics of grievance and victimization have not made Americans any more tolerant, any more compassionate, or any more sensitive to the volatile issues that quickly erupt into nasty recrimination. Our rights consciousness has awakened an appetite for things no viable democracy can offer—the simultaneous expansion of the law and the demand to be free from abuses of the law.

The result is the further weakening of community institutions, an increasingly litigious and arbitrary society, and the steady shrinking of public space. The space that is truly voluntary and consensual, where people of intelligence and goodwill can join together in rational deliberation, disappears. Meanwhile, the spheres of society where decisions are made on the basis of regulation and power expand. Public space ceases to be public when it has become an arena of competition and conflict among individuals who recognize only individual rights and demands, rather than transcendent moral values.

Reliance on law alone to secure freedom ultimately leads to a dramatically expanded law along with restricted freedom. The law is forced to enter where manners and social norms retreat, resulting ultimately in an erosion of human dignity and freedom. The handshake gives way to the omnipresence of the law. The legal system, in turn, becomes overworked and arbitrary. The courts become clogged. Democracy becomes, as George Weigle put it, "an ensemble of procedure for the imperial self."

Absent the restraining influence of moral and cultural norms, the expansion of liberty becomes a zero sum game in which one person's legal gain becomes another person's loss. The rush to use the law against others has evolved into a costly and destructive legal "arms race." People expect the law to simultaneously confer the right to sexual freedom and the right to protection from unwanted sexual advances; to guarantee gender and racial advantage for some and protection against reverse discrimination for others; to protect the rights of criminal offenders and the rights of the offended; to guard the rights of free speech but initiate new rights against the insults of hateful speech; to defend the rights of individuals and also the rights of communities, and so on.

The law has always been expected to strike careful balances in these areas, but never before has it been called on to split conflicting demands with such exasperating precision. This degree of harmony is, of course, beyond the capacity of the law and legal institutions to achieve. The law begins to resemble a harried referee who has the impossible task of policing a sport that is both choked by rules and overwhelmed by infractions of those rules. The pursuit of a just society is reduced to fighting over rules. The consequence is that we are all forced to live in a politically organized society in which all are pitted against all and much of society becomes obsessed with the pursuit of happiness through power. By encouraging excessive and contradictory claims, legal nihilism erodes the legitimacy and effectiveness of the rule of law itself.

It should go without saying that the alternative to a preoccupation with rights is not a determination to curtail them. The solution is a countervailing restraint on "rights consciousness" through a promotion of the common good and an expansion of the social space where the pursuit of common purposes can be carried out. An additional remedy is the wider use of voluntary social restraints in the form of manners and moral norms as the means of protecting liberty and social order. This would include voluntary methods of conflict resolution.

There need not be a dichotomy between the individual and society, as is often assumed in public debates over social policy, or between freedom and order. Liberty and civic community are partners, not implacable foes, in a society of ordered freedom. The preservation and enjoyment of liberty are not possible without strong communities and civic institutions.

Stable communities and mediating associations are a part of the substructure of an enduring freedom. A society in which only individuals and the state advance while the mediating associations of civil society retreat is one that is inching toward authoritarianism. When the horizontal ties of civic cooperation fray, the vertical ties of authority must be strengthened. Legitimate social authority is not the first step toward state authoritarianism, as some fear; it is the first step in its prevention.

The challenge is to restore an ordered freedom while resisting abuses of either freedom or order. Some have used freedom to advance a radical expressive individualism that completely dismisses concern for the moral ecology of society. Conversely, order has increasingly been abused in cases, for example, of warrantless searches, vigilantism, and the National Guard policing urban housing projects.

Lastly, the conduct of politics itself has a direct impact on the health of civil society. Politicians themselves carry much of the responsibility for eroding healthy social institutions and democratic values. Political conduct regularly contributes to the erosion of public respect for democratic institutions. The many maladies of politics, including the flouting of ethics, needless polarization, and the rise of a prosecutorial politics that presumes ideological opponents to be morally defective, have all been addressed extensively elsewhere. Still, it is important to acknowledge that the abuse of power, based upon a rampant utilitarianism, is an abuse of people. It turns citizens into pawns in a power game in which only a select few benefit.

Worse than the politicians themselves is an entire class of professional managers that sees politics as little more than an arena of crass calculation and public manipulation. Accountable to none, these unelected political handlers are responsible for advancing the no-holds-barred, winner-take-all mentality that mobilizes the few while driving the many from electoral participation.

The result has been a declining devotion to democratic citizenship among ordinary people. Fewer and fewer Americans recognize either the utility or the moral necessity of voting. They perceive that their government—originally "of, by and for the people"—has now evolved into a plutocracy of narrow and noisy interest groups that are drowning out the voices of ordinary citizens.

The world of practical politics must be reformed, but just as urgent is the need for politicians to preserve the legitimacy and vitality of other spheres of society that serve as buffers between the individual and the state. Formal politics is not and cannot be the only, or even the major, form of civic participation in our society.

When mediating and moderating associations collapse, human passion asserts itself through power, not reasoned argument and consensual interaction. The role of civic community in promoting deliberation and cooperation toward common ends among ordinary citizens must be expanded. Civic community offers alternative venues for public conversation and cooperative problem solving. It is a place where passions are moderated, attitudes are reformed, and ideas are enlarged.

The Market

The third major moral actor in society, in addition to the culture and the state, is the market. To suggest that the free-market economy has a major impact on civil society, both for good and for bad, is not intended as a thoroughgoing indictment of market capitalism. As the twentieth century draws to a close, market capitalism is almost universally accepted as the most effective and efficient system for the production and distribution of goods, services, and ideas, and has few serious foes.

In spite of its faults, the free market is the favored economic system on both practical and moral grounds. Free economic exchange provides the foundation for intellectual, political, and religious freedoms. The twentieth century has produced ample evidence that economic freedom and a host of other personal freedoms go hand in hand.

But standing on its own apart from a rigorously enforced ethical system, market capitalism can easily generate a preoccupation with material things, yielding a materialism not unlike its philosophical opposite, socialism. The market can easily succumb to, and perpetuate, utilitarian reasoning and values. The ethical grounding that free societies and free markets require may have been weakened as much in the West by utilitarian values as by conscious destruction by dictators elsewhere. The utilitarian individualism that is eroding the authority centers of civil society and consuming the moral capital of American democracy, as discussed above, is also the driving force in American economics.

As the twentieth century has made abundantly clear, the good society is not constructed on the foundation of free markets alone—far from it. For one, it has become fairly obvious that economic prosperity is not the social panacea it was once assumed to be. Economic expansion is certainly to be preferred over economic stagnation, but it is not an engine that drives general social improvement in a host of areas to the degree that many had assumed. American social institutions at the end of the twentieth century have never been weaker, and our continued struggle with crime, educational decline, and multiple problems afflicting children, youth, and families are perhaps most remarkable for their persistence amidst plenty, and to some extent because of material bounty.

Children are dramatically worse off today than in previous generations, in spite of record prosperity and jobs. Possibly no other generation of young people in an affluent country has been so vulnerable to the social and psychological risks frequently associated with having parents that are dysfunctional, divorced, or simply distracted by the pursuit of more prosperity.

General prosperity also does little by itself to ensure the preservation of moral virtues and habits. Some evidence suggests it may actually undermine them. Moral and social malaise are as prevalent in market-oriented societies as in state-dominated countries. Drug and alcohol abuse, for example, may be intractable problems within the middle class primarily because of an excess of disposable funds.

There can be little doubt that a culture dominated solely by the market principle awakens permissive attitudes toward consumption, amusement, and immediate gratification. Columnist and political philosopher George Will chastises some advocates of free markets, who

> see no contradiction between the cultural phenomena they deplore and the capitalist culture they promise to intensify; no connection between the multiplying evidence of self-indulgence and national decadence, and the unsleeping pursuit of ever more immediate, intense, and grand material gratifications.[10]

The ethical supports for economic life have steadily yielded to a view of economic freedom as an end in itself. The market is often defended on the grounds that it is a morally neutral means of exchange and thus preferred over the arbitrary distribution of wealth by state bureaucrats. However, there are many aspects of society that are not morally neutral, and thus should not be decided by the market alone. Market logic is fine when applied to markets, but when the "art of the deal" mentality is applied to marriage, family, culture, community, and the lives of citizens, it corrupts social life and undermines its own foundations. Self-interest is not the primary motive of the citizen, the parent, or the volunteer; self-sacrifice is.

Much of the recent market myopia was brought to the fore by a group of economic utilitarians, commonly known as libertarians. Richard Cornuelle, both a libertarian and an advocate of moral community, chastises fellow libertarians for having no "distinct vision of community" or conception of the "social as distinct from economic process." He adds that "the alluring libertarian contention that society would work better if the state could somehow be limited to keeping the peace and enforcing contracts has to be taken largely on faith."[11]

We have marketized nonmarket sectors of society to ruinous effect. Americans have come to rely too much on the impersonal mechanism of the market to satisfy human wants and aspirations. The idealization of markets as the soul arbiter of human relationships can easily produce an instrumental means of reasoning that is applied to everything. Religious and moral dogma is quickly replaced by economic dogma, and everything becomes valued in accordance with its price in a system of market exchange. The good society—a society of mutual care, respect, and obligation—cannot be constructed by self-maximizing individuals alone.

For much of our history, Americans were actually morally ambivalent about the pursuit of material wealth. On the one hand, the acquisition of property and wealth was seen by the founders as a safe and socially beneficial activity into which the passions and energies of a restless immigrant people could be channeled. Animosity growing out of ethnic differences and moral factions would be tempered to some extent by peaceful competition. A dynamic and competitive society would constantly create new winners and destroy settled social classes and ranks; no one group would possess special advantages.

As John Locke and Adam Smith understood it, the pursuit of economic interests, properly guided, clearly offers benefits in which all could share. Whatever its downside, economic competition would raise us above our worst tendencies. The social good would be served as each vigorously sought to advance his own interest. The quest for material satisfaction, in that sense, served noble purposes.

This, however, assumed a certain type of ethically grounded society, and a particular kind of individual living out a particular view of freedom. The same formula, lacking the ethical foundations, yields the utilitarian individualism we have today. Certainly, there has always been a powerful strain of individualism centering on personal improvement and rugged self-reliance. Until very recently, however, there have also been other powerful countercurrents. These included the influence of the early Puritans, the Protestant work ethic, and the search for deeper understanding of the self embodied in much of American folklore and literature, such as in the writings of Emerson, Thoreau, and Hawthorne. All of these strains saw the self as situated in a moral universe. Utilitarian individualism with its creed that material self-interest is an unambiguous good has not always been the norm.

In the past, the pursuit of wealth was evaluated against its tendency to corrupt. It was assumed that the hunger for material gain would be strongly moderated by spiritual and ethical principles. There was a time when religious values were confidently asserted as a factor in economic life. The impression frequently given that the idea of economic freedom as an end in itself originated in early American Protestant teaching is a distortion of reality. Recent scholarship bears evidence of the opposite. The dominant Protestant heritage of the eighteenth century was one of local democratic communalism. The sermons and political writings of the day were filled with warnings against narrow self-interest and the dangers of exalting the individual over the community.

Commerce without a moral compass, as the early Protestants saw it, can easily degenerate into a scramble for wealth with little regard for honest work, industry, thrift, and deferred gratification. Clear limitations were placed on the individual through admonitions to respect the corporate bonds of family, kin, and community and to seek the common good. The craven pursuit of riches rather than the pursuit of satisfaction through vocational calling violated the core tenets of Christian grace, which attributed all success in life to the grace of God. Worth was to be found in work and especially in the practice of one's vocation, not merely as a means to personal prosperity, but as an end to be valued in itself.[12]

Tocqueville was concerned about the American tendency to settle for the lowest common denominator in pursuing "petty and paltry pleasures." The rational, self-interested man too easily degenerates into the self-absorbed, narcissistic man, lacking a spiritual or ethical core, as well as affection for others or concern for their interests. This type of man was thought unfit for a self-governing society. Jefferson believed that if people lost themselves "in the sole faculty of making money," the future of the republic was bleak and tyranny was likely.[13]

The Left has long been critical of the market for encouraging selfishness and the abuse of workers. A longer tradition operating on the Right, though largely dormant at present, has criticized the market for corrupting personal virtues and cultural values. Political scientist Mark Henrie has described market individualism as one of "the two homogenizing powers" in modern society; the other being the rights-based politics of the liberal state.[14] The negative effects of each on civil society and on such mediating structures as strong families and autonomous communities are the same, he maintains.

Other prominent conservatives, like the late Russell Kirk, have pointed out how excessive commercialism can undermine the virtues of service and sacrifice that nourish community and undergird the commercial enterprise itself. Kirk criticized the blind supporters of the market for too frequently viewing markets as the ultimate value and "ultimate arbiter of values." The result, he says, is that we commit "taxidermy on moral categories," draining them "of their richness and stuffing them full of the sawdust talk of rights, interests, and interstate commerce."[15]

Capitalism, in other words, easily evolves into more than a system for the ownership, distribution, and production of goods. It becomes a faith system and a way of life. As H. Richard Niebuhr puts it, faith in wealth can easily be seen "as the source of all life's blessings and as the savior of man from his deepest misery. It is the doctrine that man's most important activity is the production of economic goods and that all other things are dependent on this."[16] This, then, becomes the message to rich and poor alike: Life consists in the abundance of things possessed; the earth is ours to do with what we want; self-interest, not the ethic of service or stewardship, is our guiding light.

Finally, markets are restless, uprooting, and relentless in their relationship to society and culture, which runs counter to many of the requirements of community. The mobility of capital in a global marketplace can exert powerful uprooting effects on communities. It is one thing to accept this "creative destructionism" as inevitable, unavoidable, and necessary for a greater good, to acknowledge the trade-offs that come with it, and to work to ameliorate its effects. It is disingenuous, however, for market advocates to voice unqualified support for global capitalism while simultaneously championing the values and habits of traditional communities, or, in other words, asserting that a liberal economy and a traditional society are entirely compatible.

Most acknowledge that a dynamic but socially disruptive global capitalism is here to stay, and in any case, there is no morally superior alternative. One can accept that the market serves important economic objectives while realizing that it can be socially disabling in some ways, and accepting that it requires a compensating solidarity in institutions of community and faith. Merely deepening our adherence to laissez-faire ideology, which some propose as the answer, may only encourage a greater blindness to its limitations.

Conclusion

The civil society debate thus far has reflected a superficial reading of the nation's social challenge, and it may ultimately represent thin gruel for a public expecting more basic change. The broad tendency today is to embrace civil society as a new paradigm that has intrinsic powers of its own to produce social renewal.

However, while civil society can certainly be an important source of social regeneration, it cannot single-handedly resist the social and cultural tide or, by itself, significantly moderate the power of the culture, the state, and the market. Whatever powers civil society possesses on its own are challenged by equally powerful forces that operate upon it from without. While communities and voluntary associations are certainly major actors in our society, they may be less powerful and less independent as moral agents, in the final analysis, than many assume.

Notes

1. Mary Ann Glendon, in *Seedbeds of Virtue: Sources of Competence, Character and Citizenship in American Society*, ed. Mary Ann Glendon and David Blankenhorn (Lanham, Md.: Madison Books, 1995), 2.

2. Robert Bellah et al., *Habits of the Heart: Individualism and Commitment in American Life* (New York: Harper and Row, 1985), 83.

3. Bellah, 81.

4. Bellah, 25.

5. Bellah, 23.

6. Os Guinness, *The American House* (New York: Free Press, 1993), 20.

7. Bellah, 76.

8. George A. Panichas, "Sapiential Voices," *Modern Age*, 39, no. 1 (Winter 1997), 48.

9. Bellah, 65.

10. Mark C. Henrie, "Rethinking American Conservatism in the 1990s: The Struggle Against Homogenization," *The Intercollegiate Review*, Spring 1993, 37.

11. Richard Cornuelle, "The Power and Poverty of Libertarian Thought," in *Cato Policy Report*, January/February 1992, vol. xiv, no. 1, 10.

12. For example, see Barry Shain, *The Myth of American Individualism* (Princeton: Princeton University Press, 1994).

13. Bellah, 31.

14. Henrie, 14.

15. Russell Kirk, *The Politics of Prudence* (Bryn Mawr, Pa.: Intercollegiate Studies Institute, 1993), 30.

16. H. Richard Niebuhr, "The Church against the World," in Charles W. Dunn, *American Political Theology* (New York, Praeger Publishers, 1984), 66.

Chapter 12

Civil Society Plus: America's Civic and Transcendent Creeds

The previous two chapters show that civil society does not exist in a moral vacuum and does not function independent of other major structures, including the culture, the market, and the state. Civil society is directly and powerfully influenced by the dominant cultural ethos of utilitarianism and individualism, and any effort to renew it must take account of many other factors and forces in American life. This chapter considers a slightly different limitation of civil society that can be stated as follows: Civil society can reinforce and inculcate a set of moral norms, but it cannot create or recreate them ex nihilo. This requires tapping into a deeper reservoir of morality vitality.

Civil society is commonly understood as the wellspring of our nation's social capital, which it certainly is. Social capital, however, is not produced out of thin air; it is not entirely self-generating and self-replenishing. Civil society draws moral authority and vitality from particular sources within its own core that are themselves essentially moral and spiritual. True social capital is drawn from our seedbeds of virtue, a rich substrata of civil society that is moral, philosophical, and religious in nature. The real seedbeds of civic community are those institutions that nourish moral habits, such as our places of worship and character-shaping institutions in the community.

To a large extent, society runs on the basis of capital borrowed from these deeper wells of social regeneration. The debate about civil society is not, and cannot become, a debate merely about the status of joining and volunteering in America, as important as these activities are. Nor can it reflect an unrealistic confidence in the innate self-sustaining, self-renewing powers of communities, as though communities operate in isolation from the rest of society. This is an inadequate understanding of how communities function, a partial reading of the American experience, and a shrunken understanding of what is often referred to as "the American creed."

America's Two-Part Creed

Nations are said to live by their myths and creeds, and this is especially true of the United States. One foreign observer who traveled throughout the country during the 1920s, G. K. Chesterton, was so impressed with the force of our basic social covenant compared to the rest of the world that he concluded: "America is the only nation in the world that is founded on a creed." That creed, he said, was so dominant that it was set forth "with dogmatic and even theological lucidity" in our founding documents.

What binds the United States together are the core myths, historical truths, and still unfolding story of free citizens. American society, as Tocqueville understood so well, is held together by core ideas, or what we might call basic propositions. As Tocqueville observed, "in order for society to exist and, even more, to prosper, it is necessary that the spirits of all citizens be assembled and held together by certain leading ideas."[1]

What are the nation's leading ideas and basic creeds? One of the most enduring and inspiring myths is the tradition of civic duty. It is a tale of robust citizenship, of helping out in times of need, of putting country ahead of self when duty calls. It is a tradition, not just of making a living, but of joining, participating, and giving. It is about our penchant for optimistic problem solving, and about the outpouring of sacrificial deeds that are displayed every time the tragedy of flood, fire, or hurricane strikes.

The American civic creed, understood this way, presents the ideal of unity grounded in solidarity, civic participation, and community problem solving. More than perhaps any other source of unity, this myth of civic generosity supplies the social glue for an ethnically and religiously diverse nation. Through the reciprocal influence we have on one another in civic community "feelings and opinions are recruited, the heart is enlarged, and the human mind is developed,"[2] according to Tocqueville. From the affiliations and affections of society's little platoons we proceed toward a love of mankind, including those having dramatically different cultural origins and stories. In the United States, civil society is the central arena in which our social creed is developed and perpetuated.

Voluntary associations, or associations of "common interest" as Tocqueville called them, serve as one of the few socially integrating and naturally ennobling forces that can be found in the United States. The United

States is not held together by common ancestry, ancient traditions, aristocracy, or ethnic or religious homogeneity. This unique American civic creed supplies the alternative, and it also goes to the core of who we believe we are.

In preserving and perpetuating this creed, both in our collective imagination and in individual practice, civil society provides much of the social capital for a functional democracy, as we saw earlier. Civil society does more than provide private charity, generate volunteers, and preserve strong neighborhoods. The institutions of civil society play an irreplaceable role in fostering competence and democratic character in individuals. By transforming children into citizens, by generating social trust, and by providing a wide range of opportunities for self-governance, civil society advances a strong democratic society.

America's Civic Creed

The country's basic civic creed—what we might call the American civic proposition—is essentially the story of cooperative civic endeavor that has been described in this book. The civic renewal movement described in these pages is powerful evidence of our still vibrant faith in America's basic civic creed, and it presents promising possibilities for reclaiming the nation's tradition of localism and volunteerism, for re-empowering civic institutions, and for regenerating communities. It must not be sold short.

It is this creed—the civic creed—that the civil society movement reflects best, in all of its promise as well as its limitations. There is much in the civic proposition that can readily be endorsed. It is rich and dynamic, to be sure. The nation's varied groups and associations are the building blocks of our social order, and they must be reinforced and revered. Few would doubt that civic community can achieve many important tasks in society, and in the process help cultivate citizens who are respectful, trustful, and helpful toward one another. Civil society represents the entire spectrum of institutions and activities that make up the social sector, apart from which our experiment in democratic self-government would not be possible. In short, this civic faith must be given fresh allegiance today as it was periodically in the past.

Nevertheless, standing on its own, the call to renew our civic creed has limits. If restoring civil society is not mostly about revitalized economics or reformed government, and not entirely about the relative size of the private or public sectors, as was discussed, neither is it solely or even primarily about recovering civic engagement. Promoting a new ethos of civic responsibility is an important but insufficient step toward renewing a nation.

America's Transcendent Creed

The civic proposition supplies only part of the content of the nation's creed. There is another American creed that has shaped our national character and that also vies for our continued loyalty, and that is what we will call the transcendent proposition. This proposition views the American experiment as fundamentally grounded in, and dependent upon, transcendent moral foundations, not merely civic action.

To suggest, as our founders did, that men and women are endowed with "certain inalienable rights" is to advance a moral and epistemological proposition. To say that we are endowed "by our creator" with these rights is to advance, in reality, a theological argument. At the outer core of the country's social and political system is a civic proposition. At its inner core is a moral and spiritual tradition that is easily forgotten and more frequently willfully discarded—what Walter Lippman referred to as "the forgotten foundation of democracy." The American experience is rooted in both a civic creed and what Lippman called a "public theology."

In accordance with this transcendent creed, Americans are called to look beyond themselves and even beyond their own communities for answers, finding strength and inspiration in unchanging ethical norms. Apart from a recovery of moral constraints and obligations that have some binding effect on each citizen, rebuilding community may not be possible. Ultimately, civic engagement requires moral determinants, and for civic institutions to be restored to their former robustness they must possess ethical substance and authority.

Civic engagement, to succeed on a large scale, must be empowered by a moral imperative. To have real public purchase, a reactivation of the nation's civic creed will require the accompanying support of a revived transcendent creed. Yet, this awareness is not at all apparent in the current civil society movement. The present civil society debate operates with an almost complete absence—indeed the near complete inadmissibility—of moral language or the transcendent presuppositions that guided our society and culture for much of its history. In fact, the fashionable habit among many of today's intellectuals and societal elite is to spread cynicism and skepticism toward American values and institutions, the consequence of which is the deconstruction of America's cultural heritage and accomplishments without affirming an alternative vision of what is good and just.

A close examination of the civil society literature indicates a near exclusive concern among its experts and advocates with the condition of our civic organizations and our proclivity for joining them. It reflects an interest mostly in knowing whether we are civicly engaged, and if not, why not. It frequently voices the belief that the chief source of social capital is simply the act of joining. Tocqueville believed, however, that although civic participation such as jury duty and volunteering on election day helped inculcate a sense of duty, activity of this kind, as important as it was, is not sufficient by itself to create a virtuous citizen.

Civic norms can become imbedded in and are partially sustained by civil society, but they are not produced there alone. In this sense, the current civil society movement wrongly identifies itself as Tocquevillian. Most current civil society advocates see themselves operating within the tradition of Tocqueville, and often refer to themselves as neo-Tocquevillians. But Tocqueville might not have approved of seeing his name invoked to legitimate a movement that issues frequent appeals to civic duty but that is timid in asserting the moral foundations of citizenship in a free society. This is a partial reading of the United States Tocqueville observed, and a distorted presentation of the American creed.

What fascinated Tocqueville the most, after all, was the central role of "mores" to the preservation of democracy in the United States. Mores, he said, were "the sum of moral and intellectual dispositions of men in society."[3] Mores include habits of the heart and mind; they entail ideas and opinions on such matters as economics, morality, and religion. To undermine these mores is to weaken the institutions of a free society, according to Tocqueville.

Mores, as Tocqueville saw them, were anything but the soft, superficial opinions and preferences that guide decisionmaking and value-formation in our society today. They bear no resemblance to the relativism that now dominates our culture and which is widely assumed by today's intellectual class to be the crowning achievement of an enlightened and sophisticated society. The mores of Tocqueville's America were powerful enough to curb individualism and egoism, whereas the social norms and regulations of today are obviously not.

In fact, what guided mores into being and kept them in place was religion, perhaps the most forbidden subject of all among many civil society intellectuals today. Religion "directs the mores," said Tocqueville, and by regulating domestic life it helps "to regulate the state." The current discussion among the vast majority of participants in civil society would appear to be tone deaf to the place of religion in the lives of most Americans, and to the role of religion as a seedbed of virtuous citizenship in a free and civil society. Tocqueville, who was sobered by the attack of French revolutionaries on tradition and religion, spared no effort to show that religion was the answer to many of America's potential excesses, not the source of them, as many intellectuals today view it.

In the United States, religion would be welcomed by revolutionary forces as a source of social order and stability, not thrown off as an impediment to human progress. Religion in Tocqueville's time was the principle source of social order. It reinforced self-control and maintained moral standards. It taught self-sacrifice and self-reliance, and fueled benevolence toward others. It can be said that religion was the principle generator of civil society.

For much of American history, religion gave birth to many of the social institutions that the civil society movement is now trying to renew, by largely secular means. According to a now largely defunct sociological tradition represented by Emile Durkheim, "nearly all the great social institutions have essentially been born in religion."[4] American civic history and religious history are inseparable.

Civic initiatives too numerous to mention here were launched during practically every period of American history. Numerous public projects that sought to improve urban or rural conditions, aid children and youth, and provide health care and education grew out of religious tendencies in the United States. Many of the nation's greatest universities, which can now be frequently heard articulating a narrow reading of the American creed, were founded by religious movements and leaders. Most of the great civic institutions launched in the nineteenth century from the YMCA and YWCA to the Salvation Army, which now constitute the backbone of civic America, were born out of religiously inspired social concern.

The American character contains much civic content, but it is also irreducibly moral and religious. Much of the country's civic creed and history are stories of the nation's enduring commitment to transcendent principles, even though frequently expressed in secular language. For example, the principle symbol of the country's civic creed is captured in the familiar symbol of the shining "city on a hill," which is nothing less than a secularized version of John Winthrop's spiritual community. For Winthrop, community was a place where, as Winthrop put it, we "delight in each other, make each others condition our own, rejoice together, mourn together, labor and suffer together, always having before our eyes our community as members of the same body."[5]

Winthrop's vision of civil society was not just about joining for joining's sake; it was about belonging to a community that possessed moral substance. Community was grounded in spiritual and ethical qualities. This form of joining together embodied the notion of commonwealth, an arrangement in which citizens combine the private pursuit of happiness with devotion to the public good, or the common weal. The fundamental criterion of success in

Winthrop's community was not material wealth or success for the individual, but rather the possibility of creating the conditions in which "a genuinely ethical and spiritual life could be lived."[6]

To fully revive the country's civic creed we must fully recover the American heritage of moral realism and spiritual values. There is such a thing as universal moral truth, and as our founders embraced the concept, that truth transcends particular religious and cultural traditions. Moral truth is not the exclusive province of a particular tradition or ethnic experience. It is accessible to every living person by virtue of his membership in the human race, and thus applicable to private and public life alike.

These universal moral principles, and not merely the country's civic creed, shaped the American public philosophy. The Western intellectual and political tradition was once assumed to be a moral and even religious tradition. Western cultures, and especially American culture, have drawn nutrients from the subsoil of religion and spiritual values. Many regard religion and culture as essentially different aspects of the same thing; culture being essentially the incarnation of a people's religious belief. As Durkheim put it: "If religion has given birth to all that is essential in society, it is because the idea of society is the soul of religion."[7] At the heart of culture is religion, and at the heart of religion are the most basic assumptions about reality and the world.

Says political philosopher Jim Skillen:

> [P]olitical and legal systems throughout the world have had their historical origins in particular religions. There is simply no way to give proper account of the emergence of contemporary political institutions and legal principles anywhere in the world apart from a recognition of their origin in Judaism, Christianity, Islam, Buddhism, Confucianism, Taoism, or a host of different cultures and religions.

Few would dispute the statement, Skillen adds, that "the United States is the product of a Protestant culture—a culture that both helped create and also struggled against various streams of the European Enlightenment."[8] Many Americans, he adds, "have little awareness of or appreciation for the imposing power that Greek thought, Roman law, and Christian faith had in shaping the western legal and political traditions."[9]

The Sacred-Secular Compromise

Our political and legal system had historical origins in a synthesis between Protestant religion and Enlightenment Humanism, each with slightly different presuppositions about human nature and society. Through compromise, the two sides settled on the notion of natural rights secured by a higher law—the laws of nature and "of nature's God." The framers unashamedly invoked, as the grounds of morality and concepts of law, the existence of a higher law that precedes and transcends the individual.

Today the original sacred-secular compromise that formed our social union has yielded to a political-cultural ethos that is aggressively secular and utilitarian. The early enlightenment philosophy that viewed religion as benign has yielded to a modern enlightenment mentality that sees the autonomy of the individual as the highest good, and thus views religion as a danger.

American public philosophy is now strained deeply between those who value religion as a source of freedom and those who see it as a threat to freedom. Kevin Hasson writes that there are "two different anthropologies" contending in the country's public philosophy today. In the first, he says, "people come with a built-in thirst for the transcendent and to express what they believe they have found. In the second, pop existential anthropology, people come with a built-in fear and alienation, and require freedom from distressing claims of morality and eternity." Which anthropology a government holds, he adds, "determines the sort of religious liberty it permits."[10]

The real question is whether the original sacred-secular compromise can be restored. The existential anthropology of which Hasson speaks, absent the transcendent anthropology, provides a weak foundation for freedom. If secular materialism provides fragile grounds for the state, it provides even shakier grounds for society and culture. A society running on a partial and selective reading of its own history is a society that will turn to partial solutions to its problems. It will seek self-renewal on the basis of a limited understanding of its own animating beliefs.

Those who stiffly resist a broader role for religion in society must ask themselves: What power could possibly compare to religion in curbing the materialism and individualism that is now sapping society of its vitality? Certainly not the civic creed standing alone. Public invocations of the civic spirit are simply not compelling enough to confront the power of modern individualism, which is based upon what Bellah calls the "improvisational self." The problem with the modern self, as discussed elsewhere, is that it "chooses values to express itself," but it is not "constituted by them as from a pre-existing source."[11]

A mass society of isolated individuals who do random and occasional civic deeds is still a weak society. The antidote to the utilitarianism that is so ruinous of the civic ethic is the animating conviction that there is a higher law, whose existence validates our human dignity and charts our moral course. As the founders understood it, basic claims to human dignity and worth are rooted safely in divine providence, and only secured by the state. The individual is not the designer of his own laws; he is not alone in the universe enjoying rights of his own construction that can be easily created today and just as easily abridged tomorrow. His rights are secure because there is such a thing as moral truth, grounded and fortified by natural laws.

The same foundations that formed our Declaration and Constitution have occasionally been invoked to correct that Constitution's defects. It was appeals to transcendent moral truths that made improvements in the Constitution possible and enabled the American democratic experiment to gain fresh bursts of legitimacy in the eyes of its citizens. It was appeals to transcendent principles that propelled the United States forward in its long march toward freedom and equality for various categories of disenfranchised and oppressed Americans. As Robert Bellah has put it, "[E]very movement to make America more fully realize its professed values has grown out of some form of public theology."[12]

American history is full of examples of how citizens have frequently been challenged to live in accordance with a better understanding of the moral principles we declare in our Constitution, and which we hope to embrace in our public life, though often imperfectly. Examples from early America up until the present include: the movement toward independence, the struggle to ratify the Constitution, the women's suffrage movement, the abolition movement, numerous moral reform movements, as well as many modern social and political movements, whether the campaign to eliminate abortion and to renew the family operating on the right, or the advocacy of government programs in the name of social justice advanced by the Left.

All of these movements have held our present conduct as Americans as deficient in light of a body of universal moral principles. Martin Luther King, an icon in the American pantheon of moral prophets, built his entire strategy for racial progress on the possibility of provoking the conscience and arousing the souls of white Americans. King knew that the only way to challenge the deficiencies of our penultimate document, the Constitution, was to invoke a power still higher, a power by which all human constitutions, in principle and practice, had to be compared and justified.

This invocation of a transcendent ethic has also helped Americans achieve difficult social progress throughout their history without going to war with each other. King's ethic for social change, rooted firmly in the transcendent creed, was essentially: "[H]im whom you would change, you must first love." This ethic inspired King to forsake a politics of resentment for a philosophy of nonviolent resistance that found its strength in spiritual, not political, power. Only through an inner spiritual transformation, he said, "do we gain the strength to fight vigorously the evils of the world in a humble and loving spirit."[13]

As King modeled out in his life, the transcendent ethic enables us to seek improvements in an imperfect world by first acknowledging our own imperfections and our own participation in and culpability for the conditions around us. When imperfect individuals acknowledge their own responsibility for the conditions around them, rather than rush to condemn another class of human beings for them, they provide the means for avoiding the re-criminations that can quickly accompany bitter public disputes.

The transcendent ethic enables us to confront a world of deep division while "bearing malice toward none," as Lincoln captured it. Says political scientist David Walsh:

> Without a pure, disinterested love from the start, we have no way of reaching it in the end; without a self-effacing modesty concerning our goal, we have no way to resist the most excessive self-aggrandizement; and without a firm recognition of the reality of good and evil, we inevitably succumb to the worst temptations of power.[14]

Fostering a spirit of forgiveness not only serves a spiritually redemptive influence; it is socially redemptive. Advocates of the American transcendent creed, such as Niebuhr and Chesterton, argued that forgiveness made it possible for opposing groups to fight to the end without denying the other's humanity. Civil society is impossible without the capacity for vigorous disagreement over basic ideas and values, while sharing enough in common over the means toward shared moral ends "to have something to disagree about."[15]

Embracing the transcendent ethic would elevate, not debase, public debate, over even the thorniest and most divisive issues of our time, because it would help us acknowledge our disagreements within a common ethical framework. Says John Courtney Murray, "The whole premise of the public argument if it is to be civilized and civilizing," he says, "is that consensus is real, that among the people everything is not in doubt, but that there is a core of agreement, accord, concurrence, acquiescence. We hold certain truths; therefore we can argue about them."[16]

Without recognizing the inherent moral worth of others, differences are never amicably settled; they only lead to the next cycle of recrimination as one side in a dispute seeks conquest over its opponents through a naked will to power. Without this sense of acknowledging the other's humanity, debates degenerate into shrill mutterings. Whoever wins, society loses, and "the barbarian is at the gates of the city."[17]

Dietrich Bonhoeffer, the German pastor who willingly faced the firing squad for resisting Hitler's atrocities, remained passionately committed to the ethic of unconditional love for all human beings, including his enemies. He warned of an irresistible pull toward a self-righteousness that destroys one's capacity to engage in heroic acts of love and mercy. This kind of judgment is "the forbidden objectivization of the other person," the result of which is the destruction of "single-minded love."

Secularism can summon no such moral conviction or civic power. It contains no grounds beyond the individual self to nourish humanitarianism, and is a feeble source of personal empathy or social sympathy. It possesses no inherent power for heroic action. It is hard to imagine American secularism summoning Americans to engage in public argument with a redemptive spirit, to fight for social change with humility and self-sacrifice, or to consistently acknowledge the humanity of others through an attitude of mercy.

Ironically, rather than acknowledging the renewing power of the transcendent creed, secularists instead direct their energies toward resisting it and what they perceive to be its dangers. As a result, the role of religion has undeniably been constricted in the West. Vaclav Havel has declared that "we live in the first atheistic civilization in human history," one that "proudly asserts that man is capable of knowing everything, describing everything, and doing everything." He said that we have "ceased to respect any so-called higher metaphysical values." Writing on the same subject Zbignew Brzezniski has said much the same thing. In surveying our moral and cultural conditions, he said that "the greatest victory for the proposition that 'God is dead' has occurred not in the Marxist-oriented states, which propagated atheism, but in western liberal democracies, which have culturally nurtured moral apathy."

Tocqueville would find these conditions remarkable. He would find even more remarkable the difficulty we currently have in publicly acknowledging religion as a primary source of civil society's renewal. Today, when the subject of religion is raised in connection with the problems of society, the immediate assumption operating throughout most of the nation's knowledge class is that it is more disease than cure for what ails our society.

The Place of Religion

The introduction of religion is assumed to represent yet another invitation to wider social divisions within the United States rather than a means to ameliorate or transcend these divisions. After all, the reasoning goes, religion certainly has been abused frequently in history, including on the European soil from which our forefathers fled in order to enjoy freedom of conscience in a new land. Why would anyone want to raise this issue?

The reason the issue is raised is because American democracy is grounded in transcendent principles, and it is through this grounding that we resist all forms of tyranny, whether religious or secular. The founders anchored their challenge to the religious oppressors of their native Europe, and their case for religious freedom in their new land, in divine law, not merely in utilitarian reasoning. Freedom was seen as a gift of God. The inalienability of freedom, equality, and independence was grounded in references to the laws of nature.

The question of how religion should or should not order our common life together is a matter of deep confusion and too frequently division—between secularists who speak the sterile language of rights and entitlements and religious movements that refuse to accommodate, in language or methods, democratic pluralism. Nevertheless, Americans remain a deeply and incorrigibly religious people, and show no signs of becoming anything else. The factor of faith is a fact of American life, and it must be recognized as mostly an aid or an impediment to social progress.

The fear and loathing that largely attend the subject of religion in the United States among public intellectuals are rooted in a flawed understanding of how religion interacted with the public order. In the United States, religion and freedom have marched hand in hand: They have not been and must not become adversaries. Tocqueville, a European who was shocked by the ferocity of the French Revolution's attack on religion, found in the United States "the spirit of religion and the spirit of freedom" both marching in the same direction. He deemed the United States one of "the freest and most enlightened nations in the world" and saw its people filled with fervor for all the "duties of religion."[18]

Tocqueville identified religion as the first political institution, not because it was the job of religious institutions or creeds to order the affairs of the state. Quite the contrary. Politics and religion "contracted an alliance" because of religion's great influence over the souls of men, and because it directed "the customs of community," producing a populace more enlightened and free than any before. The job of religion was one of nourishing the habits of restraint, industry, and tranquillity that were thought necessary to maintain republican institutions.

In other words, religion was a welcome source of influence in the shaping of civil society and the broader culture. Religion's influence over manners and morals—the habits of the heart—was vast. However, it maintained a cautious distance when it came to political parties and public affairs. In the United States, said Tocqueville, religion "exercises but little influence upon the laws and upon the details of public opinion; but it directs the customs of community; and, by regulating domestic life, it regulates the state."[19]

Religion's indirect influence was considerable; its direct influence minimal and guarded. Ministers "eschewed all parties," filled no public appointments, and were "eschewed by public opinion from serving in legislatures."[20] In short, the job of religion, as Tocqueville saw it, was to order our souls, and by extension society; not to directly rule over the state.

This is the understanding that is missing today across the entire spectrum of debate on religion and society. Confusion exists and mistakes have been made by partisans on both sides of the church-state debate. Too many secular partisans have sought to marginalize religion, and even worse, to render publicly expressed religious belief illegitimate by groundlessly suggesting that advocates of moral and religious values seek a merger of church and state.

The separation of church and state originally meant no more than the fact that the state must refrain from sanctioning a particular religion. In a mistaken application of church-state separation, the state has moved to construct a wall around the practice and expression of religion and spiritual values in society and politics. This does violence to the original meaning of religious liberty and weakens the transcendent foundations of our culture. Religion, both in private practice and public affirmation, must be honored, and its moral voice must be heard, on even the most difficult issues.

The recommendation here is not for a governmental embrace of sectarian religion or state favoritism in religion. What is being suggested, in addition to wider freedoms of expression and participation for religious citizens, is the acknowledgment that religious belief has played a constructive and pivotal role in shaping our culture and union, and that it still exists as a socially renewing power in spite of attempts to partition it off from society and politics.

Publicly sanctioned religion was never seriously regarded as an option in the United States, even during an earlier period of religious homogeneity. The brief experiment in church-state entanglement that took place in colonial

America was abandoned in fairly short order after it proved unworkable. It was problematic in design, it proved unworkable in accommodating diverse new populations as they arrived, and it was ultimately judged contrary to the principle of religious liberty by religious practitioners themselves. The hunger for religious liberty, and the desire to preserve freedom from state control, proved to be far more powerful and appealing, then and now.

No major body of American believers today wish otherwise. While most acknowledge that religion should be more widely affirmed as socially beneficial and that the state should be less hostile to it, few expect the state to elevate religion in public, and especially a particular religion, to the place it once had. For one, religious diversity mitigates against it. Most agree that Protestant hegemony over culture is gone forever, thanks both to the rise of secularism and the emergence of newly influential religious minorities. The search is now on for a framework that draws persons of all faiths into a common understanding of morality and common public language.

It is furthermore doubtful that modern and postmodern individuals will submit themselves again to the constrictions of religiously grounded social mores. According to Robert Bellah, many perceive a return to traditional forms as representing a return to "intolerable discrimination and oppression."[21] Moreover, Bellah doubts whether the older civic and biblical traditions have the capacity to reformulate themselves in such a way that is congenial to Americans while "remaining faithful to their own deepest insights."

Where does this leave American moral foundations, which are widely recognized to be in need of repair? All of these realities and more are used by postmodernists skeptics who would have everyone believe an alternative secular creed: that universal moral principles never governed our democracy, and if they did they shouldn't have, and that neither moral norms nor cultural authority, of any kind, can possibly be recovered.

The alternative to the public sectarianism that secularists fear is certainly not the public secularism they propose. When society can't draw moral meaning and direction from religious belief, it draws it from other sources. For one, it comes to rely on the market and the principle of self-interest, and becomes increasingly materialistic. The nation's common moral heritage becomes subjugated to the cant and calculation of self-interest.

When religion and morality atrophy are forcibly subordinated, citizens increasingly take their cues from a mass culture, which runs on the impulse toward amusement, self-indulgence, and vice. Society becomes driven by Nielsen ratings, quarterly profit statements, two-year election cycles, the Dow Jones Industrial Average, or any other ephemeral source of direction.

When the transcendent ethic declines, society becomes subsumed by the state, where all matters, including those that are irreducibly moral, are decided on the basis either of majoritarianism or judicial fiat. As discussed previously, when moral consensus is weak or nonexistent, political and judicial authorities try in vain to split differences on the basis of prevailing public or judicial opinion.

The state has a very difficult time finding compromise on matters that go to the core of our moral understandings. Usually, it amounts to winner take all, as numerous judicial decisions recently testify, which only deepens the cultural conflict that gave rise to the legal dispute in the first place. The state is also incapable of satisfying our natural desires and need for meaning. The alternative belief system of secular materialism attempts to substitute economic prosperity, technological prowess and progress, and the modern state for spiritual truth.

It takes us precisely to where we are today. This reductionist tendency of subjecting the human person to the tools of scientific analysis and management is spiritually impoverishing and socially corrupting. The result is a restless search for human progress through political mechanisms alone, a clamor for governmental solutions, and the elevation of human desires and longings into inalienable rights. The lack of happiness is assumed to be linked to some injustice, missing expert assistance, or properly designed public program.

Yet another result of the collapse of transcendence is the rise of ethnic and racial division. When the nation's heritage of moderated cultural and religious pluralism dies off as a centripetal force, society yields instead to the divisive dictates of group separatism, a powerful centrifugal force that will balkanize the United States if not reversed.

Our capacity to embrace diversity is itself a product of our country's unique moral and intellectual tradition—a tradition that is all too often denigrated by a misguided multiculturalism. Religious beliefs and traditions forbid believers from killing or hating persons of other colors and creeds, as discussed above. The transcendent creed, drawn from religious pluralism, provides the *unum* in *E Pluribus Unum*, and protects us against the ugly results that flow from glorifying our differences.

The point is, citizens place their faith in one belief system or another. When the humanitarian ethic of the transcendent creed is not supplying the direction for society, religious truth becomes replaced by economic, scientific, and political truth, which carries the consequences described above. The collapse of the American social and political "center" is largely a function of the decline of the nation's core creeds—civic and transcendent.

The emergence of religious and ideological conflict in the United States is a reflection of misdirected faith and of the collapse of an American public philosophy that integrated these things to the satisfaction of most. Public discourse has become strained in part because of differing conceptions of moral authority and belief. It is important to confront, rather than evade, these core differences. There is no avoiding this debate, any more than we can ignore the basic character of the United States. It is, in fact, the absence of this debate among the American elite that contributes like no other factor to tensions and produces a cultural stalemate.

The answer to the problem of religion and public life is neither running away from the conversation, as many would hope; nor is it the hot rhetoric of culture wars, as others might suggest; nor is it thinking that government can resolve this for us as a people, as still others seem to believe. Agreement around elementary moral principles is both necessary and achievable, but this agreement cannot and must not be established through plebiscitary majorities. What is needed is an honest and reasoned debate with the aim of restoring a genuine democratic pluralism, along with a fresh affirmation of the role of religion in American society.

Such a conversation must be based upon a deep and abiding respect for all persons—persons of every race, color, class, and creed. It must be carried out with humility and mutual regard, never with sanctimony and self-righteousness. Secularists must be called upon to acknowledge our basic religious nature and heritage, and religious believers must be called upon to honor persons of all faith and of no faith at all. Both must seek to develop and articulate a public philosophy that can express commonly held social values. A genuinely American public philosophy would attempt to advance a shared vision for the common good, producing a truce between those who would impose religion and those who would remove it.

An honest and respectful debate among people of goodwill on the subject of religion in the United States at the end of the twenty-first century could yield surprising results. At a minimum it could resolve what is presently seen as a source of social friction, and a challenge to civil society. A more optimal outcome would be the melding of our religious and cultural differences in a shared vision for the common good.

This job will not be easy. The substantive moral disagreements that exist today will take decades to sort through, and will never be resolved to everyone's satisfaction. To some extent the stalemate that currently exists in this area is a function both of a profound ignorance and a willful mis-representation of the intentions of one side in the religious-secular debate by the other. To listen to the religious and secular antagonists one would expect an imminent apocalyptic collapse of democracy into either a religious or secular form of tyranny or even totalitarianism. This extreme debate must be understood for what it is: It is a distortion of fact, frequently done in a deliberate attempt by one side or the other to preserve the status quo.

With very rare exceptions, religious believers are not only not promoting a religiously governed democracy, they would stiffly resist such an idea on precisely the same grounds that they advance religion, namely that true religion requires real freedom of conscience. A prominent feature of American history, largely lost in current debates, is the conscious decision of religious bodies, including such large conservative Protestant denominations as the Southern Baptist Convention, to stake their very existence on fairly strict notions of church-state separation.

Similarly, few civil liberty advocates honestly hope to see religion's demise or the loss of religious freedom. What they frequently advocate is the prevention of a dominant religion from seeking advantages through government favor or special recognition. In the realm of state power, this resistance to government favoritism often translates into a strictly enforced state neutrality and even state prohibition against religious practices in publicly funded institutions that may offend religious minorities.

The argument over the relationship of religion to social and political life is not about to go away, nor should it. But there are really two, separable issues that must be addressed by religious and nonreligious Americans alike. The first, and more difficult issue, concerns the relationship of religion to politics and the state. Here, the question is whether to maintain the existing regime of strict governmental neutrality toward religion in matters of the state, for reasons cited above.

The second issue, both more important and less problematic, concerns whether to welcome a far broader role for religion in the noncoercive realm of civil society, premised upon an acknowledgment of pluralism. The argument over the relationship of religion to democratic politics need not impede the deeper engagement of religious faith in the work of rebuilding the character-forming institutions of democratic society within the non-authoritative realm of civil society. As Tocqueville formulated the issue, this is precisely where the role of religion, religiously inspired moral norms, and religiously directed social movements fit best in the American system.

Neither of these debates need slow the advance toward recovering widely shared ethical norms. As shown in the next chapter, the greater challenge is for people of intelligence and goodwill to find a common moral language for public life, one which maximizes our faith in universal moral principles, and minimizes antagonisms based upon our respective religious creeds. On this, the future of democracy may rest.

Conclusion

The United States was never a creed-less, norm-less society, and cannot succeed by attempting to become one. It is animated by a civic and transcendent creed. The early shapers of the civic vision held also to the transcendent proposition and it's assumption that the grounds for our existence and our mutual civic obligations is transcendent moral truth.

The American experiment is fundamentally grounded in, and dependent upon, transcendent moral foundations. Much of our cultural story and symbols are religious. Much of the country's self-renewing capacity is linked to the power of religious revival and the social reforms that often accompany it to periodically transform our society.

In the final analysis, the civic story depends, for binding effect, on moral claims. The current movement to recover the civic creed would be more fruitful if it were linked more directly to the transcendent proposition. What is that transcendent proposition? That our democracy has a soul, that our nation has a creed, that our institutions must possess moral cohesion, and that American renewal draws its inspiration and power from our country's venerable heritage of religious faith.

Notes

1. Alexis de Tocqueville, *Democracy in America*, vol. 2, trans. by George Lawrence (New York: Anchor, 1969), 433.

2. Tocqueville, 434.

3. Robert Bellah et al. *Habits of the Heart: Individualism and Commitment in American Life* (New York: Harper and Row, 1985), 37.

4. Robert Bellah, *On Morality and Society* (Chicago: University of Chicago Press, 1973), 191.

5. Bellah, *Habits of the Heart*, 28.

6. Bellah, *Habits of the Heart*, 29.

7. Bellah, *On Morality and Society*, 231.

8. Jim Skillen, *Recharging the American Experiment: Principled Pluralism for Genuine Civic Community* (Grand Rapids: Baker Books, 1994), 30.

9. Skillen, 55.

10. Quoted in column by William Raspberry, *Washington Post,* 20 October 1997.

11. Bellah, *Habits of the Heart*, 80.

12. Robert Bellah, "Religion and Legitimation in the American Republic, *Transaction*, vol. 15 (1978), 21.

13. See Martin Luther King's early sermon, "The Transformed Nonconformist."

14. David Walsh, *After Ideology* (San Francisco: HarperCollins, 1993), 68.

15. John Courtney Murray, *We Hold These Truths: Catholic Reflections on the American Proposition* (New York: Sheed and Ward, 1960), 11.

16. Murray, 11.

17. Murray, 11.

18. Alexis de Tocqueville, *Democracy in America*, vol. 1 (New York: Vintage Books, 1945), 319.

19. Tocqueville, 315.

20. Tocqueville, 320.

21. Bellah, *Habits of the Heart*, 144.

Chapter 13

Toward Moral Realism and Republican Character

The civil society debate, of necessity, involves a deeper debate about elementary moral and ethical principles that must be operative in society. Chief among the objectives of the movement will be forging a new consensus over the basic values upon which a free society rests.

That debate will either divide or unify, attract or repel, depending upon whether the protagonists in the debate have in mind forging a new American public philosophy or simply winning the next round of partisan conflict. Anxiety about public and private morality runs across the political spectrum, and there is much at stake for everyone, regardless of religion or ideology. The debate concerns the kind of society all Americans, whatever their party registration, live in.

The urgent need is to recover a moral order larger than the individual. Individualism has come under increased focus as a leading cause of civic decline. But it is important to acknowledge that the United States has always placed a premium on the individual, perhaps more so than any civilization. What must be recognized is that two forms of individualism have vied for acceptance: One "is moral, ultimately grounded in religion, according to which life is sacred and each person is unique, irreplaceable and priceless; the other is rational and utilitarian, in which the social good is whatever best satisfies the preferences of individual actors."[1]

As we discussed earlier, this latter form of utilitarian individualism, combined with moral relativism, has not been friendly to the institutions the civil society movement seeks to renew. In fact, the pervasive moral skepticism and doubt of our time comes as close as any other factor to being the chief cause of the near collapse of the authority and legitimacy that institutions need to function in a society.

Since the 1960s, says Amitai Etzioni, "many of our traditions, social values and institutions have been challenged, often for valid reasons." But, he adds, the end result is that "we live in a state of increasing moral confusion and social anarchy."[2] At the core of the chaos-producing trends is a philosophical utilitarianism that may be leading the United States away from the possibility of a peaceful and enduring public order.

Philosophical Corruption

Many of the dominant philosophies operating in the United States have significantly altered the relationship of individuals to one another in society and to social institutions. Utilitarian individualism has maintained that the problems of society can be solved by autonomous individuals exercising private choice in a market economy and procedural state. But if morality is completely contingent upon human choice, and not binding on all citizens in any meaningful way, then we must all resign ourselves to the possibility of continued social decline.

Modern philosophy, according to James Q. Wilson, author of *The Moral Sense*, with some exceptions, represents a fundamental break with philosophical traditions of the past that held individuals capable of, and responsible for, acting morally toward one another. For the last century, he says, "few of the great philosophical theories of human behavior have accorded much weight to the possibility that men and women are naturally endowed with anything remotely resembling a moral sense." Moral philosophy fell to a "relentlessly materialistic doctrine in which morality, religion, and philosophy have no independent meaning."[3] People are understood to have instincts and appetites, but no "moral sense."

As a result of this, says Wilson, "man is adrift in an uncharted sea, left to find his moral bearings with no compass and no pole star, and able to do little more than utter personal preferences, bow to historical necessity, or accept social convention." The result is "hollow men" drifting through "lonely crowds" in "an age of anxiety" that has "no exit."[4]

The philosophical doctrine of Logical Positivism, in particular, sought to establish a radical distinction, in the name of scientific objectivity, between facts and values. Facts existed in the objective realm of research and observation. Values were assigned to the subjective category of feelings, preferences, and tastes. This attitude became especially pervasive in educational fields as schools and universities could find no basis for including a place for morality within secular sciences. Many concluded that belief in values was essentially unscientific, more akin to religious faith. Moral education was assumed to involve indoctrination and was thus inconsistent with cultural diversity and intellectual freedom.

Another trend, and an extension of the first, has been what Thomas Lickona calls "personalism." Unlike relativism, which simply argues against the notion of objective truth, personalism celebrated the subjective self. Personalism exalted the individual over society and asserted freedom from moral norms. Older substantive notions of character lost out to more superficial categories such as "personality," which concerned itself with style and image, not the pursuit of knowledge or truth.[5] Not only is morality thought to lack objective grounding, the search for moral meaning within one's self is pursued with self-reverential fascination. Values, to be held and applied, must be "authentically mine" whether or not they are anyone else's.

Personalism was fueled by various education movements such as the values clarification movement and self-esteem programs. Unlike previous concepts of self-respect, which insisted on respect for others as well as one's self, these movements presented the self as separated from others, "narcissistic and solipsistic," according to Gertrude Himmelfarb. These new notions of self-fulfillment, self-expression, and self-realization derived "from a self that does not have to prove itself by reference to any values, purposes, or persons outside of itself." Esteem was presumed, she says, to "adhere to the individual regardless of how he behaves or what he accomplishes."[6]

A final factor in the erosion of moral consensus was an accelerating and intensifying pluralism. As the United States became more culturally diverse, public leaders became less, not more, inclined toward asserting a common culture consisting of core values. For society in general and schools in particular, this represented a dramatic departure from the original vision and central mission of public institutions: assimilation.

But most have come to acknowledge the inadequacies of this approach. There are signs that moral belief is being recovered as a defensible intellectual posture. The moral subjectivism school has declining adherents, both because old philosophical schools are slowly dying out and because, even within the most insulated intellectual circles, there is a dawning realization that society is sinking into the Hobbesian swamp. Most of us would rather not live in a society in which all are at war, each person against another, and life is "solitary, poor, nasty, brutish and short."

Life in the United States certainly hasn't approached this point, but the palpable sense of raw cynicism and anger that many detect in the streets of the United States has caused even the moral agnostic among us to suddenly discover some utility in moral principle, whether the grounding of those moral principles are essentially religious or essentially reason-based. As stated elsewhere, this is the primary mission that most Americans believe the civil society should be about. While civil society has meant different things to different people at different times and places, its early development in the seventeenth and eighteenth centuries was offered in resistance to "state of nature."

We are "in the middle of a paradigmatic struggle," says Amitai Etzioni, author of *The Moral Dimension*. Coming under increased challenge, he says, is "the entrenched utilitarian, rationalistic-individualistic, neoclassical paradigm which is applied not merely to the economy but also, increasingly, to the full array of social relations, from crime to family."[7] At the core of this old philosophical system is the assumption that "freestanding individuals are the decision-making unit, the actors" and that community and society count for nothing.[8] The silencing of the moral voice leaves us with only two alternatives, says Etzioni: "a police state, which tries to maintain civic order by brute force, or a moral vacuum in which anything goes."[9]

Living in a state of absolute freedom is not freedom at all; in fact, as Dostoevsky put it, "to begin with unlimited freedom is to end with unlimited despotism." All societies need a moral code. Political and moral philosopher Vaclav Havel, who spent his life searching for ways to recover moral transcendence, first as a writer and now as president of the Czech Republic, believes that human civilization will only be possible if "we all accept a basic code of mutual coexistence, a kind of common minimum we can all share, one that will enable us to go on living side by side."[10]

Havel maintains that while we may need to continue to expand the combined traditions of classical, Judaic, and Christian belief systems, we must find somewhere in the foundations of religions and cultures "respect for what transcends us; certain imperatives that come to us from heaven, or from nature, or from our own hearts; a belief that our deeds will live after us; respect for our neighbors, for our families, for certain natural authorities; respect for human dignity and for nature: a sense of solidarity and benevolence towards guests that come with good intentions."[11]

It is time to reconstruct social values, says Etzioni, not along the lines of traditional authority of the 1950s, but along lines which nevertheless have us once more providing "moral affirmation."[12] Moral affirmation requires recovering a "moral voice," one that does not merely censure, but which "blesses." We affirm moral action in community when "we appreciate, praise, recognize, celebrate, and toast those who serve their communities, from volunteer fire fighters to organizers of neighborhood crime watches."[13]

Confidence that there are such things as moral facts, which can be discovered, approved, and broadly applied within the human community, is returning. The evidence from human history that core values are indispensable to the function of society is ample. There is a fairly settled body of fixed opinion and long-standing practice across civilizations holding that certain moral propositions are true.

Foundations for Moral Life

What are the sources of moral guidance? Confusion over what moral education and character development entail often leads to doubts and arguments over the question of whose values should be upheld.

One source of moral truth, of course, is religious belief, as we discussed extensively in the previous chapter. Religion has a mixed record of tolerating divergent beliefs in history, but most religious believers need little encouragement to avoid behavior that is hateful, hurtful, or destructive to the public order. They are forbidden from violence or killing, not because there is a law against it, but because of a divine sanction against it that they violate at the risk of their own souls. Believers generally don't need to be told about right and wrong, justice and injustice; they usually recoil in horror at stories of starving children, religious persecution, or ethnic violence, because each violates the divine dictate to honor and respect all human life.

But as discussed in the previous chapter, religion is not likely to again find wide acceptance in public institutions. The debate over the relationship of religion to politics and the state should not set back the search for a moral framework that joins secular and religious adherents. There are other foundations for moral life that are operative beyond revealed religion, which can be applied to restoring society.

One of them is what James Q. Wilson calls "the moral sense." "People," he says,

> have a natural moral sense, a sense that is formed out of the interaction of their innate dispositions with their earliest familial experiences. To different degrees among different people, but to some important degree among almost all people, that moral sense shapes human behavior and the judgments people make of the behavior of others.[14]

The second foundation for a new moral realism, then, is the existence of an innate moral "sense" that exists independent of cultures and moral codes.

Universal moral laws are a third foundation for moral life. For those concerned that a system of values cannot be constructed or taught without favoring one religion or culture over another, they have not considered the existence of a uniform set of moral principles that transcend cultures. Many moral claims are self-evidently true; for example, that honesty and kindness are good, and that a long series of offenses against man and nature are wrong: murder, slavery, sexual exploitation, spouse or child abuse, slaughtering endangered species, or dumping toxic substances into streams. These things are simply wrong, anywhere and under all circumstances. There is no known society in the world that does not consider Mother Teresa a saintly hero, and Hitler a heinous murderer. Things may blur a bit when we enter less clear-cut categories, but the point here is that moral assertions have always been made, and must be made.

C. S. Lewis, himself a devout Christian, pointed out in the *Abolition of Man* that there are certain universal ideas of right and wrong that recur in the writings of ancient Egyptians, Babylonians, Hebrews, Chinese, Norse, Indians, and Greeks, along with Anglo-Saxon and American writings. Lewis called these transcendent principles the Tao, a term borrowed from the Chinese that means simply "the way." Rooted in the laws of nature, the Tao is a road that leads to the good life, and to harmony with nature and its maker. This concept bases such moral imperatives as the care for the young and veneration of the old, not on subjective human psychology, but in universal principles of justice that transcend individuals and cultures.

Among these universal laws, according to Lewis, are the laws of beneficence, of justice, of good faith and veracity, of mercy, magnanimity, and of duty to family. That these core principles emerged around the globe throughout the millennia, independent of one another, on vastly different soil, producing the same successful civilizations regardless of race or religion, confirms Lewis' suggestion that they are rooted in natural laws of the universe, not just Judeo-Christian doctrines found in divine revelation, for example.

These universal principles embodied what Lewis called "a common human law of action which can overreach rules and ruled alike." Belief in the Tao is necessary to "the very idea of a rule which is not tyranny."[15] To abandon them, says Lewis, is to sap a civilization of its dynamism, creativity, and coherence. When societies abandon the Tao, according to Lewis, they produce "men without chests," of whom society vainly expects "virtue and enterprise." To step outside the Tao, says Lewis, is to have "stepped into the void"—it is socially suicidal.[16]

The common core virtues that C. S. Lewis identifies are not

ethnocentric; they span time, cultures, and religions. Many of the purveyors of these human values on the American continent were originally "white European males," as today's multiculturalists would describe them, owing to the homogenous makeup of the United States at the time of the country's founding. Yet the framers were drawing from a deeper and more diverse well of antiquity than simply European culture. The virtues not only transcend cultures, they predate the Victorian age and terms like *bourgeois* by thousands of years.

In other words, rather than magnifying differences, a recovery of the moral principles that transcend cultures can be applied as the answer to a divisive multiculturalism. The rich heritage and contributions of all immigrant groups can be honored, and no group has a monopoly on virtue or a special exemption from human vice. Human accomplishments in science, arts, and enterprise come in all colors and creeds.

A fourth foundation for moral life would be found in a search for core principles or practical "laws of living" that are ethically grounded and proven to work in ordinary daily living. Stephen Covey, the popular author, maintains that personal effectiveness flows from the consistent application of principles that are universally found in the human experience. Covey describes principles as "deep, fundamental truths, classic truths, generic common denominators. They are tightly interwoven threads running with exactness, consistency, beauty and strength through the fabric of life."[17] These principles for living, says Covey, have natural and unavoidable consequences: positive consequences when we are living in harmony with them, negative consequences when we spurn them. They apply to everyone, whether or not they live in awareness of them, but, Covey adds, "the more we know of correct principles, the greater our personal freedom to act wisely."[18]

Covey uses the example of "the law of the farm." In nature, the practice of cultivating the land is governed by natural processes and principles, and these principles determine outcomes. He asks, "Can you imagine forgetting to plant in the spring, flaking out all summer, and hitting it hard in the fall—ripping the soil up, throwing in the seeds, watering, cultivating—and expecting to get a bountiful harvest overnight?" Covey maintains that this kind of "cramming" not only fails in the natural world, it ultimately fails in a social system as well. Societies require careful conscientious cultivation. In the long run, the "law of the farm" governs in all arenas of life.[19]

Stories of heroism and virtue, and of right and wrong lived out in the drama of life, are a fifth source of moral life. Bill Bennett, in his best-selling *Book of Virtues*, attempts to recover the tradition of telling stories about the lives of ordinary Americans who did heroic deeds through self-sacrifice. A hero, says education scholar Dennis Denenberg,

> is an individual who can serve as an example. He or she has the ability to persevere, to overcome the hurdles which impede others' lives. While this intangible quality of greatness appears almost magical, it is indeed human. And it is precisely because of that humanness that some individuals attain heroic stature.[20]

Once upon a time, says Denenberg, "kids had heroes, and lots of them." They were everywhere: They were part of curricula, of textbooks and kids reading materials, in movies and in daily folklore, from which kids drew their values for life. Today, he says, truly legendary heroes have become virtually displaced persons, disappearing from view, replaced often by the latest "kid-culture fad hero."[21]

A similar form of moral storytelling is recalling the story of the country's founding. The nation's founders, such as Thomas Jefferson and George Washington, had a lot to say about what virtue was and how it connected to the life of a nation. Washington maintained that we would not manage to maintain a free republic without a lot of it. Freedom without virtue is impossible, he said.

Ben Franklin went well beyond theorizing about virtue. He developed and promulgated a comprehensive list, drawing from many of the same sources cited here. Franklin's list of virtues—temperance, silence, order, resolution, industry, sincerity, justice, moderation, cleanliness, tranquility, chastity, and humility—are virtues that humane societies everywhere have sought to keep in wide practice. These were thought to be virtues that nourished human civilization. Only the modern mind would view them skeptically and consider itself wise enough to invent principles that are newer and better. The ancient Greek term for this scale of self-confidence is *hubris*.

A sixth and final approach to recovering the moral life is to cultivate personal character as a primary goal in civic renewal. At the core of character are the notions of respect and responsibility. To act with responsibility for one's actions, one must be willing to take into account the consequences of one's behavior toward others. To act consistently with respect toward others, one must have high regard for their inherent worth, which is acquired through the character-shaping institutions of society, but especially in the family. Families and communities, according to John Gardner, are "the ground-level generators and preservers of values and ethical systems," without which no society can remain vital.[22]

Strategies for renewing character must be consistent and comprehensive, which means that certain primary institutions such as family and kin are vital. Countless studies confirm the basic conclusion that human bonds—primarily those of family—are indispensable to achieving emotional and cognitive well-being. Through a fairly complex developmental process in early childhood, families help individuals control impulsiveness and develop a capacity for empathy toward others. The most extreme forms of antisocial behavior, such as ruthless crime, are often explained by the absence of caring, competent parents, especially the father.

The cultivation of character is less a function of indoctrination than of reinforcing positive habits. Moral virtues, such as courage and honor, come about as a result of habit, according to an older Aristotelian tradition. Sound character, according to this school, is acquired through the development of sound habit, or through "habituation." We become just "by doing just acts, temperate by doing temperate acts, brave by doing brave acts."[23]

Character development is not just an individual process, nor is it simply a function of pedagogy. The human person does not stand alone in a universe of moral abstractions and impersonal forces; he or she is a social and moral being who comes by moral development through a process that is inherently social. In a free and democratic society, the individual and the society influence each other. The root meaning of the Greek word for ethics (*ethikos*) signifies an ethos that is rooted in community and transmitted through customs.

The problem with many efforts to guide moral reform, according to Amitai Etzioni, is that they address moral life as though it is simply a matter of developing individual conscience on one's own. Says Etzioni, "Many Americans disregard the crucial role of the community in reinforcing the individual's moral commitments."[24] Individuals are powerfully affected by "the approbation and censure" of others, especially those with whom we have close relations, such as family and neighbors. A society that wishes to preserve character, then, will encourage these voices in the community to speak in "unison and with clarity" in a way that strengthens individual judgments about right and wrong.

Character is caught from life and from social institutions—from family, teachers and peers, places of worship, athletics, the media and the popular culture. Culture exerts a powerful force over the entire enterprise of character formation. Culture functions as society's thermometer and thermostat: It shapes and reflects society's deeper values and meaning. Thus the content of culture can easily overwhelm other functions in society by its force, as most parents and teachers will readily acknowledge.

A healthy culture is not indifferent to its effect on individual character. Culture either elevates or debases, summons the noble or ignoble, generates public spiritedness or self-absorption. In other words, culture either cultivates or corrupts character. If the aim is to recover a civil and humane society, Americans must create a culture of character operating throughout all spheres—the home, neighborhood, schools and workplace, and the powerful character-shaping institutions of media and entertainment.

Individuals and society interact. C. S. Lewis said that moral principles are learned indirectly from others around us—moral exemplars—and that it was difficult to preserve virtuous individuals apart from a virtuous society. According to Gertrude Himmelfarb:

> Individuals, families, churches, and communities cannot operate in isolation, cannot long maintain values at odds with those legitimated by the state and popularized by the culture. It takes a great effort of will and intellect for the individual to decide for himself that something is immoral and to act on that belief when the law declares it legal and the culture deems it acceptable.[25]

Values, she says, require legitimization.

For values to be re-legitimized, the United States needs a more honest and productive debate about the core moral principles that are required in a free society. This debate will necessitate doing away with a radical ethical pluralism that holds that no ideal is superior to another and that building the good society can be done without any basic agreement on the rules. But asserting values cannot be confused with a call to simply assert power. Attempts at restoring declining cultural values and order through power frequently only provoke and exacerbate the conflict. The search for an underlying consensus over substantive moral principles must avoid a winner-take-all majoritarianism.

The United States also needs a new venue for discussing values as well as a new language—more civic and less sectarian, more civil and less belligerent. The debate about values for society is not about single issues, or even predominantly about legislative conflicts. The American renewal movement that is coming will not focus predominantly on political ideology or partisanship for the simple reason that neither is capable of social or moral regeneration. Citizens and leaders alike from all sectors of society will be needed to rebuild moral consensus around the tripod of character, culture, and community.

Civic Republicanism

As growing numbers of Americans are beginning to realize, progress is not possible without civil society, and civil society is not possible without functioning social institutions firmly anchored in moral foundations. Born of a growing dissatisfaction with prevailing approaches, growing numbers of political theorists and social critics are turning to a tradition that has historically been a strong competitor to liberal individualism—civic republicanism.

The preservation of virtue was thought by many of the nation's founders to be a central concern of statecraft. As originally designed by the framers and as observed over the years by visitors to the United States such as Tocqueville and Chesterton, citizenship and character were the very centerpiece of the American creed. The founders understood that self-interest in pursuit of private advantage was a natural impulse that could be socially beneficial if matched by an equal effort by society to instill civic virtue. Combined, commerce and character would build a civilization rich in opportunity and civil in its manners and mores.

The existence of self-interest as a motivating force was taken as a given; as the founders saw it, rooted in nature. But neither was there any doubt, given man's natural tendency toward vice and faction, that society had to take the necessary steps to preserve character. The thought that the pursuit of virtue could be abandoned entirely for the pursuit of interests alone would have been considered inconceivable. Yet, with very few exceptions, politics in recent decades has given scant recognition to the republican virtue thought so central to American success. Current ideologies appear either unwilling or incapable of commanding unselfish devotion to anything that might be defined as the common good.

National progress is not widely thought today to be related to character, but rather improvement in material conditions. The vision of progress that has dominated Western imagination ever since the Enlightenment has been one of "unending technological, industrial, social and political progress."[26] The search for human progress in the form of technical and material advances, and the neglect of spiritual and social health, have created a society wedded to the pursuit of happiness through power, litigation, and crass consumerism. The result has been the triumph of the private over the public, the individual over the community, the secular over the sacred, and commerce over character.

Civic republicanism offers a vision for the reordering of society, not merely reforming government. It is a vision for achieving social change, not just ballot box victories for partisan majorities. It is a vision for empowerment, not only of individuals but of communities. Civic republicanism affirms the spiritual dimensions of the country's longing for renewal and seeks to confront the power of secular ideologies and intellectual paradigms that crowd out the sacred from community life.

Civic republicanism replaces a humanism that is secular with a humanitarianism that embraces the whole person, including his or her spiritual and social nature. Society is a spiritual community, said Edmund Burke. It is not an artificial construction; it is a spiritual partnership, not just between those who are living, but "between those who are living, those who are dead, and those who are not yet born."[27]

The search for transcendent foundations for law, politics, economics, and society need not be a sectarian undertaking. Civic republicanism offers a framework for transcending religious and ideological factionalism by reviving a language that is neither secular nor sectarian. It is a language of social fraternity, strengthened neighborhoods, and shared values. Above all, it places the focus of concern on the strengthening of those institutions that mediate between the individual and the state—family, religious, civic, and voluntary associations.

Generating social change will require resuscitating an older and richer concept of both citizenship and politics—a tradition rooted in character. The true citizen does more than participate in elections. He or she organizes his or her community against crime, develops strategies against teen pregnancy, volunteers at local charities, and joins the PTA. The true politician is a public servant who does more than simply attend to the affairs of government; he or she leads efforts to strengthen the character-shaping institutions of civil society.

The restoration of character throughout society will require new social movements that are committed to transcending an exhausted ideological politics that defines all social and cultural problems as the appropriate target for legislative agendas, not civil society, to solve.

The pattern of the past suggests that change begins when growing numbers of people are appalled enough at disorder to reassert time-tested notions of informal social control against a too dominant libertine subculture. Values of permissiveness are forced to yield to values emphasizing the mastery of passion out of respect for the good of the society.

Until very recently, the work of moral uplift for the sake of society was thought by the cultural elite to be progressive, not reactionary, work. A good, progressive, and compassionate society was one that bothered to solicit good character in its citizens. Because preserving morality was not assumed to be coercive or mostly the business of government, with the possible exception of public schools, it was reinforced predominantly through voluntary means throughout all sectors of society.

During the nineteenth century, Americans created hundreds of new voluntary associations and societies aimed at social reform and moral uplift. There were spiritual awakenings, temperance movements, private charity campaigns, and children's aid societies. For the churched, there was the Sunday school movement; for the unchurched, there were YMCAs and rigorous character education programs in the public schools.

Works of charity treated the whole person. Temperance cadets took aim at morally reckless youth. Poorly socialized young males were mentored by adult men. Churches did not wait for a change in Congress to rescue neglected and abandoned children. The unemployed were drawn into church-sponsored training programs that developed the habits of self-motivation as well as the skills of industry.

What made the difference during previous periods of American history was the development of voluntary societies and social reform movements that sought to socialize males, curb adolescent crime, and take sterner measures to protect vulnerable citizens. The results of these voluntary social movements were to restore personal restraint, which resulted in substantial declines in alcohol consumption, criminality, sexual license, and a host of other social problems.

Conclusion

The term *civil society*, after an extended period of neglect, has returned to our vocabulary. The civil society debate in the United States has raised expectations for social renewal. But much has changed since Tocqueville's time, and any movement to renew American society and culture must take full account of the difficulty posed by these changes. The world has been transformed economically and structurally, but it has also been transformed ideologically.

The differences between the United States today and the old world of Tocqueville's time are many, but the greatest difference is a difference of spirit. In many ways, the tendencies that Tocqueville worried about on the American scene are now operating in full force as we enter the twenty-first century. Freedom is no longer tied to religion and tradition and has thus become a more libertine freedom. Various forms of social authority have been leveled by a driving appetite for emancipation from authority. Strict codes of morality have been replaced by the rise of the autonomous self, in which love of self replaces love of something larger than self for many.

What is at stake are the values and beliefs of an entire culture. Thus, what the current civil society debate is mostly about is whose values and beliefs will be operative within the culture at large. As polls indicate, this is what concerns the public most. Many of the solutions to our country's weaknesses lie in the civic, cultural, and moral realms where government solutions are often deficient and unworkable. What is needed to save families, make neighborhoods friendly and safe, and restore lost virtues are dynamic new social movements centered on the restoration of character such as have come along periodically in American history, each aiming to recover moral norms upon which an ordered society depends.

Democracy is a noble experience, but history suggests that with neglect democratic societies falter. The United States, with all of its strength and astonishing prosperity, is no exception; there are too many signs of it subsiding into decay. Democracy was made for democrats, and derives its strength from character-shaping institutions in civic community, and the health of the surrounding culture. For the American democratic experiment to be reborn, we must first recover the transcendent moral principles upon which it was founded and on which it still depends.

Notes

1. Robert Bellah et al., *The Good Society* (New York: Alfred A. Knopf, 1991), 114.

2. Amitai Etzioni, *The Spirit of Community* (New York: Touchstone, 1993), 2.

3. James Q. Wilson, *The Moral Sense* (New York: The Free Press, 1993), 3.

4. Wilson, 5.

5. From Don Eberly, ed., *The Content of America's Character: Recovering Civic Virtue* (Lanham: Md.: Madison Books, 1995), 14.

6. Eberly, 14.

7. Amitai Etzioni, *The Moral Dimension: Toward a New Economics* (New York: The Free Press, 1988), ix.

8. Etzioni, *The Moral Dimension*, 10.

9. Etzioni, *The Moral Dimension*, 37.

10. Address by Vaclav Havel, Harvard University, Cambridge, 8 June 1995.

11. Havel.

12. Etzioni, *The Spirit of Community*, 12.

13. Etzioni, *The Spirit of Community*, 24.

14. Wilson, 2.

15. C. S. Lewis, *The Abolition of Man* (New York: Macmillan, 1947), 84.

16. Lewis, 77.

17. Stephen Covey, *The Seven Habits of Highly Effective People* (New York: Simon and Shuster, 1989), 122.

18. Covey, 123.

19. Covey, 55.

20. Dennis Denenberg, "The Role of Heroes and Heroines in the American Story," in *Building a Community of Citizens: Civil Society in the 21st Century*, ed. Don Eberly (Lanham, Md.: University Press of America, 1994), 108.

21. Denenberg, 109-110.

22. Etzioni, *The Spirit of Community*, 31.

23. James Q. Wilson, "Public Policy and Personal Character," in *Thinking about America: The United States in the 1990s*, ed. A. Anderson and D. L. Bark (Palo Alto, Calif.: Hoover Institution, 1988), 493.

24. Amitai Etzioni, "Restoring our Moral Voice," *The Public Interest*, Summer 1994, 109.

25. Gertrude Himmelfarb, "A Demoralized Society: The British/American Experience," *The Public Interest*, Fall 1994, 74.

26. David Walsh, *After Ideology* (San Francisco: HarperCollins, 1993), 3.

27. Russell Kirk, *The Conservative Mind* (Washington, D.C.: Regency Books, 1986), 17.

Chapter 14

A Call to Civil Society:
Why Democracy Needs Moral Truths

Author's note: What follows is a statement that was drafted and signed by a distinguished and ideologically diverse group of scholars and public leaders under the leadership of the Council on Civil Society. The purpose of *A Call to Civil Society* was to draw together in one document the core concerns of leading civil society theorists regarding the state of American culture and society, to identify areas of common ground, and to identify ways to recover community, character, and public morality in the United States. The Council on Civil Society is affiliated with the Institute for American Values. The "Call" was released to the nation on May 27, 1998. The author contributed to *A Call to Civil Society* as a member of the drafting committee.

Why We Come Together

We come together as citizens of diverse beliefs and differing political affiliations to issue an appeal for the renewal of the American experiment in self-governance.

We come together as Democrats, Republicans, and Independents, agreeing to put aside partisan political disputes in order to rediscover our primary institutions and shared civic story. We come together as people of various ethical and faith traditions, agreeing to set aside theological differences in order to rediscover the public moral philosophy that makes our democracy possible.

What is the state of our union? Certainly there is much good news. The

United States is the longest-lasting constitutional republic in history. Across the planet, opponents of freedom are on the defensive, as the American idea increasingly becomes the world's idea. Today the United States is not only the world's outstanding superpower, but more importantly, the world's great exemplar of democratic civil society.

But let us be honest. In what direction are we tending? In our present condition, are we likely to remain the best hope for a world in which so many human beings still endure neglect and injustice? Are we likely to sustain our commitment to freedom and justice for all, so that those in our midst who are suffering might yet be lifted up by our democratic faith and practice?

No. Notwithstanding the achievements of which we are properly proud, our democracy is growing weaker because we are using up, but not replenishing, the civic and moral resources that make our democracy possible. This is why we come together. This is why we issue this call.

The Public Verdict

What is our most important challenge at the end of this century? Is it governmental? Many people believe so. Indeed, at various points in this century, our society has turned to government to remedy social problems and achieve great tasks. Government, many of us have believed, must be a front line of defense against social distress, a guarantor of personal security, perhaps even our basic force for ethical decency and concern. Only government, in this view, is powerful enough to guide the market forces that generate benefits for many, but not for all.

Is our core challenge economic? Many people believe so. Wanting to reap the rewards of self-discipline and hard work, our society in this century has consistently relied upon economic growth as a primary means of spreading prosperity and underwriting equality of opportunity. Moreover, economic freedom can help to secure political freedom, since only in a dynamic market economy are economic relationships independent enough to limit the centralizing, power-assuming tendencies of government.

These issues are important. But the core challenge facing our nation today is not primarily governmental or economic. Neither government action on its own, nor economic growth on its own, nor the two in tandem, can cure what most ails us.

To understand the nature of our challenge, we begin by listening respectfully to public opinion. According to leading analysts, the citizens of our nation have reached two conclusions about our current direction. First, we suffer from growing inequality. And second, we suffer from moral depletion.

As we become an increasingly fragmented and polarized society, too many of our fellow citizens are being left behind, not participating in the benefits of economic growth and free society. And as our social morality deteriorates, life becomes harsher and less civil for everyone, social problems multiply, and we lose the confidence that we as Americans are united by shared values. These two closely related conditions endanger the very possibility of continuing self-governance.[1]

Our fellow citizens are especially alarmed and overwhelmingly agreed about the problem of moral decline. Consider a few recent measurements. The analyst (and member of this council) Daniel Yankelovich reports in 1996 that

> public distress about the state of our social morality has reached nearly universal proportions: 87 percent of the public fear that something is fundamentally wrong with America's moral condition, up from 76 percent a year ago. In general, a widespread feeling of moral decline has sharply expanded within the public over the last two years, regardless of gender, age, race or geographical area.[2]

According to a Gallup poll, 78 percent of the public rates "the state of moral values in this country" as either very weak or somewhat weak. About 76 percent believe that moral values have deteriorated in the past 25 years.[3] An analysis of current adult attitudes toward teenagers similarly concludes that the public's core concern "is not youngsters' health problems, safety, or poverty rates. Rather, Americans are deeply troubled by the character and values exhibited by young people today."[4]

When citizens worry about "moral decline," what do they mean? Do they want, as we so often hear, to "roll back the clock"? Return to the 1950s? Reverse the gains made by women and minorities?

No. Racism and sexism remain serious problems in our society. Yet with each passing year, Americans express growing intolerance for segregation, bigotry, prejudice against minorities, or restricting opportunities for women in public life. Despite widespread concern about our moral condition, there is little desire to "go back" to some earlier era.

Let us listen to what people actually say. First, the public understands weakening morality as behavior that threatens family cohesiveness. Teenage pregnancy, unwed childbearing, extramarital affairs, easy sex as a normal part of life—majorities of Americans view each of these trends as evidence of deteriorating social morality.[5] When a polling firm recently asked

Americans to identify the part of our society where "an effort to do better" would "make the biggest difference," the most frequently chosen answer (27 percent) was "strengthening the family."[6]

Second, the public understands weakening morality as behavior that is increasingly uncivil—that is, behavior that reflects a rejection of legitimate authority and a lack of respect for others. Neighbors not being neighborly. Children disrespecting adults. Declining loyalty between employers and employees. The absence of common courtesy, such as indifference from retail clerks, or being treated like a number by impersonal bureaucracies. Drivers who menace and gesture at other drivers. In general, people who tend to push others aside, looking out only for themselves. Nearly 90 percent of the public believes that this type of incivility is a serious national problem. About 80 percent believe that the problem has gotten worse in the past ten years.[7]

Finally, the public understands moral decline as the spread of behavior that violates the norm of personal responsibility. Public examples abound. A pro baseball player spits on an umpire and nothing much happens. A pop star announces that she wants a baby but not a husband. An adroit political consultant turns a personal scandal into a lucrative book deal.

Do these high-visibility cases signal a deeper trend? Yes. According to a Chilton Research Services poll, 67 percent of the public believe that "the U.S. is in a long-term moral decline." By a margin of 59 percent to 27 percent, Americans believe that "lack of morality" is a greater problem in the United States than "lack of economic opportunity."[8]

Here, then, is the public's basic judgment of our current predicament: growing inequality, surrounded and partly driven by moral meltdown. Declining morality is reflected primarily in the steady spread of behavior that weakens family life, promotes disrespect for authority and for others, and insults the practice of personal responsibility.

The social manifestations of this crisis are everywhere around us. Let us summarize its basic dimensions:

- Declining child and adolescent well-being
- Continuing disintegration of marriage and the family
- Unacceptably high (though now declining) levels of violence and disorder
- Deteriorating educational systems
- An unraveling of many aspects of civic engagement and voluntary association
- A growing sense that we are not responsible for or accountable to

one another
- A growing sense that relations between races, economic classes, and generations are not guided by attempts at shared understanding
- An increasing coarseness and harshness in popular culture, politics, and public discourse
- A spreading abdication of adult responsibility and an increasing acceptance of the adult as a perpetual adolescent
- An increased tolerance for self-centered and selfish behavior in all spheres of life
- A growing belief that success should be measured by how much money we have and how much we can buy
- A dramatic undermining of the distinction between right and wrong
- The loss of confidence in the possibility of public moral truth.

The Civil Society Proposition

As awareness of this crisis spreads across the political spectrum, a new term has emerged in our public debate: civil society. Fairly suddenly, the prosaic world of civic participation, family dinners, PTA meetings, and youth soccer has acquired a profound public significance. Despite a partisan and often rancorous political climate, Democrats and Republicans alike now extol the concept of civil society. Indeed, civil society is increasingly touted as a newfound wonder drug for curing any number of problems, from fragmenting families to the decline of voter participation. Yet at present, the term is a bit like a Rorschach test: It can mean whatever anyone wants it to mean.

To us, civil society refers specifically to relationships and institutions that are neither created nor controlled by the state. The essential social task of civil society—families, neighborhood life, and the web of religious, economic, educational, and civic associations—is to foster competence and character in individuals, build social trust, and help children become good people and good citizens.

Ultimately, civil society is a sphere of our communal life in which we answer together the most important questions: What is our purpose, what is the right way to act, and what is the common good. In short, it is the sphere of society that is concerned with moral formation and with ends, not simply administration or the maximizing of means.

We call ourselves a Council on Civil Society because we hope to contribute to the debate in the United States about the meaning and potential of civil society. We view civil society as the best—not perfect, but best—conceptual framework for understanding and responding to the most urgent challenge facing our society: the moral renewal of our democratic project.

Seedbeds of Virtue

Are Americans competent to govern themselves? This question has vexed us from the beginning. In 1788, in *Federalist 55*, James Madison wonders whether there is "sufficient virtue among men for self-government." Reflecting upon those "qualities in human nature which justify a certain portion of esteem and respect," Madison reminds us: "Republican government presupposes the existence of these qualities in a higher degree than any other form."[9]

An unfree society has much less need of virtuous or civic-minded people. But a democracy, the Founders insisted, depends decisively upon the competence and character of its citizenry. What are those ways of life that self-governance requires? What are those "qualities" that the Constitution "presupposes" in the American people? They are precisely those qualities that are currently disappearing from our society.

Their disappearance is primarily philosophical, hence also institutional. The qualities necessary for self-governance take root in individuals essentially due to the influence of certain moral ideas about the human person and the nature of the good life. The primary exposure to these ideas comes from certain forms of association, beginning with the family. Together, these moral ideas and person-to-person associations have historically constituted our seedbeds of civic virtue—our foundational sources of competence, character, and citizenship. There are at least twelve of them.

The first and most basic is the family. Why? Because self-governance begins with governing the self. In this sense, the family is the cradle of citizenship, since it is in the family that a child first learns, or fails to learn, the essential qualities necessary for governing the self: honesty, trust, loyalty, cooperation, self-restraint, civility, compassion, personal responsibility, and respect for others. As an institution, the family's distinguishing trait is its powerful combination of love, discipline, and permanence. Accordingly, families can teach standards of personal conduct that cannot be enforced by law, but which are indispensable traits for democratic civil society.

The second is the local community or neighborhood. All people need safe, stable environments in which they can play in parks, go to the library, walk out the front door to be with other people, help each other, offer guidance to each other's children, and participate in the various other community activities and relationships that help to make life meaningful. Historically, the United States has always been an amalgam of diverse and vital neighborhoods, in this sense more a community of communities than a unitary national culture.

Democracies require communities of this sort. These local environments in which community members maintain a common life, often rooted in collective memory and shared values, constitute precisely those ecologies in which men, women, and children are most likely to thrive. These are places where parents can confidently tell their children: "Go outside and play."

The third is faith communities and religious institutions. A great majority of Americans consider religion to be of great importance in their lives. During any given week, United States church and synagogue attendance exceeds total attendance at all United States sporting events by an estimated factor of 13 to one, while voluntary financial contributions to houses of worship exceed total ticket revenue from professional sports by an estimated factor of 14 to one.[10] United States faith communities also form the spiritual and institutional backbone of the nation's sizable philanthropic and charitable sector.

If a central task of every generation is moral transmission, religion is a primary force in American life—historically, it has probably been the primary force—that transmits from one generation to another the moral understandings that are essential to liberal democratic institutions. Religion is especially suited to this task because it focuses our minds and hearts on obligations to each other that arise out of our shared createdness. By elevating our sights toward others and toward ultimate concerns, religious institutions help us turn away from self-centeredness, or what Tocqueville terms "egotism," democracy's most dangerous temptation, through which "citizens have no sympathy for anyone but themselves."[11]

At their best, then, our houses of worship foster values that are essential to human flourishing and to democratic civil society: personal responsibility, respect for moral law, and neighbor-love, or concern for others. These same values also help to drive progressive social change. In this sense, it is no accident that organized religion, animated by personal devotion, has been at the heart of arguably the two most important social movements in American history: the abolition of slavery and the Civil Rights movement.

Many of the essential rituals of civil society are enacted in our houses of worship. Baptisms, bar and bat mitzvahs, weddings, funerals, and other social expressions of the religious impulse connect us to one another and reflect our moral imagination. By helping us to transcend mere economic and political arrangements, our faith communities can guide us toward a common moral life.

The fourth is voluntary civic organizations. Here are what Alexis de Tocqueville famously called our "voluntary associations," describing them in the 1830s as a hallmark of American exceptionalism and as a defining trait of American civil society. As he put it in *Democracy in America*: "Americans of all ages, all conditions, and all dispositions, constantly form associations. They have not only commercial and manufacturing companies, in which all take part, but associations of a thousand other kinds—religious, moral, serious, futile, extensive or restricted, enormous or diminutive."[12]

Consider just a few current examples: book clubs, Little League, the Future Farmers of America, the Kiwanis Club, the Girl Scouts, the Chamber of Commerce, the Advertising Council, and the National Association for the Advancement of Colored People.

Our reliance upon voluntary associations to achieve social goals stems from the widespread division and dispersal of authority in the United States. A prime example of this phenomenon is our dependence upon private religious associations to guide our public moral philosophy. Another example is philanthropy. In most modern societies, when the issue is distributing money to projects aimed at social betterment, government is usually in the lead. The United States, with its thick diversity of private philanthropies, is a notable exception. Much of the dynamism and variety of American society stems from this unique structure of dispersed philanthropic authority. In this sense, voluntary associations are custodians of pluralism, undergirding the democratic idea by limiting the homogenization of culture and the centralization of authority.

The fifth is the arts and art institutions. Music, poetry, literature, dance, theater, painting, sculpture, architecture, and the other arts are crucial legends and components of civil society. Fundamentally, they are statements of meaning and aspiration. They also inevitably ask and answer moral questions: what is good or bad, what is true or false. Toward these purposes, the arts provide us with cognitive and sensual experiences that are otherwise unavailable to us. Much of what we know by way of art is only knowable through art.

At their best, the arts and art institutions affirm core values of civil society: good craftsmanship, sensitivity, creativity, and integrity of materials and expression. In a pluralistic society, the arts can serve as universal languages, permitting authentic cultural exchanges that penetrate to the core of human feeling. The arts can elevate public discourse by providing models of beauty and standards of clarity. They can activate the imagination. Education in the arts can root children in their cultural traditions; such education is essential to the task of cultural transmission. In these ways, contemplation of the arts permits us to transcend the utilitarian preoccupations of everyday life.

The sixth is local government. Closely related to voluntary civic organizations, and a partial exception to the thesis that our basic challenge is not governmental, the structures of participatory local government—school boards, recreation boards, town meetings, and other forms of face-to-face civic engagement—are primary incubators of civic competence. Structures of local government activate the potential for civic engagement. They model and transmit not only a general sense of civic responsibility, but also the particular skills of citizenship: deliberation, compromise, consensus building, and reason giving.

The seventh is our system of primary and secondary education. Especially in democracies, which must continually nourish their comparatively few founts of common culture, a basic responsibility of schools is cultural transmission: passing on to students a civilizational story in which they all can share, in part by teaching them the skills to participate in and help shape that story.

In addition to teaching basic intellectual skills, schools in self-governing societies are called upon to embody and require basic standards of good conduct: personal responsibility, respect for teachers' authority, and respect for other students. Also, educational institutions sustain democratic culture by helping students attain civic literacy, including knowledge of their country's constitutional heritage, respect for the lives of national heroes, including great dissidents, a comprehension of what good citizenship is, and an appreciation of their society's civic and moral ideals.

The eighth is higher education. If you could look only in one place to take the deepest measure of our civilization, where would you look? Some members of this council would choose to look at our religious ideas and institutions. Others would choose our system of higher education. Especially in our era, when the social authority of religious belief has weakened, and when more young people than ever go on to some form of higher education, the modern university may be our truest cultural barometer, our most accurate indicator of who we are becoming.

The rise of the modern university, originating in part from the intellectual demands of theological inquiry, roughly accompanies the rise of modern democracy. Both have roots in a common set of civilizational values, including intellectual freedom, a reliance upon reason and the scientific method, a belief in the objectivity of truth and knowledge, and confidence that the diffusion of knowledge contributes to civic virtue.

The ninth is business, labor, and economic institutions. Business and economic institutions play an increasingly prominent role in civil society. For millions of Americans today, the workplace is a primary source of personal identity and a central venue for social relationships. Indeed, for many people, the workplace may be more influential than neighborhood, house of worship, or even family. Americans have also long believed that the experience of work itself—of giving honest value in return for fair reward—can build good character.

Similarly, while private firms in free market economies operate in part according to a calculus of rational self-interest, they are also pervaded by dense webs of moral ties and associations. Consequently, private firms in free societies are major custodians—and can themselves become major creators or destroyers—of social competence, ethical concern, and social trust.

Why? Because work is intrinsically social. Work is bound up with self-interest, but it also typically points past itself, toward service, cooperation with others, and the common good. Employment is thus partly a private relationship, but also one with intrinsic dignity and a substantial public dimension. For this reason, business, labor, and economic institutions do not exist apart from the rest of civil society. That the economy is part of civil society also demonstrates that it is part of our moral order as well—not some extrinsic force, and certainly not an end in itself, but rather a major reflection of our judgments about the conditions for human flourishing and the larger meanings of our common life.

The tenth is media institutions. Here is the seedbed that is most rapidly expanding in size and influence. It is also the business institution that Americans most universally criticize as undermining civic life. From a parent's perspective, one of the most important changes in family life in the second half of this century has been the growing influence of the media in the socialization of children.

Great majorities of parents now believe that the cultural values promulgated by broadcast, cinematic, and other electronic media are overtly and increasingly hostile to the values that parents want their children to acquire.[13] Despite (and perhaps partly because of) the new television ratings system, so recently announced and applauded by politicians and industry executives, the rapid vulgarization of this season's television programming, much of it aimed at children, has been sad and even sickening to behold.[14] From a Democrat's perspective, the growing dominance of the entertainment media in our national life, including the collapse of any boundary between entertainment and journalism, is now on almost everyone's short list of what to blame for many of the ills of our democracy, including the rise of cynicism, the decline of face-to-face civic engagement, and the spread of incivility.[15]

The eleventh is a shared civic faith and a common civic purpose. What is our nation's purpose? What brings us together and defines us as a people? Unlike most countries, our answers to these questions are primarily philosophical. We are a nation dedicated to certain propositions. As the Founders put it: "We hold these truths."

The civic truths that we hold—and that hold us together—are those of Western constitutionalism, rooted in both classical understandings of natural law and natural right and in the Judeo-Christian religious tradition. Our founding idea is liberty, guided by the proposition that all people are created equal. Our shared civic faith is one of republican self-governance. The juridical principles that define us as a people are those of the American Constitution. Our common civic purpose is a government that secures the blessings of liberty, including the freedom to search together for a workable understanding of equality. The briefest expressions of this civic creed are inscribed on our coins: "Liberty" and "E Pluribus Unum" ("From many, one").

The United States was born, and from time to time is reborn, largely around these basic civic truths. At their best, they guide us toward a story of robust citizenship and cooperative civic endeavor, embodied in the notion of the commonwealth, in which citizens combine the private pursuit of happiness with devotion to the public good.

The twelfth is a public moral philosophy. Because our civic truths are largely constitutional and procedural, they do not tell us how to pursue happiness or how to live a good life. Instead, they establish principles of justice for a society in which pluralism is a fact and freedom is a birthright. In addition to civic truths, then, our democracy depends upon moral truths.

The moral truths that make possible our experiment in self-governance are in large part biblical and religious. They are also strongly informed by the classical natural law tradition and the ideas of the Enlightenment. They are what the Founders called "laws of nature and of nature's God" and what Martin Luther King, Jr., called "higher law." The most eloquent expressions of our reliance upon these truths are found in the Declaration of Independence, Washington's Farewell Address, Lincoln's Gettysburg Address and Second Inaugural Address, and King's Letter from the Birmingham Jail. The briefest expression of this reliance is inscribed on our coins: "In God We Trust."

These truths authorize the possibility of our democracy. Without them, all of our democracy's seedbeds, including our civic truths, atrophy. First, our moral truths underwrite our social well-being, primarily because they teach us to govern our appetites and to transcend selfishness. Only our moral truths insist that we Americans understand freedom, our primary civic end, as an ethical condition—not simply as immunity from restraint, but instead as the morally defined mean between license and slavery.

Second, our moral truths underwrite our political freedom. In some societies, there is only one master-organizing device for society: the state. In this sense, all of life's questions, including what is virtue and what is a good life, are political questions, answered ultimately by government. Our tradition resists this unitary model of society, insisting in particular upon the disestablishment of religion and the right of religious freedom. This change serves to relativize the political domain, in part by limiting the power and reach of the state, and in part by causing government itself to draw legitimacy from, and operate under, a larger moral canopy that is not of its own making. This relativization of politics also places a special responsibility on the morality-shaping institutions of civil society.

Finally, our moral truths underwrite the very rationale for democratic civic engagement. In this sense, they are guarantors of our civic well-being. For here is the first philosophical prerequisite for robust civic engagement: the belief that your opponent is not your enemy, and that you and your opponent are more alike than different. And why is that?

For many of us, the answer is that all people, as persons created in the image of God, possess transcendent human dignity, and that consequently each person must always be treated as an end, never as a means. The Founders affirmed as "self-evident" this moral idea that all persons possess equal dignity.

And here is the second and most fundamental prerequisite: the belief that moral truth exists and that it is accessible to people of reason and goodwill. Otherwise, why have any faith at all in democratic civic engagement? For these reasons, reverent regard for a public moral philosophy—an ensemble of knowable, objective moral truths—is our democracy's most indispensable foundation.

The Moral Crisis

No nation on earth has so thoroughly staked its success on the functioning of free and voluntary civic associations. Yet during the past three decades in the United States, at least some of these primary institutions of civic engagement have significantly eroded. For this reason, a number of leading analysts has recently suggested that our fundamental challenge today is re-empowering local civic organizations and renewing face-to-face civic interaction throughout our society.

In this view, if we would spend less time as workers and consumers, and more time as citizens and neighbors; if we would vote and volunteer and participate more, and watch TV less; if we would recognize those among us who suffer not primarily as clients of the state, but as neighbors in need—if we would do these things more often and energetically, we would finally be engaging our deepest problems. In brief, our core imperative is democratic renewal through civic engagement.

There is much to commend in this vision. Our local associations help us to attain a sense of purpose and belonging by anchoring us in particular loyalties and specific relationships. They nourish the habits and skills of citizenship. Through their diversity and through their independence from the state, they also embody cultural pluralism and help to safeguard political freedom.

Yet this conception of the solution—democratic renewal via civic engagement—ultimately ignores as much as it illuminates. This idea tends to ignore the family, almost certainly civil society's most important institution. It also tends to ignore the role of business, labor, and economic institutions in creating or depleting social capital.

More fundamentally, it ignores a key question: What would make anyone want to participate in civic life in the first place? And what would enable anyone to distinguish between "good" civil society, such as efforts to start a hospital or help the homeless, and "bad" civil society, such as private militias or efforts to exclude racial minorities?

Civic participation, as an independent imperative, is more about process than substance. It is ultimately a means, not an end in itself. Put differently, effective civic engagement in a democracy presupposes, and depends on, a larger set of shared ideas about human virtue and the common good. In short, effective civic engagement requires a public moral philosophy. Absent a guiding set of shared moral truths, voluntary civic associations can be just as harmful to human flourishing as any big government bureaucracy or big business bureaucracy.

Moreover, while our civic truths depend upon moral truths, the latter cannot be derived from the former. Our public morality (essentially religious, philosophical, and extra-legal) constitutes something over and above our civic norms (essentially constitutional, juridical, and procedural).

To imagine otherwise—to suppose that a free society can derive its public morality from a strictly civic realm—is to fall precisely into that unitary view of society in which everything is ultimately political, decided by the state. If independent moral truth does not exist, all that is left is power. Such a view of reality is, among other things, antithetical to the Western ideal of human freedom. In the long run, it is likely to prove fatal to the project of republican self-governance.

What ails our democracy is not simply the loss of certain organizational forms, but also the loss of certain organizing ideals—moral ideals that authorize our civic creed, but do not derive from it. At the end of this century, our most important challenge is to strengthen the moral habits and ways of living that make democracy possible.

The Moral Economy

The economy exists to support human flourishing. It is not an end in itself. For this reason, our political economy is inextricably linked to our moral economy, and it is therefore impossible to speak responsibly of moral renewal without addressing its economic dimensions.

For example, the weakening of civil society, including its moral foundations, is closely connected to the persistence and spread of economic inequality. The connection flows both ways. Urban joblessness, diminished economic prospects for poorly educated, low-income minority youth, parents who have less time for their children because they are spending so much time at work in order to keep ahead of the bill collectors—these are clearly examples in which material conditions can worsen civil society and deplete moral and social capital.

Conversely, a fragile civil society worsens material conditions. The depletion of civic faith, especially our belief that we are one people, with obligations to one another, surely helps to cause (and also excuse) the spread of inequality. The erosion of our seedbed institutions—such as nuclear families and kin networks whose members can support each other economically and help their young people to find jobs—clearly contributes to the deteriorating economic prospects facing many of our citizens.

More broadly, our economic and family values are not so easy to disentangle. When, for example, we come to believe as employers and employees that relationships are typically short-term, that loyalty is outdated, and that "me first" is the final rule, should it surprise or even concern us when these same principles come to dominate our understandings of marriage, parenthood, and civic life?

Is it merely a coincidence that, for most Americans in recent decades, our roles as workers and consumers have gotten thicker and more dominant, while our roles as family members and neighbors have grown thinner and weaker? No. These various dimensions of our lives are not separate spheres, divergent questions; they are different ways in which we confront the same basic questions.

Part of the challenge of renewing civil society, then, is to relativize economics, recognizing that free markets and cost-benefit analyses are primarily means, not ends. They can tell us how, but not what or why. Economic activity within democratic civil society is not a definition of, but an opportunity for, moral responsibility and authentic self-determination. For precisely the same reason, however, another aspect of renewing civil society is recognizing the moral bases of economic activity. Consider just a few obvious examples. The increasingly crude use of sex by corporate advertisers to sell products. Our seeming complacency in the face of jolting new disparities between the most successful and the most shattered among us. Our frequent desire to believe that whatever the free market produces must be valid. Our tendency to treat other people, and at times even view ourselves, primarily as consuming objects who purchase an identity in the marketplace. In each case, it is clear that our economic activities and institutions are not exempt from the need for moral renewal.

The Human Person

In large measure, to affirm the existence and importance of moral truth is to confirm a particular understanding of the human person. Indeed, regarding many cultural issues today, from doctor-assisted suicide to cloning to divorce, it may increasingly be our answer to this upstream question—what is a person?—that ultimately guides our downstream conclusions. For this reason, defining the human person may be where America's civil society debate is ultimately headed.

According to many people—perhaps in some respects according to most Americans today—we humans, at least in the United States, are autonomous units of desires, rights, and legitimate values of our own choosing. We are self-originating sources of valid claims,[16] essentially unencumbered, self-owning, and auto-teleological. For short, call it a philosophy of expressive individualism, or a belief in the sovereignty of the self—a kind of modern democratic equivalent of the old idea of the divine right of kings.

We view this understanding of the human person as fundamentally flawed. We understand human beings as free, reasonable, and therefore responsible beings with a basic drive to question in order to know. Deliberating, judging, and choosing—having reasons for what we value and love—are characteristic human activities. For this reason, what we value and love is intelligible and therefore public. What is reasonable transcends our purely private imaginings; it is something in which all persons have the potential to share. Our capacity for reasonable choosing and loving is what allows us to participate in a shared moral life, an order common to us all.

For these reasons, we understand humans as intrinsically social beings, not autonomous creatures who are the source of their own meaning and perfection. We humans only live in communities, through which we are talked into talking and loved into loving. Only through such connectedness can we approach authentic self-realization.

From this perspective, the basic subject of society is the human person, and the basic purpose of government—and all other institutions—is to help foster the conditions for human flourishing. In turn, the essential conditions for human flourishing are the elements of what we are calling democratic civil society, anchored in moral truth.

A Strategy for Renewal

At the end of this century, America's primary challenge is the moral renewal of our democracy. Toward this end, we propose three major goals:

First, to increase the likelihood that more children will grow up with their two married parents.

This goal recognizes the steady breakup of the married couple child-raising unit as the leading propeller of our overall social deterioration and the necessary starting point for any strategy aimed at recovery. Reversing the trend of family fragmentation is a necessary (though not sufficient) step toward the larger goal of strengthening the ability of parents to raise healthy, caring, productive, and morally grounded children.

Second, to adopt a new "civil society model" for evaluating public policies and solving social problems.

Regarding any public policy proposal, the first question should be: Will this policy strengthen or weaken the institutions of civil society? Regarding any major societal goal, the first question should be: Can this goal be achieved by utilizing and empowering the institutions of civil society?

The old model is essentially mechanistic, relying on government regulation or economic incentives. As public policy, the old model tends toward centralized authority and direct intervention. It is largely problem-oriented. By contrast, the new model is essentially ecological. It strives to view social environments the way ecologists view natural environments. Accordingly, it tends toward decentralized structures of authority and a rich diversity of approaches. It is largely prevention-oriented, seeking not so much to specify outcomes as to shift probabilities, primarily by protecting and, when possible, enhancing the overall "climate" of institutions and ideals that constitute civil society.

The old model is a stool with two legs: government and economics. The new model adds the missing third leg: social institutions and values. The old model both presupposes and (often unintentionally) depletes social capital. The new model seeks directly to protect and nourish social capital. In the old model, society consists of its individual members. In the new model, society consists of individual members who are encultured by institutions and obligated to the common good. The old model is aggressively secular, often influenced by a professional social work or "client" approach, and is typically reluctant to employ moral reasoning or offer moral judgments. The new model, while strictly protecting religious freedom, is more accommodating to faith-based activism and public service, favors community-based mentors and citizen leaders over outside professionals and experts, and, as a result, is more able to rely upon moral reasoning and to exercise moral judgment.

Third, to revitalize a shared civic story informed by moral truth.

This final goal is the most important. Regarding our civic faith, our main challenge is to rediscover the democratic bonds that, amidst and because of our differences, unite us as one people. Regarding our public moral philosophy, our main challenge is to rediscover the existence of transmittable moral truth.

Recommendations

The Family

1. We call upon all of us who are parents to rededicate ourselves to spending more time with our children and providing them with greater moral guidance.

2. We hope that we as parents will strive to strengthen the bonds of community and mutual support with our neighbors and with other parents, and nurture the marriage bond as the first and most important gift we give to our children.

3. We hope that parents will more strongly resist the pressure to acquire more and more material things, and will increasingly join with other parents

to stand against the forces of materialism that can pollute our children's moral environment.

4. We recommend that public policy at all levels seek explicitly to recognize and protect marriage as a social institution.

5. We recommend that the federal tax code recognize the family, not just the individual, as a basic unit of taxation. Specifically, we recommend that the tax code treat the married-couple family household as a single unit of taxation; end the "marriage penalty" in the tax code by permitting married couples to split (share equally) their income for purposes of taxation; avoid creating tax incentives for unwed childbearing or divorce; avoid creating tax disincentives for within-wedlock childbearing or for parental care of children and other unpaid labor in the home or community; and support the rearing of children through generous and universal per-capita deductions, exemptions, and credits.

6. Through the federal tax code, we recommend the creation of new educational credits or vouchers for parents who leave the paid labor force for a period of time to care for young children. These credits could be used for high school, vocational, college, graduate, or post-graduate education. This reform would improve child well-being and strengthen family life by encouraging more parental care of young children. It would also enhance human and social capital through continuing education. Finally, this reform would honor the parental vocation, in part by reducing the long-term educational, training, and labor force disadvantages of at-home parental care of children.

7. We urge clergy and communities of faith to devote prayerful attention and greater resources to programs of premarriage counseling and education, marital enrichment, marriage mentoring, and help for marriages in crisis, as well as to the development of community marriage policies in which a diversity of clergy and congregations in a community commit to lowering the divorce rate and creating a culture of marriage within congregations and in the larger community.

8. We hope that state legislatures will consider reforming no-fault divorce laws. The twin purposes of reform are lowering the divorce rate and improving the quality of marriage. Ideas for reform include: extending the waiting period for divorce; establishing incentives or requirements for premarital education and for marital counseling in cases of at-risk marriages; and, in cases in which only one spouse wants the divorce, requiring the establishment of fault. Another potentially promising reform is "covenant marriage" legislation, recently adopted in Louisiana and now being considered in other states, which permits individual couples to opt out of the

no-fault system and enter into a legally more binding marriage.

9. We recommend that the United States Congress repeal federal regulations that currently prevent local school districts from taking actions to discourage unwed teen childbearing. Some schools may wish to adopt new policies stating that students who become pregnant, or who impregnate someone, are thereafter ineligible for extracurricular school activities, such as sports, glee clubs, or homecoming awards. Other schools may wish to use incentives rather than disincentives. Consistent with the mandate to educate all young people, federal regulation should encourage local experimentation in this area rather than prevent it.

10. As part of their newly reformed welfare programs, we urge governors and state legislatures to remember the fathers and to promote marriage. Too often in welfare reform, the priority of economic self-sufficiency for single mothers has overshadowed the priority of strengthening fragile families. Specifically, we recommend that states establish preferences for low-income married couples in the distribution of limited, discretionary benefits such as public housing units and Head Start slots. We also recommend that, whenever possible, states expand their welfare-to-work programs to include low-income males, especially those who are married fathers.

The Local Community or Neighborhood

11. We hope that neighborhood and civic leaders, philanthropies, communities of faith, and others will support and participate in efforts aimed at community empowerment and community organizing—efforts that, in some of our nation's poorer and more marginalized communities, are developing new local leaders and rebuilding society.

12. One promising new civil society entity for saving and building affordable housing is the nonprofit community development corporation, or CDC. There are about 2,000 CDCs in the United States today, building and rehabilitating housing for poorer families who are under-served by current landlords and private, for-profit developers. CDCs are rooted in communities and typically sponsored by neighborhood associations, churches, social agencies, tenant groups, and unions. They focus not only on physical issues such as open space and density, but on other factors that influence housing choices, such as drugs, crime, transportation, retail development, and city services. In these ways, CDCs not only build and fix up houses; they also build the social trust and fix up the community networks which are essential for turning houses into stable homes in good

communities. We recommend that new United States federal housing policies recognize and support the work of effective CDCs in rebuilding battered communities.

Faith Communities and Religious Institutions

13. The sina qua non for American renewal is the renewal of a common moral life. Such a renewal will not take place unless faith communities and religious institutions play a leading role, since vigorous communities of faith are vital to the discernment and transmission of moral truth. For this reason, we urge religious institutions to recognize their crucial role and oppose the trends that would push religion to the fringes of American public life.

14. We call upon religious institutions to take more seriously the work of helping to strengthen families, including supporting parents in the day-to-day work of raising their children and helping families to recover and live out a sense of the sacred in everyday life.

15. We urge faith communities to step up their efforts to help families resist the growing pressures of materialism and the growing penetration of commercial values into family life. As one step, we urge faith-based organizations to follow the lead of the Roman Catholic Church, which recently called upon business advertisers to "respect the dignity of the human person" and accept moral responsibility for "what they seek to move people to do."[17]

16. We hope that more religious organizations across the country will begin working actively with state welfare agencies and juvenile justice officials, providing mentoring and other services, all aimed at reducing poverty and helping fellow citizens in need. Examples of this type of church-based witness and community service include a mentoring program for juvenile offenders in Richmond County, South Carolina, and a mentoring program for families on public assistance in Ottawa County, Michigan.

17. We recommend that the president and the Congress strengthen and expand the 1996 "charitable choice" legislation which permits faith-based organizations, without denying or relinquishing their religious charter, to compete on equal terms with other private groups for government contracts to deliver welfare services to the poor. We hope that an expanded charitable choice provision will apply to all federal laws which currently authorize government at any level to contract with nongovernmental organizations to provide services.

Voluntary Civic Organizations

18. We recommend that the United States Congress create a new federal tax credit for individual contributions of up to $500 ($1,000 for married couples) to charitable organizations whose primary purpose is the prevention or alleviation of poverty. The goals of this reform are to stimulate individual giving to a wide diversity of anti-poverty initiatives, and to shift a modest but measurable proportion of overall authority for antipoverty resource allocation and service provision from the federal government to the institutions of civil society. We recommend that state governments consider adopting a similar policy.

19. We hope that sports and youth organizations will reexamine their attitudes and policies, deepening their commitment to the ideals of sportsmanship, fair play, and respect for others. We hope that these associations will reaffirm the proper place of all sports within the larger civic realm—a realm that ought, in a civil society, to transcend and relativize the realms of entertainment and revenue generation. Such a rediscovery would surely foster much greater discipline regarding the reality of athletes as personal heroes and civic role models. This work has already begun through organizations such as the Citizenship Through Sports Alliance, convened by the United States Olympic Committee.

The Arts and Art Institutions

20. We recommend that parents, public officials, artists, and educators take concerted action to restore arts to the schools and high standards to arts education. In recent decades, despite the proliferation of local arts institutions, the growth of public and private funding for the arts, and greater public access to diverse artistic traditions, audiences for serious music, theater, poetry, literature, and visual arts remain small. In cases such as music and literature, audiences are actually graying and dwindling. Moreover, with each passing year, popular entertainment in almost all its manifestations grows coarser and more harmful to society. These failures are partly rooted in the failure of arts education. In many public school districts, arts programs have been eliminated entirely. Even in school districts that still devote resources to these programs, arts educators today increasingly strive for "relevance" (i.e., connection to contemporary youth culture), typically act as if spontaneity of student expression is the highest value, and focus largely on the therapeutic value of arts activities. What gets lost are the lodestars of genuine arts education: training children in technical

sophistication, exposing them to historical masterworks, and aesthetic cultivation. This is a shame. Especially for growing numbers of secularized young people, the arts may represent the last real avenue to moral and spiritual elevation.

Local Government

21. We recommend that the Congress and state legislatures consider litigation reform that would reimpose limits on the duration and content of federal court decrees in areas of local government such as housing, special education, and crime control. The civil society purposes of this reform are to help reverse the current trend of judicial displacement of local government, and to help protect the separation of powers. In our democracy, we rely on courts to protect constitutional rights, not engage in comprehensive, long-term oversight of the structures of local government.

Primary and Secondary Education

22. Too many of America's schools are currently unsuccessful in teaching the basic skills of literacy. We recommend that parents, educators, and public officials join together to create a stronger emphasis upon literacy as a primary educational goal.

23. We hope that educators and parents will implement character education programs in schools. These programs have been developed by nonprofit organizations such as the Character Education Partnership, Character Counts, the Jefferson Center for Character Education, the Josephson Institute of Ethics, and others.

24. We hope that innovative parents and educators, empowered when necessary by state regulatory reform, will create special charter schools devoted to the ideals of civil society and liberal education. An example of such an experiment is the City on a Hill School in Boston, Massachusetts.

25. To enhance parental authority in the upbringing of their children, and to improve education by enhancing accountability, we urge government at all levels to expand the ability of parents to choose the schools their children attend.

Higher Education

26. Liberal democracies require colleges and universities that provide a liberal education. Yet on too many campuses, both the ideals and realities

of a general or liberal education are getting weaker. Too often, higher education may actually erode our sense of common humanity, neglect or disdain the intellectual inheritance of our civilization, narrowly politicize intellectual discourse, and assault even the possibility of discerning truth. In such cases, higher education undermines the bases of liberal education and liberal democracy. We hope that colleges and universities will act with urgency to renew their commitment to liberal education, inquiring into the ways in which they can strengthen the structure, improve the content, and increase the rigor of that general education which is a paladin of our civil society.

Business, Labor, and Economic Institutions

27. Free markets, like the free societies they are intended to support, depend for their existence on the overall health of civil society. As they make future decisions, we hope that business and labor leaders will remember this truth. Economic activities that weaken communities or assault the integrity of childhood might not always reveal their ill effects in the short run, but the task of sustaining civil society requires a disciplined commitment to the long run. We especially urge leaders in business to recognize the moral dimensions of the decisions they make. We hope that they might act as if their own children were the ones most directly affected by these decisions.

28. Wherever possible, we urge employers to expand opportunities available to employees for flexible workplace arrangements, including tele-working, job sharing, compressed work weeks, career breaks, job protection and other benefits for short-term (up to six months) parental leave, and job preferences and other benefits, such as graduated reentry, for long term (up to five years) parental leave. The main civil society goal of these new opportunities is to permit parents to spend more time with their children.

29. While some members of this council would not wish to trade the flexibility of U.S. labor markets for those of Japan or Europe, United States employers often have more leeway than they might suppose in their treatment of workers. Even in strict economic terms, the companies that do best are often those that do not treat their workers like replaceable commodities. Regarding downsizing or replacing permanent employees with independent contractors, temporary workers, or so-called perma-temps, "tough-minded" often turns out to be weak-minded—an example of bad civil society generating bad economics. Wherever possible, we recommend

significantly expanded opportunities for employee ownership, employee participation, employee training, workplace organizing and associations, and other policies aimed at enhancing employee loyalty and building human and social capital.

30. While some members of this council are critical of some current trade union practices, we understand the essence of collective bargaining as a system of private ordering which gives the parties directly involved both the opportunity and responsibility to decide the rules that most directly touch the day-to-day conditions of employees. In this sense, trade unions are classic institutions of civil society. We also note that, as workplace organizing and the practice of collective bargaining have receded in recent decades, government intervention in the employment relationship has increased. Unions and collective bargaining can also serve as a nongovernmental means of reducing inequality, especially for minorities, while offering individuals an important means to engage in grassroots self-determination. We believe that trade unions could, and hope that they will, play an important role in renewing civil society.

31. We regret what appears to be a widespread refusal of corporate philanthropies even to consider financial support for faith-based organizations whose mission is to serve the poor and renew civil society. The topic is complicated, but this policy, or at least this attitude, should be reconsidered. There is nothing inherently illegitimate about religiously informed work for social betterment. The proof should be in the pudding. The a priori denial of corporate support to faith-based organizations is largely arbitrary and almost certainly counterproductive.

Media Institutions

32. We recommend that the broadcast industry voluntarily readopt "Family Hour" policies through which networks agree to exclude inappropriate violence and sexual content from programming at least during the first hour of prime time, usually 8:00 to 9:00 p.m., the hour with the highest concentration of child and teenage viewers. We view the recovery of the "Family Hour" policy as a small but valuable first step toward greater civic responsibility within the broadcast industry.

33. We urge the National Association of Broadcasters, the trade association of television networks and local television stations, to refurbish and readopt a voluntary "Television Code" that establishes minimum industry standards regarding the content and frequency of television advertising and the content of television programming. The NAB voluntarily

adopted a Television Code in 1952, but abandoned it in 1983, partly due to an antitrust challenge from the United States Justice Department regarding the industry's collective oversight of advertising. Abandoning this code was a serious, far-reaching mistake. It ought to be reversed.[18] To alleviate fears of antitrust litigation, we recommend that the Congress pass special legislation to permit this industry to readopt a voluntary code of conduct without fearing that such a code might be judged as anticompetitive by the United States government.

34. If the National Association of Broadcasters declines voluntarily to adopt and enforce an ethically serious code of conduct, we urge parents and other consumers collectively to exercise the power of boycotts to make their views known to industry executives and public officials.

35. We hope that our fellow citizens will consider supporting National TV-Turnoff Week, sponsored by TV-Free America.

A Shared Civic Faith and a Common Civic Purpose

36. We recommend that educators and parents reexamine current practices and pedagogies in an effort to attain higher standards of civic literacy in education. These changes would focus on transmitting to students a knowledge of their country's constitutional heritage, an understanding of what constitutes good citizenship, and an appreciation of their society's common civic faith and shared moral philosophy.

37. We urge governments, educators, and private employers to reform, but not abolish, special efforts to reach out to lower-income African-Americans and other low-income citizens. One hopeful approach, termed "developmental" (as opposed to "preferential") outreach, focuses on special opportunities for performance enhancement among minority and lower-income students and employees without either lowering standards or creating racially based differential standards. The civil society purpose of this form of affirmative action is simple and urgent: racial reconciliation and reaching out with generosity toward what is often called the "underclass," or those of our fellow citizens who are most in need of justice and civic friendship.

38. We hope that local governments, social work and human service professionals, communities of faith and others will seek to strengthen and expand the institution of adoption, including transracial adoption. Adoption is an important institution of civil society, yet significantly weakened in recent years. The reasons for strengthening it today are to insure that more children will grow up with two married parents, and to challenge ourselves

and one another to reach out to children in need and to overcome parochialism, including racial parochialism.

A Public Moral Philosophy

39. The insensitivity in the recent past of the United States Supreme Court toward the influence of religion in public life has weakened our civil society. Some Supreme Court decisions seem to have been based on the idea that a modern state implies or requires a society sanitized of public religious influence, a society in which religion is forcibly reduced by law to a purely private role. We reject this idea. As one example for the future, we hope that the Court will no longer stifle creative local experiments with church-provided services in poor communities, and more generally, will recognize anew the vital role that religion plays in helping people to help themselves.

40. In addition to its increasingly evident economic and social disadvantages, the civic values that are reflected in state sponsorship of lotteries are inimical to the values necessary for self-government. Democracy requires an ethic of sacrifice and responsibility. State lotteries, backed by massive public advertising campaigns, purvey a counter-civics ethic of escapism and false hope, in which our fortunes in life depend on luck. (The motto of New York's lottery is "You never know!") Government at all levels should cease this harmful practice. Despite the tax revenue involved, we also urge states to discontinue the growing practice of licensing—and therefore indirectly collaborating with—casino gambling and video poker.

41. We hope that all of us, including our society's leaders, might strive to understand morality less as a question of individual taste and more as a question of what is true. Transmittable moral truth is the essential product and foundation of democratic civil society.

Conclusion: Summary Propositions

- Democracy depends upon moral truths. Because our access to truth is imperfect, most moral disagreement calls for civility, openness to other views, and reasonable argument in the service of truth.
- Democracy embodies the truth that all persons possess equal dignity. Civil society embodies the truth that we are intrinsically social beings, cooperating with one another in order to know who we are and how to live.
- Democratic civil society is a way of living that calls us fully to pursue,

live out, and transmit moral truth.

Members of the Council on Civil Society

Enola Aird, activist mother (Cheshire, CT)

John Atlas, Executive Director, Passaic County Legal Aid Society; Founder, National Housing Institute (New Jersey)

David Blankenhorn, President, Institute for American Values

Don S. Browning, Alexander Campbell Professor of Religious Ethics and the Social Sciences, University of Chicago Divinity School

Dan Coats, United States Senator, Indiana

John J. DiIulio, Jr., Professor of Politics and Public Affairs, Princeton University

Don Eberly, Founder and Chairman, National Fatherhood Initiative; Director, Civil Society Project (Lancaster, PA)

Jean Bethke Elshtain (Chair), Laura Spelman Rockefeller Professor of Social and Political Ethics, University of Chicago

Francis Fukuyama, Omer and Nancy L. Hirst Professor of Public Policy, George Mason University

William A. Galston, Professor at the School of Public Affairs, University of Maryland

Claire Gaudiani, President, Connecticut College

Robert P. George, Princeton University

Mary Ann Glendon, Learned Hand Professor of Law, Harvard University

Ray Hammond, Pastor, Bethel A.M.E Church (Jamaica Plain, MA)

Sylvia Ann Hewlett, President, National Parenting Association

Thomas C. Kohler, Professor of Law, Boston College Law School

Joseph Lieberman, United States Senator, Connecticut

Glenn C. Loury, Professor of Economics, Boston University

Richard J. Mouw, President, Fuller Theological Seminary (Pasadena, CA)

Margaret Steinfels, Editor, *Commonweal*

Cornel West, Professor of Philosophy of Religion and Afro-American Studies, Harvard University

Roger E. Williams, Executive Director, Mount Hermon Association, Inc. (Mount Hermon, CA)

James Q. Wilson, Collins Professor of Management and Public Policy, Emeritus, UCLA

Daniel Yankelovich, President, Public Agenda

Notes

1. See Daniel Yankelovich, "Three Destructive Trends," *Kettering Review,* Fall 1995, 6-15.

2. Daniel Yankelovich, "Trends in American Cultural Values," *Criterion* 35,

no. 3 (Autumn 1996), 2-9.

3. CNN/*USA Today*/Gallup poll, 9-12 May 1996. By margin of 53 to 42 percent, Americans believe that our moral problems today are more serious than our economic problems. About 60 percent believe that solving our economic problems would solve none or only a few of our moral problems.

4. *Kids These Days: What Americans Really Think about the Next Generation* (New York: Public Agenda, 1997), 8.

5. Daniel Yankelovich, "Trends in American Cultural Values," 6.

6. Peter D. Hart and Robert Teeter, *Wall Street Journal*/NBC News poll, 5-8 December 1996.

7. "On Civility in America," *The Public Perspective*, December/January 1997, 62-65.

8. "Real National Unease—Especially on 'the Moral Dimension,'" *The Public Perspective,* October/November 1996, 24.

9. *The Federalist* (New York: The Heritage Press, 1945), 376.

10. National and International Religion Report, 2 May 1994.

11. Alexis de Tocqueville, *Democracy in America*, vol. 2 (New York: Schocken Books, 1961), 123. Tocqueville also writes (vol. 1, 362): "Religion in America takes no direct part in the government of society, but it must nevertheless be regarded as the foremost of the political institutions of that country; for if it does not impart a taste for freedom, it facilitates the use of free institutions."

12. Tocqueville, vol. 2, 128-129.

13. See Dale Kunkel, Kirstie M. Cope, and Carolyn Colvin, *Sexual Messages on Family Hour Television: Content and Context* (Santa Barbara: University of California Department of Communications, December 1996).

14. According to Nielson ratings, about one million children each week watch *The Jerry Springer Show*, arguably the most corrupt and corrupting show now on television.

15. See Robert D. Putnam, "The Strange Disappearance of Civic America," *The American Prospect* 24 (Winter 1996), 34-48.

16. This phrase is from John Rawls, "Kantian Constructivism Moral Theory," *Journal of Philosophy* 77 (September 1980), 543.

17. Pontifical Council for Social Communication of the Roman Catholic Church, Ethics in Advertising (1997), reprinted in *Advertising Age*, 10 March 1997, 26.

18. In light of current programming, the now discarded Television Code makes for fascinating reading. For example: "Accordingly, in selecting program subjects and themes, great care must be exercised to be sure that treatment and presentation are made in good faith and not for the purpose of sensationalism or to shock or exploit the audience or appeal to prurient interests or morbid curiosity." Indeed, if we simply delete the words "in good faith and not" for the above-quoted sentence, we get an excellent idea of the reigning goals and sensibilities of current TV programming.

Select Bibliography

Aaron, Henry J., Thomas E. Mann, and Timothy Taylor, eds. *Values and Public Policy*. Washington, D.C.: Brookings Institute, 1994.

Anderson, A., and D. L. Bark, eds. *Thinking About America: The United States in the 1990s*. Palo Alto, Calif.: Hoover Institution, 1988.

Bellah, Robert. *On Morality and Society*. Chicago: University of Chicago Press, 1973.

———. *The Good Society*. New York: Alfred A. Knopf, 1991.

Bellah, Robert, et al. *Habits of the Heart: Individualism and Commitment in American Life*. New York: Harper & Row, 1985.

Berger, Peter, and Richard John Neuhaus. *To Empower People: The Role of Mediating Structures in Public Policy*. Washington, D.C.: American Enterprise Institute for Public Policy Research, 1977.

Blankenhorn, David. *Fatherless America*. New York: Basic Books, 1995.

Blumin, Stuart. *The Emergence of the Middle Class: Social Experience in the American City, 1760-1900*. Cambridge: Cambridge University Press, 1989.

Bronfenbrenner, Urie, et al. *The State of Americans*. New York: The Free Press, 1996.

Brookings Institute. *Values and Public Policy*. Washington, D.C.: Brookings Institute, 1994.

Covey, Stephen. *The Seven Habits of Highly Effective People*. New York: Simon and Schuster, 1989.

Dunn, Charles W. *American Political Theology*. New York: Praeger Publishers, 1984.

Eberly, Don E., ed. *Building A Community of Citizens*. Lanham, Md.: University Press of America, 1994.

———. *Restoring the Good Society*, Grand Rapids, Mich.: Hourglass Books, 1994.

———. *The Content of America's Character*. Lanham, Md.: Madison Books, 1995.

Etzioni, Amitai. *The Moral Dimension*. New York: The Free Press, 1988.

———. *The Spirit of Community*. New York: Touchstone, 1993.

Fukuyama, Francis. *Trust*. New York: The Free Press, 1995.

Geyer, Georgie Anne. *Americans No More: The Death of Citizenship*. New York: Atlantic Monthly Press, 1996.

Glendon, Mary Ann, and David Blankenhorn, eds. *Seedbeds of Virtue*. Lanham, Md.: Madison Books, 1995.

Guinness, Os. *The American House*. New York: The Free Press, 1993.

Gurstein, Rochelle. *The Repeal of Reticence*. New York: Hill and Wang, 1996.

Himmelfarb, Gertrude. *The De-Moralization of Society: From Victorian Virtues to Modern Values*. New York: Alfred A. Knopf, 1994.

Hunter, James Davison. *Culture Wars: The Struggle to Define America*. New York: Basic Books, 1991.

Kirk, Russell. *The Conservative Mind*. Washington, D.C.: Regency Books, 1986.

Kunkel, Dale, Kirstie M. Cope, and Carolyn Colvin. *Sexual Messages on Family Hour Television: Content and Context*. Santa Barbara: University of California Department of Communications, 1996.

Lewis, C. S. *The Abolition of Man*. New York: Macmillan, 1947.

McManus, Michael J. *Marriage Savers*. Grand Rapids, Mich.: Zondervan, 1995.

Murray, John Courtney. *We Hold These Truths: Catholic Reflections on the American Proposition*. New York: Sheed and Ward, 1960.

Nisbet, Robert. *The Quest for Community*. San Francisco: Institute for Contemporary Studies, 1990.

———. *The Sociological Tradition*. New York: Basic Books, 1966.

O'Sullivan, John. *The Loss of Virtue: Moral Confusion and Social Disorder in Britain and America*. New York: National Review Books, 1992.

Pearlstein, Mitchell B. *From Moynihan to "My Goodness": Tracing Three Decades of Fatherlessness in the United States*. Minneapolis: Center for the American Experiment, 1995.

Popenoe, David. *Life Without Father*. New York: The Free Press, 1996.

Putnam, Robert D. *Making Democracy Work: Civic Traditions in Modern Italy*. Princeton: Princeton University Press, 1993.

Ryan, K. and G. F. McLean, eds. *Character Development in Schools and Beyond*. New York: Praeger Publishers, 1987.

Sandel, Michael. *Democracy Discontent: America in Search of a Public Philosophy*. Cambridge: Harvard University Press, 1996.

Schlesinger, Arthur. *The Disuniting of America: Reflections on a Multicultural Society*. New York: W. W. Norton, 1992.

Shain, Barry. *The Myth of American Individualism*. Princeton: Princeton University Press, 1994.

Skillen, Jim. *Recharging the American Experiment: Principled Pluralism for Genuine Civic Community*. Grand Rapids, Mich.: Baker Books, 1994.

Sorokin, P. A. *The Crisis of Our Age*. New York: E. P. Dutton, 1943.

Tocqueville, Alexis de. *Democracy in America*. Translation by Henry Reeve. New York, n. p. 1954.

———. *Democracy in America*. Translation by Philips Bradley. New York: Vintage, 1990.

———. *Democracy in America*. Garden City, NY: Doubleday Anchor Books, 1996.

Vanourek, Gregg, Scott W. Hamilton, and Chester E. Finn, Jr. *Is There Life After Big Government? The Potential of Civil Society*. Indianapolis: The Hudson Institute, 1996.

Valsh, David. *After Ideology*. San Francisco: HarperCollins, 1993.

Vashington, George. *Rules of Civility and Decent Behaviour in Company and Conversation*. Mount Vernon, Va.: The Mount Vernon Ladies Association, 1989.

Wilson, James Q. *The Moral Sense*. New York: The Free Press, 1993.

Wolfe, Alan. *Whose Keeper?: Social Science and Moral Obligation*. Berkeley: University of California Press, 1989.

Index

Abolition of Man, 206
A Call to Civil Society, 217
Acton Institute, 63
Adams, John, 13, 98
Advertising Council, 224
Aird, Enola, 243
Alcoholics Anomymous, 84
Alexander, Lamar, 61–62
Alliance for National Renewal, 89
American Association of Retired
    People (AARP), 24, 85
American Civic Forum, 97, 100
American Enterprise, 53
American Enterprise Institute, 53
American Legion, 82
American Prospect, 30
American Red Cross, 130
American Unum Project, 23
*Americans No More: The Death of
    Citizenship*, 38
*A National Conversation on
    American Pluralism and
    Identity*, 99
Anderson, Kenneth, 134
Aristotle, 156, 160
Atlantic Monthly Magazine, 49
Atlas, John, 243
Baldrige, Letitia, 114–115
Balz, Dan, 46
Barber, Benjamin, 97
Baumeister, Roy, 119
Beem, Christopher, 106
Bellah, Robert, 38, 108, 164, 167,
    188–189, 194

Bennett, William, 26, 31, 71, 88,
    106–107, 115, 118, 121, 130,
    166, 207
Berger, Peter, 62–63
Bethel A.M.E. Church, 243
Betrayal of Democracy, 108
Blankenhorn, David, 49, 51, 55,
    243
Blumin, Stuart, 77
Bly, Robert, 109
Bonhoeffer, Dietrich, 191
Book of Virtues, 207
Boys and Girls Clubs of America,
    130
Boston College Law School, 243
Boston University, 43, 119, 243
Boy Scouts, 21, 77–78
Boyte, Harry, 97
Bozell Worldwide, 111
Bradley, Bill, 26
Bradley Foundation, 61
Brooks, David, 31, 130
Browning, Don S., 243
Brzezniski, Zbignew, 191
Budziszewski, J., 114
*Building Communities from the
    Inside Out*, 88
Burke, Edmund, 212
Califano, Joseph, 120
Callecoat, Michael, 46
Call for a New Citizenship, 97
Carnegie Council on Adolescent
    Development, 41
Carter, Stephen, 108

Capital Research Center, 63
Case Western Reserve University, 119
Catholic Charities, 69
Center for Effective Compassion, 63
Center for Urban Affairs, 88
Chamber of Commerce, 224
Character Counts Coalition, 127, 130, 238
Character Education Partnership, 131, 238
Chesterton, G. K., 125, 182, 190, 211
Chilton Research Services, 220
Christian Coalition, 24
Chronicle of Philanthropy, 70
Citizenship Through Sports Alliance, 237
City on a Hill School, 238
Civic Declaration, 97
Civic Practices Network, 90
Civicus, 90
Civil Society Project, 243
Clark, John, 71
Clinton, Bill, 42, 50, 65, 67, 99, 116
Coats, Dan, 61, 68, 71, 243
Cohen, Jean, 28–29
Coleman, James, 47
Committees of Correspondence, 77
Commonweal, 243
Communitarian Network, 88
Communities of the Future, 90
Community of the Future Network, 90
Connect America, 89
Connecticut College, 243
Cornuelle, Richard, 152, 175
Council on Civil Society, 51, 106, 217, 221
Council on Families, 51–52
Covey, Stephen, 207
Croly, Herbert, 64

Culture of Disbelief, 108
Culture Wars, 109
de Civiltate, 111
Democracy in America, 224
Democracy on Trial, 98, 142
The De-moralization of Society, 108
Denenberg, Dennis, 208
Dewey, John, 64
DiIulio, John J., 243
Dionne, E. J., 27, 37, 80
Distinctions, 115
Dole, Bob, 116
Dostoevsky, Fëdor Mikhailovich, 204
Drucker, Peter, 138
Durkheim, Emile, 47, 186–187
Eberly, Don, 243
Eberly, Sheryl, 115
Edelman, Marian Wright, 130
Ehrenhalt, Allen, 8–9, 11, 81
Elks, 78
Elshtain, Jean Bethke, 29–30, 43, 51, 98, 127, 142–143, 243
Emerson, Ralph Waldo, 176
Erasmus, Desiderius, 111
Etzioni, Amitai, 88, 108, 121, 129, 202, 204, 209
4H, 130
Family Independence Center, 60
Fatherless America, 49, 55
Federalist 55, 222
Focus on the Family, 54
Fordham University, 42
Franklin, Benjamin, 208
Frum, David, 31
Fukuyama, Francis, 44–45, 121, 138, 243
Fuller Theological Seminary, 243
Future Farmers of America, 224
Gallagher, Maggie, 52
Gallup, George, 111, 128
Gallup Organization, 86
Gallup Poll, 111, 219

Galston, William, 49–50, 81, 88, 91–92, 136, 243
Garden Clubs, 78
Gardner, John, 141, 152, 208
Gates, Chris, 23
Gaudiani, Claire, 243
Gauld, Joseph, 131
George, Robert P., 243
George Mason University, 243
Gerson, Mark, 68
Geyer, Georgie Anne, 38
Gingrich, Newt, 63, 67
Girl Scouts, 21, 77, 224
Glendon, Mary Ann, 135, 153, 163, 243
Gramm, Gerald, 77
Greenberg, Paul, 105
Guinness, Os, 13, 167
Gurstein, Rochelle, 110–111
Habermas, Jürgen, 14
Habitat for Humanity, 87
Habits of the Heart, 38
Hackney, Sheldon, 99–101
Hammond, Ray, 243
Harvard University, 20, 24, 44, 76, 82, 84, 116, 135, 153, 161, 163, 243
Harwood, Richard C., 96, 98, 141
Hasson, Kevin, 188
Havel, Vaclav, 16, 146, 191, 204
Hawthorne, Nathaniel, 176
Heclo, Hugh, 14
Henrie, Mark, 177
Heritage Foundation, 62–63, 71
Hernandez, Lesvia, 46
Hewlett, Sylvia Ann, 243
Himmelfarb, Gertrude, 28, 31, 108–109, 203, 210
Hitler, Adolf, 191, 206
Horn, Wade, 54
Howard, John, 157
Hudson Institute, 64, 71
Huffington, Arianna, 63, 118
Hunter, James Davison, 109, 133

Hyde School, 131
Institute for American Values, 51, 217, 243
Institute for Global Ethics, 131
Integrity, 108
Jefferson Center for Character Education, 130–131, 238
Jefferson, Thomas, 177, 208
Johnson Administration, 48
Johnson Foundation, 90
Johnston, Henry, 118
Josephson Institution of Ethics, 130, 238
Joyce, Michael, 63, 137
Kaiser Foundation, 117
Kass, Leon, 53
Kennedy, Jacqueline, 114
Kettering Foundation, 91, 95, 99
Kettering Review, 99
King, Martin Luther, 14, 189–190, 227
Kirk, Russell, 177
Kiwanis, 77, 224
Knight Foundation, 100
Kohler, Thomas C., 243
Krauthammer, Charles, 106, 121
Kristol, Irving, 49
Kunkel, Dale, 117
Laconte, Joe, 71
Ladd, Everett, 85
Lasch, Christopher, 108
Leo, John, 118
Lewis, C. S., 114, 206–207, 210
Lickona, Thomas, 119, 126, 203
Lieberman, Joseph, 243
Life Without Father, 55
Lincoln, Abraham, 23, 133, 190, 227
Lions, 77
Lippman, Walter, 64, 184
Little League, 85, 224
Locke, John, 176
Los Angeles Times, 120
Losing Ground: American Social

Policy, 1950-1980, 49
The Lost City, 8
Loury, Glenn, 43, 243
Madison, James, 134, 222
Mansfield, Harvey, 116
Marriage in America, 51–52
Marriage Savers, 52
Marriage Savers, 52
Marshall, Will, 97
Martin, Judith, 113–114
Masons, 77
McKnight, John, 88–89
McLaughlin, John, 27
McManus, Michael, 52–53
Mead, Margaret, 54
Meilaender, Gilbert, 114
The Moral Dimension, 108, 204
The Moral Sense, 108, 202
Morin, Richard, 46
Morris, James, 113, 118
Morone, James, 30
Mother Teresa, 206
Moulton, John, 112
Mount Hermon Association, Inc., 243
Mouw, Richard, 243
Moyer, Bill, 49
Moynihan, Daniel Patrick, 48–49, 166
Murray, Charles, 49, 60
Murray, John Courtney, 101, 190
National Association for the Advancement of Colored People, 224
National Association of Broadcasters, 240–241
National Center for Fathering, 55
National Center for Neighborhood Enterprise, 63, 89
National Civic League, 23, 89
National Commission on Children, 49
National Commission on Civic Renewal, 26, 28, 81, 88, 90

National Commission on Philanthropic and Civic Renewal, 61–62
National Endowment for the Humanities, 99
National Fatherhood Initiative, 54–55, 243
National Housing Institute, 243
National Institute for Responsible Fatherhood, 55
National Issues Forum, 90, 99
National Parenting Association, 243
National Parents Association, 115
National TV-Turnoff Week, 241
National Rifle Association, 24
The Negro Family: The Case for National Action, 48
Neuhaus, Richard John, 62–63
Newsweek, 37, 115
New Yorker, 37
New York Times, 120
Niebuhr, H. Richard, 177, 190
Nisbet, Robert, 12, 63, 136, 151, 153
Northwestern University, 88
Novak, Michael, 135
Nunn, Sam, 88
Odd Fellows, 77
Olasky, Marvin, 63–64
Paglia, Camile, 28, 31
Panichas, George, 167
Parent-Teacher Association (PTA), 21, 26, 82, 84–85, 212, 221
Passaic County Legal Aid Society, 243
Pew Center for Civic Journalism, 100
Pew Charitable Trust, 90
Pew Partnership for Civic Change, 90
Points of Light Foundation, 89
Policy Review: The Journal of American Citizenship, 62

Pollitt, Katha, 82
Pope John Paul II, 106
Popenoe, David, 50, 52, 55, 79
Post-Modernity Project, 133
Powell, Colin, 26, 62, 67, 89, 115
Princeton University, 86, 243
Progressive Policy Institute, 63, 97
Project for American Renewal, 61
Project on Public Life and the
    Press, 100
Promise Keepers, 54, 84, 87
Public Agenda, 99, 243
Public Interest, 53
Putnam, Robert, 20, 24, 26, 44–45,
    76–79, 81–85
Quayle, Dan, 49–50
The Quest for Community, 63, 151
Rahn, Wendy, 45, 48
Rand Corporation, 44
Raspberry, William, 54, 107
Reagan, Ronald, 31, 89
Reiff, Philip, 13
The Repeal of Reticence, 110
The Revolt of the Elites, 108
Rimel, Rebecca, 100
Rivers, Eugene, 68
Rockefeller IV, Jay D., 49
Rockwell, Norman, 29
Roper Center for Public Opinion
    Research, 85
Rotary, 77
Rousseau, Jean Jacques, 109
Royal, Robert, 23
*Rules of Civility and Decent
    Behaviour in Company and
    Conversation*, 115
Salvation Army, 21, 186
Samuelson, Robert J., 85
Sandel, Michael, 12, 139–141, 144
Schambra, Bill, 65, 142, 145
Schlesinger, Arthur, Jr., 38, 143,
    160
Schroeder, Patricia, 26
Seducing the Samaritan, 71

Shain, Barry, 140
Sierra Club, 24
Silber, John, 116–117
Skillen, Jim, 187
Skocpol, Theda, 20, 82
Smith, Adam, 138, 176
Smyre, Rick, 90
Sons of Liberty, 77
Sorokin, P. A., 161
Southern Baptist Convention, 197
Steinfels, Margaret, 243
Stengle, Richard, 87
Talent, Jim, 61
Taylor, Frederick, 137
Teen Challenge, 61
*The Tragedy of American
    Compassion*, 63
Thoreau, Henry David, 176
Tocqueville, Alexis de, 12, 21–24,
    45, 48, 71, 75, 77–79, 84, 140,
    143, 146, 159, 177, 182,
    185–186, 191–193, 197, 211,
    213, 223–224
To Empower People, 62
True Love Waits, 87
TV-Free America, 241
United States Olympic Committee,
    237
United Way, 86, 130
University of California at Los
    Angeles, (UCLA), 243
University of Chicago, 138, 243
University of Chicago Divinity
    School, 243
University of Maryland, 46, 50,
    243
University of Minnesota, 45, 97
University of Texas, 114
University of Virginia, 109, 133
Uslaner, Eric, 46
U. S. News and World Report, 68,
    111, 118
Walsh, David, 190
Walzer, Michael, 20

Washington, George, 115, 208, 227
Washington Post, 27, 46, 85
Watts, J. C., 61
Webster, Noah, 165
Weekly Standard, 31
Weigle, George, 171
West, Cornel, 243
Whitehead, Barbara Dafoe, 49, 52
Who Cares, 90
Wiesel, Elie, 106
Williams, Roger E., 243
Will, George, 101, 175
Wilson, James Q., 108, 129, 145, 202, 205, 243
Wilson Quarterly, 113

Wilson, William Julius, 80
Wingspread Journal, 90
Winthrop, John, 186–187
Wolfe, Alan, 22, 28, 29, 39, 138–139
Woodward, Kenneth, 37
Wuthnow, Robert, 86
Yankelovich, Daniel, 9, 83, 126, 219, 243
Young Men's Christian Association (YMCAs), 77, 87, 130, 186, 213
Young Women's Christian Association (YWCAs), 186
Zinsmeister, Karl, 80–81

About the Author

Don Eberly has written or edited four books and speaks widely on topics of American society and culture. He directs the Civil Society Project and serves in roles with the Council on Civil Society and the National Commission on Civic Renewal. He is founder and chairman of the National Fatherhood Initiative and is an affiliate scholar at the Institute for American Values. His work is regularly reported on by national media outlets.